Wolfgang Spießl

Assessment and Support of Error Recognition in Automated Driving

Wolfgang Spießl

Assessment and Support of Error Recognition in Automated Driving

When the machine fails

Südwestdeutscher Verlag für Hochschulschriften

Impressum/Imprint (nur für Deutschland/only for Germany)
Bibliografische Information der Deutschen Nationalbibliothek: Die Deutsche Nationalbibliothek verzeichnet diese Publikation in der Deutschen Nationalbibliografie; detaillierte bibliografische Daten sind im Internet über http://dnb.d-nb.de abrufbar.
Alle in diesem Buch genannten Marken und Produktnamen unterliegen warenzeichen-, marken- oder patentrechtlichem Schutz bzw. sind Warenzeichen oder eingetragene Warenzeichen der jeweiligen Inhaber. Die Wiedergabe von Marken, Produktnamen, Gebrauchsnamen, Handelsnamen, Warenbezeichnungen u.s.w. in diesem Werk berechtigt auch ohne besondere Kennzeichnung nicht zu der Annahme, dass solche Namen im Sinne der Warenzeichen- und Markenschutzgesetzgebung als frei zu betrachten wären und daher von jedermann benutzt werden dürften.

Coverbild: www.ingimage.com

Verlag: Südwestdeutscher Verlag für Hochschulschriften GmbH & Co. KG
Dudweiler Landstr. 99, 66123 Saarbrücken, Deutschland
Telefon +49 681 37 20 271-1, Telefax +49 681 37 20 271-0
Email: info@svh-verlag.de

Approved by: München, LMU, Diss., 2011

Herstellung in Deutschland:
Schaltungsdienst Lange o.H.G., Berlin
Books on Demand GmbH, Norderstedt
Reha GmbH, Saarbrücken
Amazon Distribution GmbH, Leipzig
ISBN: 978-3-8381-2925-9

Imprint (only for USA, GB)
Bibliographic information published by the Deutsche Nationalbibliothek: The Deutsche Nationalbibliothek lists this publication in the Deutsche Nationalbibliografie; detailed bibliographic data are available in the Internet at http://dnb.d-nb.de.
Any brand names and product names mentioned in this book are subject to trademark, brand or patent protection and are trademarks or registered trademarks of their respective holders. The use of brand names, product names, common names, trade names, product descriptions etc. even without a particular marking in this works is in no way to be construed to mean that such names may be regarded as unrestricted in respect of trademark and brand protection legislation and could thus be used by anyone.

Cover image: www.ingimage.com

Publisher: Südwestdeutscher Verlag für Hochschulschriften GmbH & Co. KG
Dudweiler Landstr. 99, 66123 Saarbrücken, Germany
Phone +49 681 37 20 271-1, Fax +49 681 37 20 271-0
Email: info@svh-verlag.de

Printed in the U.S.A.
Printed in the U.K. by (see last page)
ISBN: 978-3-8381-2925-9

Copyright © 2011 by the author and Südwestdeutscher Verlag für Hochschulschriften GmbH & Co. KG and licensors
All rights reserved. Saarbrücken 2011

*Ambition is the path to success,
persistence is the vehicle you arrive in.*

– William Eardley IV –

To my family.

Preface

This dissertation has been written in partial fulfillment of the requirements for the Degree of Doctor of Natural Sciences in the Department of Mathematics, Informatics and Statistics at the University of Munich (Ludwig-Maximilians-Universität München).

From September 2007 to March 2010 I was a graduate student at the Ludwig-Maximilians-Universität München. All research described in this work has been carried out at the research and development facilities of BMW Group Research and Technology in cooperation with the chair of Media Informatics (LFE Medieninformatik) at the Ludwig-Maximilians-Universität München.

A dissertation work cannot be created in isolation without the input and support of many people contributing in various ways. Every decision in this work has not been made at the sole discretion of myself, but is the result of intense communication and discussion. Especially in the automotive domain, there are so many limitations and constraints to be considered that cannot be overlooked by a single person. In all stadiums of this work, the initial phase, through the process of ideation, in numerous brainstorming sessions, in the conception of solutions, during the preparation of experiments and the interpretation of the results, professional as well as unbiased feedback and experiences from colleagues and other researchers were invaluable and always very welcome. Also in the practical part, implementation, testing, data analysis, etc., I was grateful for every helping hand.

Therefore I decided to write this document using the scientific plural, accounting for the support and counseling that helped to shape this work.

Acknowledgements

First of all I want to thank my supervisor Heinrich Hußmann for his willingness to support my dissertation project. He was also the one who gave me the idea of such an undertaking. Despite his many duties he always managed to find time for discussion, counseling and detailed feedback on my work. But he also gave me the freedom of pursuing my work in an industrial environment. Thank you very much for the encouragement. I also would like to thank my second supervisor Klaus-Josef Bengler for the initial shaping of the topic and his support. We have been working together for almost two years and I am grateful for his persistence in making me present my work.

Special thanks go to Albrecht Schmidt who was not only my supervisor during my studies and the initial phase of this work, but also became a friend. He made it possible for me to go to places, I would not have gone otherwise which was always an enriching experience. He always pushed me a little further than I thought I could go. I am deeply grateful for this.

During my work at BMW Research and Technology, I had many discussions with my superiors Bernhard Niedermaier and Dirk Wisselmann whom I thank for their courtesy and support in difficult questions. Furthermore, I want to thank my technical advisers Stefan Hoch and Mehdi Farid. Mehdi was a very valuable discussion partner and gave my work the necessary little push into the right direction.

Furthermore I'd like to thank all my colleagues, fellow doctorands and students at BMW who made the time during my promotion work worthwhile. Particular thanks go to the students who were directly involved in my topics, namely Felix Schwarz, Marion Mangold, Michael Bunk, Christina Kreuzmair, Niklaus Voellmy, Arne Albrecht, and Tessa-Virginia Hannemann for their help. Also thanks to Thomas Schaller, Michael Ardelt, Thomas Bleher and Andreas Thönnessen for their support. I owe a great debt of gratitude to the team operating the BMW driving simulation centre. Without Alex, Toni, Martin, Svenja, Stefan, Uli, and Sebastian it would not have been possible to conduct my experiments. Thank you very much for your helpfulness.

Personally, I want to express the deepest gratitude to my family for their endless support during all my life and for always providing a place to come home. You helped so much with this work, probably without even knowing. Cordial thanks to my sister Evi for proof-reading and actually 'understanding' my thesis.

Preface

The ultimate appreciation I give to my wife Martina. She has been the most important person in my life during the last years. I thank you for your faith in me, for staying awake with me in times of self doubt, taking me for a walk after long hours of work, and above all, for just being there. Thank you for all your love.

Abstract

Technical progress in the field of automated driving research is about to alter the way of driving from manual control toward supervision of automated control. The increasing dissemination of advanced driver assistance systems brings more and more people into contact with (semi-)automated systems that do not only warn against certain dangers and intervene if necessary, but are also able to take over parts of the driving task. Automated vehicles have the potential to increase traffic safety, efficiency and to reduce the driver's workload. This requires systems working with absolute perfection that sense and interpret the environment correctly at any time and transform this information into adequate actions. However, such systems are not yet available today. Therefore it is necessary that the driver supervises automated vehicle control systems in order to be able to recognise automation errors and to intervene. Even if there is still a long way to go, it is worth taking a look at the ramifications an automated driving task implies. Currently, there is no methodical approach for a systematic assessment of human error recognition capabilities in the context of automated driving. The Lane Change Test is a standardised and well known method to measure driver performance under varying side conditions. In this thesis, this test has been further developed into the Automated Lane Change Test (ALCT). The ALCT allows the measurement of error recognition performance during an automated drive in a driving simulation environment using a set of objective metrics (mean response time, missed errors, false interventions). In several studies, this method has been assessed for objectivity, reliability and validity. It proved sensitive for different secondary task conditions. Tasks requiring active engagement showed the most prominent effect on error recognition and response. Haptic feedback through the steering wheel showed a positive effect on error recognition performance. There are more potential measures imaginable in order to improve the recognition of automation errors, in particular the difficult situation of slowly drifting out of the lane. After a discussion of these measures for effectiveness and acceptance, the most promising idea for improving this situation has been implemented, a prospective driving path display that visualises the vehicle's trajectory in the near future based on sensor data. By comparing the predicted path with the actual course of the road, a deviation caused by erroneous automation behaviour can be recognised earlier and potentially critical situations can be avoided. A user study showed that such a display should be realised in the form of a contact analogue head-up display following the paradigm of Augmented Reality, since the error recognition results were best in this condition.

Zusammenfassung

Die Forschung auf dem Gebiet des automatisierten Autofahrens macht enorme Fortschritte. Durch die zunehmende Verbreitung von Fahrerassistenzsystemen kommen immer mehr Menschen in Berührung mit (teil)automatisierten Systemen, die nicht nur in kritischen Situationen warnen und unterstützend eingreifen, sondern sogar Teile der Fahraufgabe übernehmen können. Autofahren kann durch automatisch gesteuerte Fahrzeuge sicherer, effizienter und weniger beanspruchend werden. Dies setzt allerdings perfekt funktionierende Systeme voraus, die die Fahrzeugumgebung jederzeit richtig erfassen, interpretieren und auf Basis dieser Informationen stets die richtigen Handlungsentscheidungen treffen können. Solche Systeme sind derzeit noch nicht verfügbar. Deshalb ist es notwendig, dass automatisierte Fahrzeugsysteme vom Fahrer überwacht werden, um Automationsfehler erkennen und ggf. korrigierend eingreifen zu können. Auch wenn automatisiertes Fahren noch in der Zukunft liegt, lohnt sich die Betrachtung der möglichen Effekte bereits heute. Derzeit gibt es keinen methodischen Ansatz, um systematisch die Fehlererkennung beim automatisierten Fahren zu bewerten. Deshalb wurde im Zuge dieser Arbeit mit dem Automated Lane Change Test (ALCT) eine Methode entwickelt, die es erlaubt, die Erkennung fehlerhafter Fahrzeugführung während einer automatisierten Fahrt in der Fahrsimulation in verschiedenen Dimensionen (Reaktionszeit, verpasste Fehler, Falscheingriffe) zu messen. Die Methode wurde in mehreren Studien nach Objektivität, Reliabilität und Validität abgesichert und zeigte sich sensitiv gegenüber unterschiedlichen Nebentätigkeiten. Gerade aktiv zu bedienende Nebenaufgaben während der automatisierten Fahrt haben einen deutlichen Effekt auf die Erkennung von Automationsfehlern. Durch haptisches Feedback über das Lenkrad konnte eine deutliche Verbesserung in der Fehlererkennungsleistung nachgewiesen werden. Um die Erkennung solcher schwieriger Fehlersituationen, insbesondere beim langsamen Abdriften von der Spur zu verbessern, sind weitere vielfältige Maßnahmen denkbar, die nach ihrer Wirksamkeit und Akzeptanz bewertet wurden. Als eine der vielversprechendsten Maßnahmen wurde eine vorausschauende Fahrpfadanzeige umgesetzt, die die auf Sensordaten basierende zukünftige Fahrzeugtrajektorie visualisiert. Durch einen Abgleich des Straßenverlaufs mit dem prädizierten Pfad ist für den Fahrer ein frühzeitiges Erkennen von Abweichungen möglich und dadurch ein früheres Eingreifen und Vermeiden von kritischen Situationen. Untersuchungen zeigten, dass sich eine kontaktanaloge Darstellung der Fahrzeuganzeige nach dem Augmented Reality Prinzip am besten dazu eignet, die Fehlererkennung durch den Fahrer zu verbessern.

Contents

List of Figures   xxi

List of Tables   xxvii

1   Introduction   **1**
- 1.1   Motivation 1
- 1.2   Focus, Research Questions and Contributions 4
- 1.3   How this Thesis is Organised 5
  - 1.3.1   Structure 5
  - 1.3.2   Conventions 6

2   Background and Related Work   **9**
- 2.1   Background on Cognitive Science 9
  - 2.1.1   Taxonomy of the Driving Task 9
  - 2.1.2   Information Processing 13
  - 2.1.3   Secondary Tasks and Driver Distraction 16
- 2.2   The Basics on Automation 20
  - 2.2.1   Definitions 21
  - 2.2.2   Taxonomies of Human-Centred Automation 21
  - 2.2.3   Application Areas and Benefits of Automation 26
  - 2.2.4   From Driver Assistance to Automation 28
  - 2.2.5   Research Programmes on Automated Vehicles 30
- 2.3   Implications of Human-Automation Interaction 33
- 2.4   Summary 38

3	Methodology and Procedure		39
	3.1	Formal Categorisation of Secondary In-car Tasks	39
		3.1.1 Secondary Task Analysis in ADAM	40
		3.1.2 Delphi Study on Secondary Task Demands	41
		3.1.3 Final Task Categorisation	43
		3.1.4 Selection of Secondary Tasks for Experiments	47
	3.2	Towards an Assessment Methodology for Error Recognition in Automated Driving	52
		3.2.1 Need for a Methodology	52
		3.2.2 Lane Change Task as Methodological Basis	54
	3.3	Towards Driver Support for Error Recognition in Automated Driving . . .	58
		3.3.1 Related Work	58
		3.3.2 Discussion of Potential Support Measures	59
	3.4	Summary	61

4	Development of the Automated Lane Change Test		63
	4.1	System Design	63
		4.1.1 Functionality	63
		4.1.2 ALCT Implementation	66
		4.1.3 Discussion of Differences between LCT and ALCT	74
	4.2	User Study 1: LO version	76
		4.2.1 Hypotheses	76
		4.2.2 Experimental Procedure	77
		4.2.3 Technical Realisation	78
		4.2.4 Sample	81
		4.2.5 Results	81
		4.2.6 Discussion of Results	93
	4.3	User Study 2: LO vs. HI version	97
		4.3.1 Experimental Goals and Hypotheses	97

CONTENTS   xix

   4.3.2 Experimental Procedure and Setup 98

   4.3.3 Sample 98

   4.3.4 Results 98

   4.3.5 Discussion of Results 108

 4.4 Methodical Discussion 111

 4.5 Summary 113

5 Magic Carpet – A Prospective Driving Path Display 115

 5.1 Development of the Magic Carpet 115

   5.1.1 Basic Principles and Related Work 115

   5.1.2 Design Process and General System Description 119

   5.1.3 Implementation 121

   5.1.4 Modelling of Automation Errors 124

 5.2 Evaluation of the Magic Carpet in a User Study 129

   5.2.1 Hardware Setup and Human-Machine-Interface 131

   5.2.2 Experimental Design and Procedure 132

   5.2.3 Metrics 135

   5.2.4 Pre-study 135

   5.2.5 Hypotheses 137

   5.2.6 Sample 137

   5.2.7 Results 138

   5.2.8 Discussion of Results 150

 5.3 Summary 155

6 Contributions and Conclusion 157

 6.1 Discussion of Contributions 157

 6.2 Conclusion and Future Work 162

A Appendix 169

Bibliography 179

List of Figures

1.1 Structure of this thesis in six chapters. 6

2.1 The 3-Level-models from Rasmussen [132] and Donges [43] related to each other (translated and redrawn from [44]). 12

2.2 Selective attention. A: The bottleneck occurs before perceptual analysis. B: The bottleneck occurs after perceptual analysis (from [89], redrawn). . 14

2.3 Performance Operating Characteristics (POC) showing two tasks performed simultaneously and the cost of concurrence (redrawn from [172]). 15

2.4 Wickens' multiple resource model (MRM), showing the different dimensions. Performance in multiple tasks is typically better when the tasks use different input-output modes (redrawn from [172]). 16

2.5 Human information processing loop (redrawn from [172]). 17

2.6 Pilot control and management continuum (from [11], redrawn.) 24

2.7 Top: H-Mode automation spectrum and seamless transitions between different LOAs (translated from [55], redrawn). Bottom: Mockup car augmented with active side stick (from [91]). 25

2.8 Car platooning using the Automated Highway System (from [93]). . . . 31

2.9 A closed control loop consisting of the controller (act), processor (interpret) and measurement device (sense). Redrawn from [61]. 34

2.10 Relationship between arousal and performance. Graphs according to Yerkes and Dodson [181] and Galley [57]. 37

2.11 Relationship between control and monitoring functions and the corresponding implications for the human operator (redrawn from [176]). . . 37

3.1 Mean results of the final Delphi rating comprising the DALI dimensions for each of the 21 tasks (standard deviation not displayed). 44

3.2	Results from the survey on desired tasks during automated driving.	48
3.3	Left: Navigation destination entry; right: Interactive map.	50
3.4	BMW iDrive controller. Push, tilt and rotate a central knob, mounted in the centre console.	50
3.5	Left: Short text reading task, single lines of text; right: long text reading task, unstructured block of text, crime short story.	51
3.6	Ballomat. A neutral-coloured ball drops to the ground. The ball then is randomly shaded with red or blue colour and starts moving towards a bucket. If the colour of the ball and the bucket do not match, the user must intervene.	54
3.7	Lane Change Task. Left: Original setup with PC and gaming wheel (from [122]). Right: Virtual LCT driving scene.	55
3.8	LCT normative path model (solid line), realistic manually driven path (dotted line), and sign distances. The lane change manoeuvre should ideally start 30 m (a) before passing the sign and completed within 10 m (b), regardless of a change across one or two lanes (from [122]).	56
3.9	When engaging in a visual task on a display, a video image of the frontal driving scene could be displayed in a splitscreen-view (montage).	61
4.1	Error categories. Left: Lane change when not supposed to (error 1); middle: no lane change when supposed to (error 2); right: change to the wrong lane (error 3).	64
4.2	Temporal course of the ALCT. At t_0 the current road sign is revealed and is visible until t_3. In case of an error an intervention takes place at t_2, which can be as late as just before the t_0 of the next sign. t_1 indicates the first glance at the driving scene.	69
4.3	Left: Kollmorgen hollow shaft motor used to apply torque on the steering wheel. Right: Schematics of the signal chain to control the motor.	72
4.4	Lane change trajectories of the ALCT HI version. The PT1-filtered lane offset is used as input for lateral control.	73
4.5	Simulink functions containing road sign computation algorithms.	74
4.6	ALCT experimental setup. Test participant driving the ALCT LO version. He is operating the interactive map using the iDrive controller and wears a head-mounted eye-tracking system.	79

LIST OF FIGURES xxiii

4.7 Schematics of hardware and software architecture in the driving simulation environment. 79

4.8 Left: Dikablis eye-tracking system. One camera tracks the user's eye, the field camera captures the environment. Properly calibrated we know what the user looks at. Right: Analysis view. The screen can be subdivided into areas of interest (AOIs). Visual markers anchor AOI positions on the screen for automated analysis. The cross-hair shows the test subject's current gaze point. 80

4.9 Mean response time and standard deviation for the baseline and all secondary tasks (sorted in ascending order). 82

4.10 Number of missed errors in each condition summed over all test subjects (sorted in ascending order). 83

4.11 Number of false interventions in each condition summed over test subjects (sorted in ascending order). 84

4.12 Mean response times in seconds and standard deviation of all conditions grouped by dimensions. 85

4.13 Mean response times in seconds and standard deviation of all conditions grouped to error categories. 86

4.14 Mean gaze times and standard deviation (in seconds) of all visual tasks for AOIs CID and FRONT, sorted in descending order. 88

4.15 Gaze analysis of missed errors summed over all participants. All missed errors, overlooked errors and errors seen but not correct. 89

4.16 Time to first fixation on FRONT in seconds and standard deviation when road signs appear (all visual tasks, sorted in ascending order). 90

4.17 Mean DALI score and standard deviation, sorted in ascending order. . . . 90

4.18 Top: Mean level of perceived fatigue and standard deviation, rated after corresponding task, sorted in ascending order. Bottom: Mean level of perceived fatigue and standard deviation, rated after corresponding task, temporal progression. 91

4.19 Mean assigned rank and standard deviation of all secondary tasks, sorted in ascending order from perceived easiest to hardest task. 92

4.20 Mean rating of interruptibility and standard deviation. Sorted in descending order, grouped by categorisation into easy and bad interruptibility. . . 93

LIST OF FIGURES

4.21 Mean response time in seconds and standard deviation for version LO and HI. Grouped by version and sorted in ascending order. 99

4.22 Mean response time in seconds and standard deviation for error categories in version LO and HI. 101

4.23 Histogram of false interventions. Number of times the automation was unnecessarily overruled by a given number of subjects. Only a single subject had no false interventions, another as much as 33. 102

4.24 Mean gaze times on CID and FRONT in seconds with standard deviation. 104

4.25 Gaze analysis of missed errors summed over all participants. All missed errors, overlooked errors and errors seen but not corrected, grouped by version. 105

4.26 Time until the first fixation on AOI FRONT in seconds and standard deviation in the visual tasks, grouped by version. 106

4.27 Mean DALI score and standard deviation, sorted in ascending order, grouped by version. 107

5.1 Sketch of a prospective driving path display. The internal representation of the vehicle's projected guidance trajectory is mapped onto the road in form of a virtual coloured area. The vehicle will take the projected path and in a few seconds reach the position where the end of the driving path currently is. 116

5.2 Milgram's Reality-Virtuality continuum (redrawn from [109]). 117

5.3 Augmented reality navigation. Left: Extra display (from [116]). Right: Contact analogue display (from [143]). 118

5.4 Contact analogue brake bar indicating the stopping distance (from [161]). 118

5.5 Sketches of carpet alternatives. Left: Wheel traces. Right: Combination of wheel traces and carpet. 119

5.6 Front view showing the carpet display. It shows the vehicle's future path and position up to three seconds ahead. 120

5.7 Realisation of the carpet in the driving simulation, overall hardware setup and information flow. 121

5.8 Vehicle trajectory determined by offset y_0, heading angle θ and curvature κ. 122

5.9 Principle how the carpet polygon is constructed. 123

LIST OF FIGURES

5.10 Lane deviation resulting from manipulated lane information visible in the carpet. 124

5.11 Simulink implementation of the generation of the data necessary to display the carpet polygon. 125

5.12 Exemplary plot of error functions with different polynomial degrees. In our case, the most adequate behaviour for the modelling of errors is reached by the squared function (red). 129

5.13 Different carpet versions. Left: Magic Carpet realised as contact analogue head-up display content merged with the driving scene. Right: Extra-display in the vehicle's centre console showing an augmented video of the driving scene with the driving path and no additional content on the front scene. 130

5.14 Driving simulator setup. Mockup car in front of a curved canvas displaying the driving scene. 131

5.15 Left: Control buttons on the steering wheel, the I/O-key (bottom left) toggles longitudinal and lateral automation. Right: Digital instrument cluster, displaying current speed and status of the automated longitudinal and lateral control system. 132

5.16 Mockup interior with the AOIs FRONT, IC, CID, and DISPLAY, and three visual markers on the dash board for automatic gaze detection. 136

5.17 Carpet deviating from the centre of the lane in a left curve (left) and in a right curve (right). 136

5.18 Pre-study: Mean reaction time in seconds and standard deviation in left and right curves. 137

5.19 Mean lane deviation and standard deviation of all errors (excluding the initial error) and the initial error (in meters), grouped by carpet version. The red horizontal line indicates the lane border. 139

5.20 Mean lane deviation and standard deviation in error situations grouped by carpet version. The initial error results in the highest, errors in right curves in the least lane deviation. The red horizontal line indicates the lane border. 140

5.21 Mean lane deviation and standard deviation in meters grouped by carpet version and curve. The red horizontal line indicates the lane border. . . . 141

5.22 Mean lane deviation and standard deviation in meters grouped by carpet version and secondary tasks. The red horizontal line indicates the lane border. 141

5.23 Plot of lane deviation during the initial contact error in the Baseline condition. The upper dashed line indicates the lane border of the right lane. . 143

5.24 Plot of lane deviation during the initial contact error in the DISPLAY condition. The upper dashed line indicates the lane border of the right lane. 144

5.25 Plot of lane deviation during the initial contact error in the HUD condition. The upper dashed line indicates the lane border of the right lane. 144

5.26 Percentage of situations successfully resolved before leaving the own lane, grouped by version. 145

5.27 Answers to the question, at what point of time did the test subjects overrule the automation in case of an error. 149

A.1 Sample of 21 questions in the Delphi study. On the right, the second Delphi round is shown with the results from the first round. 169

A.2 Computation of road sign contents implemented as Stateflow chart. 170

A.3 Second ALCT experiment: Interaction Version × error category. 173

A.4 Carpet error computation as implemented in Simulink, depicted for the squared error function $y = b \cdot x^2$. 174

A.5 Carpet experiment: Interaction Carpet version × Type of curve. 176

A.6 Carpet experiment: Interaction Carpet version × Type of secondary task. . 176

A.7 Carpet experiment: Interaction Type of secondary task × Type of curve. . 177

List of Tables

2.1 Driving-related information as perceived by human sensory channels (translated from [162]). The visual channel is clearly dominant. 13

2.2 Endsley's hierarchy of levels of automation with intrinsic functions [50] (H = Human, C = Computer). 23

2.3 Selection of common driver assistance systems currently available in modern cars and the provided degree of assistance. 29

3.1 Secondary tasks selection used in the ADAM project (from [17]). 41

3.2 List of tasks rating in the Delphi study. 42

3.3 Categorisation of secondary tasks according to the dimensions modality, degree of interaction, interruptibility and information encoding. 46

4.1 Possible manoeuvres in the ALCT and the corresponding target lanes in case of error category 1, 2 or 3. n/a means that this error is not applicable for this manoeuvre. 65

4.2 Overview of the differences between the LCT and the ALCT implementation. 75

4.3 Total summed gaze times, mean gaze times and maximum gaze times (in seconds) on the AOIs CID and FRONT for all visual tasks. 87

4.4 Lane changes overlooked, summed over all test subjects. 88

4.5 Correlations of response times within the different secondary tasks (Pearson-r). The table shows correlations between tasks in the LO version (lower left), between tasks in the HI version (upper right) and pairwise compared between the versions (diagonally). 100

4.6 Number of missed errors and false interventions in each condition summed over all participants. 102

4.7 Correlations response times to age (Pearson-r). 103

4.8 Total summed gaze times, mean gaze times and maximum gaze times on the AOIs CID and FRONT for all visual tasks in both versions, in seconds. 104

4.9 Number of lane changes overlooked, summed over all test subjects. 105

4.10 Ranking of tasks regarding the perceived difficulty. 108

5.1 Correlations between lane deviation and response time, Pearson-r. 138

5.2 Situations successfully resolved (and percentage) before leaving the own lane, grouped by version. 145

5.3 Mean gaze time in seconds and mean gaze distribution in % (with standard deviation) during phone call and navigation task grouped by carpet version. 146

5.4 Descriptives of gaze data in the DISPLAY condition over the whole experiment. The values show enormous individual differences. 147

A.1 Permutation of secondary tasks during the test runs in seven variants in the first ALCT experiment. 171

A.2 Permutation of secondary tasks during the test runs in the second ALCT experiment. Light cells indicate the LO version, dark cells indicate the HI version. 172

A.3 Permutation of secondary tasks during the test run in 12 variants in the carpet experiment (N = navigation, T= phone call). 175

Chapter 1

Introduction

1.1 Motivation

Individual mobility is one of the highest goals but also greatest challenges in modern societies. According to the latest traffic report of the German Federal Statistical Office, the traffic volume on Germany's roads has grown by 250% since 1970[1]. By that time, for each 100,000 vehicles, there were 102 road fatalities per year. This number has been continuously reduced by stricter traffic regulations and **passive safety** measures in cars such as seat belts, head rests, airbags, crumple zones and structurally improved car bodies. Increasingly, cars have been equipped with **active safety** systems that support the driver in stabilising the car for instance in slippery road conditions. Today, advanced driver assistance systems (ADAS) are able to sense the environment and offer intelligent cruise control, lane keeping assistance, automatic parking support, etc. Those systems provide safety and comfort by active control and by warning the drivers against potentially dangerous conditions and situations, such as forward and lateral collisions. These systems have contributed to reduce road fatalities by 92% compared to 1970.

The report also reveals that 86% of all road accidents are caused by incorrect driver actions. The rest was mainly due incorrect behaviour of pedestrians, adverse road conditions and lack of vehicle maintenance. This finding is not really surprising. So for a further increase of traffic safety, a potential measure could be to reduce the human factor in road traffic by increasing the degree of automation. In theory, vehicles driving automatically could increase the safety and efficiency of the whole road traffic system. With no human in the control loop, accidents because of inattention, fatigue,

---

[1] http://www.destatis.de/jetspeed/portal/cms/Sites/destatis/Internet/DE/
Content/Publikationen/Fachveroeffentlichungen/Verkehr/Verkehrsunfaelle/
Unfallentwicklung5462401099004,property=file.pdf

misjudgement, or overlooking of other road users could be eliminated and many lives could be saved. Vehicles communicating and cooperating with each other would allow minimal safety margins with even increased speed, since no adverse driver behaviour could interfere with steady traffic flow. This could even have a positive ecological effect on the environment by the decreasing energy consumption due to the better predictability of future vehicle actions.

It must be noted that automation has progressed dramatically in the past decades in all parts of our lives. With the technological and computational advances more and more work is done by machines, robots and computers. Especially in transportation we have seen remarkable effort to reduce routine actions for human operators. Autopilots for aircrafts and ships have existed already for decades [97, 176], and also for cars, we have seen numerous research projects and activities from the industry in the recent past addressing the field of fully automated driving. The most known initiatives are the DARPA Challenges, competitions that target driverless vehicles navigating autonomously to a given destination on regular roads, difficult terrain and even urban areas (cf. 2.2.5). Since the 1980's, a number of research institutes have shown cars that were able to drive partially or fully automatically, equipped with increasingly complex technology, beginning with simple monochromatic cameras up to fusioning multiple arrays of laser scanners, radar, lidar, etc.

Experts usually fail to predict when a future vision will ultimately arrive [102]. So despite technological advances, fully automated systems will probably stay at research stage for a long while. For this to become reality, the way road traffic works today would have to change profoundly, because all vehicles would have to be able to cooperate with each other. From a present-day perspective, this is not yet realistic, because also inter-vehicle communication is still in research. Car manufacturers are facing so many technical, economical and legal challenges that fully autonomous driving is not – at least not yet – their ultimate goal. In fact, some manufacturers are quite successful in selling manual driving with their car as a desirable and enjoyable activity. For a considerable number of drivers this is the most important reason to buy a car. So a more pragmatic approach is to not to automate driving generally, but only when manual driving is just not enjoyable. Letting an automated system take over control for example in monotonous and unpleasant driving situations (such as stop-and-go traffic) seems promising. The attractiveness of this thought is caused by the unattractiveness of those driving situations [93, 100]. It has been shown that in strenuous control tasks automated systems can contribute substantially to reducing stress [184], and can outweigh the hedonic quality of

1.1 Motivation

manual driving [174]. Through the absence of immediate and permanent control tasks, mental resources normally needed for manual driving become free. It is then not unlikely that a mental shift towards other activities happens, intentionally or unintentionally (e.g. [131]).

Nevertheless, one of the major challenges in automation in general is its potential failure, regardless of the application domain. At the present day, there is a considerable chance that sensors and cameras cannot detect the environment correctly all the time, e.g. the lane markings, which may result in a potential incorrect action taken by an automated system, such as leaving the lane. When automation fails, for whatever reasons, the human operator must take over manual control again. So, the primary task is no longer active control, but to supervise the correct execution of the driving task by the automated system, to **recognise errors** that are not recognised by the automation itself, and to act appropriately if necessary (*supervisory control* [146]). So, one of the central topics in this thesis is optimal support for humans in supervising automation under the assumption of potential failures of the automated system.

With the broad availability of autopilots for airplanes, the effects of automation and shared control between machines and human operators have been intensely researched. It could be assumed that effects of automation in aviation apply to automated driving as well. For some basic results this might be true, but there are numerous differences that have to be considered. The overall traffic situation in the air is very different from the road. Planes are meticulously scheduled, surveilled and guided by air traffic control in the air as well as on the ground. Professionally trained pilots (often two at a time) are prepared for every situation that might occur during a flight, landing or take-off. When an intervention becomes necessary with an active autopilot system (e.g. avoiding to cross another plane's path), the time frame for this usually comprises a few minutes.

All this is not the case with driving a car. On the road, vehicles follow each other in a distance of only a few seconds, driving past each other with a few meters distance. Thus the time to react in case of need is dramatically shorter, several seconds at most. That means, it is much more difficult to take over a car than a plane if the autopilot fails, because of the time component [37]. In airspace, there are no other traffic participants but planes, whereas car drivers must also have consideration for pedestrians and bicyclists (so-called vulnerable road users, VRUs). There is also no central supervisory authority communicating and guiding road vehicles safely to their destinations. Although there are international traffic rules, it is not uncommon that drivers from a foreign country do not know those rules or have a different interpretation of them. Therefore dedicated research on the failure of automated driving systems and the consequences is essential.

1.2 Focus, Research Questions and Contributions

In this work, we target specifically the problem of human recognition of failing automation, because this is a very central issue in the topic of automated driving. We do not assume fully autonomous vehicles, but systems that are able to take over permanently certain parts of the driving task, i.e. they take over longitudinal and lateral control, by keeping the vehicle at a certain speed, distance to other vehicles and within its current lane (semi-automated systems, cf. 2.2.4). The problem arises when the automated system does not work as intended and the driver must detect incorrect system behaviour. Errors in automated longitudinal control result in inappropriate speed adaptation, whereas incorrect automated lateral control manifests in erroneous steering behaviour. Automated longitudinal control systems have been in the markets for years (e.g. Adaptive Cruise Control) and are widely accepted. Permanent automated lateral control systems are still very rare and almost unknown to most drivers. Also the lateral distance to other vehicles is mostly much smaller than longitudinally, so that errors in lateral control can become critical very quickly. Recent work also focuses on lateral control errors (e.g. [131]). That is why we will focus on imperfect automated *lateral* vehicle guidance in this work. Currently there are no dedicated methodological means available that allow the assessment of error recognition by humans in an automated driving context with varying conditions. Furthermore, it is not known what can be done in order to support humans in the recognition of occurring automation errors during an automated drive. It is also not clear to what degree the previously mentioned mental shift towards secondary activities, such as phoning, takes place with an only supervisional driving task. Based on this, we state the following main research questions:

1. **By which methodology can human recognition of automation errors in an automated driving situation be suitably assessed?**

2. **By which means can human recognition of automation errors in an automated driving situation be supported?**

3. **To what extent do secondary activities influence humans in the recognition of automation errors in an automated driving situation?**

The answers to these questions can be briefly summarised by the following main contributions made by this thesis that are explicated in detail in section 6.1:

1. We have created and evaluated a systematic methodology with objective measurements for assessing error recognition in a simulator-based automated driving scenario. This method specifically addresses errors in automated lateral control. We gained insight into how different conditions can influence the performance of humans in error recognition.

2. We provide a discussion of potential measures to support the recognition of automation errors, again with the focus on incorrect lateral control. Tactile feedback conveyed through the steering wheel proved to be a valuable information channel. Another promising approach – a prospective driving path display – has been implemented in two different versions in a driving simulation environment and evaluated as a proof of concept under varying conditions.

3. We have created a systematic categorisation of secondary activities relevant to the driving context based on human information processing principles. This categorisation has been verified using the created assessment methodology, and has also been applied in the course of the evaluation of the driving path display. The role of secondary tasks in the context of automated driving has been addressed specifically in all studies reported in this work.

1.3 How this Thesis is Organised

1.3.1 Structure

Below we present a brief outline of this work, also graphically depicted in Fig. 1.1.

- Chapter 1 gives an **introduction** to the context of the thesis. We present the motivation, the goals and the contributions that came out of this work.

- In chapter 2 we cover relevant **related work** on basic principles of the driving task, information processing, automation in general and in the automotive context. We also discuss automation trust, failure and their implications of human-machine interaction.

- Chapter 3 covers preliminary work and reflections on the two main topics of this work: the **assessment** and **support** of error recognition in automated driving, as well as the subtopic of the influence of **secondary tasks** on error recognition as the cross-cutting topic in this work. We discuss the methodologies, procedures, results and decisions that led to the work done on that topics, which is then presented in chapters 4 and 5, also with respect to secondary tasks.

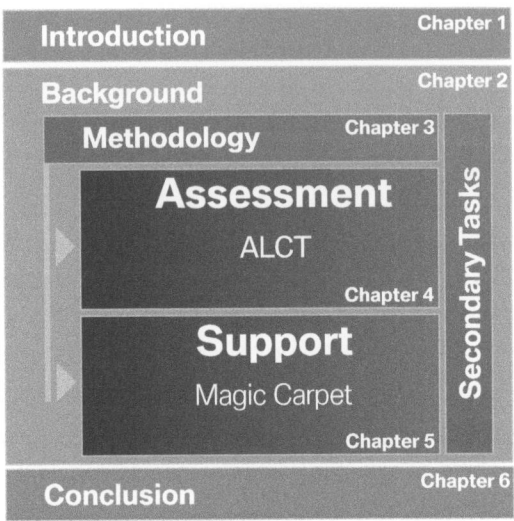

Figure 1.1: Structure of this thesis in six chapters.

- Chapter 4 describes the development and the evaluation of the **Automated Lane Change Test** (ALCT), a novel methodology to assess error recognition in automated driving. We present two user studies conducted with the ALCT. The first study focuses on secondary tasks simultaneously performed when driving automatically and the influence on error recognition. In the second study, we examine different versions of the ALCT and the influence of tactile feedback on error recognition manifesting in different measurements.

- In chapter 5 we present the **Magic Carpet**, a prospective driving path display that supports the recognition of automation errors. We describe the development, the technical background, and a comprehensive user study conducted with different instantiations of the driving path display.

- Chapter 6 summarises and discusses the contributions of this thesis, refers to future work and opens directions for further research in the field of automated driving.

1.3.2 Conventions

Statistics This work presents a series of studies and experiments in the chapters 3, 4 and 5. Results are reported with common statistical notation and depiction. We would like to give a very brief definition of the basic terms and how they are used in this work.

1.3 How this Thesis is Organised

Calculated mean values of data on a metric scale are denoted as M, together with the declaration of the standard deviation (SD) of the mean value as a measurement of variance. The standard deviation (s) is defined as the square root of the variance (s^2) [14]:

$$s_n = \sqrt{s^2} = \sqrt{\frac{1}{N}\sum_{i=1}^{N}(x_i - \bar{x})^2}$$

with $\{x_1, x_2, \ldots, x_N\}$ representing the observed values of the sample items and $\bar{x}$ the mean value of the observed values. The standard deviation is usually depicted in charts as error bars, both positively and negatively displayed from the mean value, with 1 SD in height.

Any statistical test used in the course of this work assumes a significance level $\alpha = 5\%$, i.e. the probability of error is less than 5%. For the definition of specific tests, please refer to relevant literature, e.g. Bortz [14].

Web References References to web addresses do not appear in the bibliography section at the end of this document, but are added directly as a footnote at the bottom of the corresponding page where they are mentioned. All cited URLs have been retrieved on 28/04/2011.

Citations Citations use article-relative pagination. For an absolute pagination, refer to the bibliography section.

Summaries At the end of each chapter, a concluding paragraph summarises the most important aspects and outcomes described in this chapter.

Chapter 2

Background and Related Work

As a basis for the work that has been done in this thesis, this chapter prepares the theoretical background. Before addressing the topic of automation, section 2.1 provides an introduction to acknowledged mechanisms occurring during information processing and sensory perception in general, during driving, and when performing simultaneous activities. Section 2.2 gives an introduction to the most important terms regarding automation and the research that has been done in this field in the past decades. Section 2.3 discusses the implications of human-automation interaction.

2.1 Background on Cognitive Science

In order to understand the complex interaction between driver, vehicle and an automated system, this section covers the fundamental principles of cognitive science in terms of information processing and the most important models describing drivers' behaviour. We refer to a comprehensive overview given by Michon [108].

2.1.1 Taxonomy of the Driving Task

The driving task is basically a feedback control activity performed by the driver [24]. Driver, vehicle, and environment (DVE) form a compound and interact with each other. Perception, processing and interpretation of driving related information from the driver's environment leads to vehicle control actions as a response to this information. Since the permanent movement of the ego-vehicle as well as of other road users result in a permanent changing constellation of sensory information [44], a permanent re-assessment of the current situation is necessary. Typical sources of immediate driving-related information are for instance the surrounding traffic, road conditions, traffic lights, pedestrians, and also the state of the ego-vehicle, e.g. speed, position within the lane, etc. Also the driver's wishes (looking for a parking spot, upcoming left turn, etc.) play an important role in this compound and influence the driver's actions. Since driving is a complex activity influenced by many factors, it makes sense to subdivide the driving task into more basic building blocks. Geiser introduced a categorisation of driving in *primary, secondary* and *tertiary* tasks [25, 58]:

- **Primary Tasks** All actions that are directly necessary for vehicle positioning. This comprises mainly longitudinal (accelerating, braking) and lateral (steering) guidance with respect to the surrounding environment.

- **Secondary Tasks** All actions that occur in the process of the primary tasks in order to ascertain safe vehicle guidance under varying environmental conditions. This includes shifting gears, operating windscreen wipers, operating headlights, but also the interaction with other traffic participants, e.g. operating turn signals, hazard lights, horn, etc.

- **Tertiary Tasks** All actions that are not directly involved in the safe operation of the vehicle, but serve the satisfaction of diverse driver needs, e.g. for comfort (climate control), entertainment (radio, music), or information (traffic information, navigation). Usually these tasks are performed simultaneously to the primary and secondary tasks, i.e. during driving.

Note: Very often, the primary and secondary tasks are aggregated simply to "tasks related to driving" or the "primary task" and the tertiary tasks then become "secondary tasks", or tasks that are not driving-related. In the course of the work we will heavily use the term *secondary task* which is to understand in the sense of tertiary tasks.

The **primary task** is often described using the **3-Level-Model** (also called *Hierarchic vehicle guidance model*) by Bernotat [9]. This model has been frequently cited and extended, e.g. by Donges [43], Michon [108] or Geiser [58]. The model comprises the following levels (cf. Fig. 2.1, right):

Navigation On the highest or most abstract level is the navigation task which comprises the selection of an appropriate route with respect to the available network of passable roads. Unexpected events, for example traffic congestion, accidents or incorrect driving actions (e.g. wrong turn) and their implications on the estimated time of arrival, potentially influence the driver's route choice. The navigation task is typically fulfilled locally or temporally discrete with the driver monitoring the adherence to the chosen route by distinctive points along the road. Michon [108] calls this level *strategic level* where

2.1 Background on Cognitive Science

general plans with low action frequency are made. This level requires the most conscious mental activity. Navigation systems aim to support the driver on this level by taking over the task of selecting a route.

Manoeuvring Subordinated to the navigation level is the manoeuvring task which implements the chosen navigational route into concrete driving manoeuvres. The driver must extract and interpret the relevant information from the current traffic situation and derive the appropriate reference variables regarding lane position and velocity. The driver anticipates the progression of these variables and intervenes appropriately in the sense of an open loop control in order to achieve the least possible deviation between the intended and actual course. Typical tasks on this level are lane changes, overtaking, or keeping constant headway. Michon identifies controlled action patterns on this level with a time constant in the dimension of seconds [108].

Stabilisation On the lowest level lies the stabilisation of the vehicle, that means the operation of pedals and steering wheel in order to implement the intended driving manoeuvres. The driver is part of a closed control loop, in which deviations from the normative values must be compensated by appropriate actions. Michon calls this level *control level* with automatic action patterns and an action frequency in the dimension of milliseconds [108].

As mentioned, this model represents a hierarchic order. The tasks on the upper levels can only be executed if the lower levels do not require mental resources in an exceeding degree, since the cognitive demands increase with each higher level. The more automated the tasks are through practice, the less mental resources are required. If the stabilisation level requires a lot of mental effort as it is the case with driving beginners, manoeuvring and navigation are very difficult. Rasmussen developed a 3-level model describing the performance of a skilled human operator [132, 133], cf. 2.1, left:

Skill-based Skill-based behaviour "represents sensory-motor performance during acts or activities which [...] take place without conscious control" [132], p. 2. This level is characterised by highly automatised stimulus-response mechanisms, resulting from long-term training processes. Those skills are most efficient, since they are often anchored in the cerebellum, and do therefore not require conscious attention. Examples are all kinds of basic vehicle operation activities, e.g. steering, clutch use and manual gear shifting, etc.

2. Background and Related Work

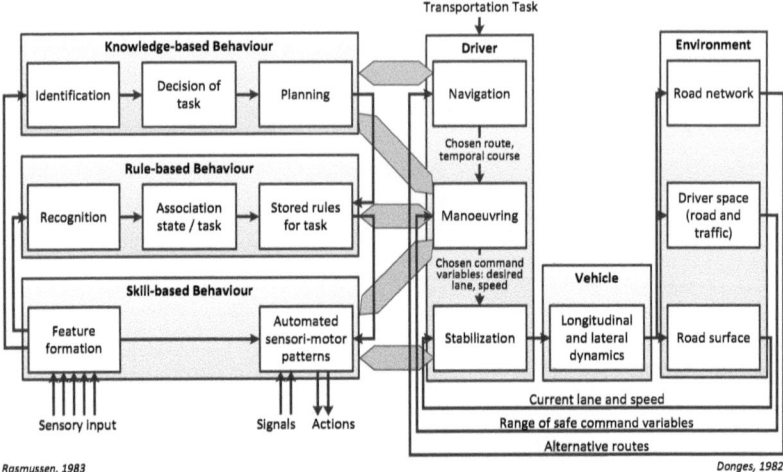

Figure 2.1: The 3-Level-models from Rasmussen [132] and Donges [43] related to each other (translated and redrawn from [44]).

Rule-based Rule-based behaviour can be described by an "if-then-relation". In a certain traffic situation (e.g. overtaking a slower vehicle) the driver retrieves stored behavioural patterns as formerly experienced in similar situations that have been successfully solved. Those patterns can only be applied, **if** the appropriate conditions are met (e.g. no oncoming vehicle in the opposite lane, no vehicle overtaking from behind). **Then** the appropriate procedures are selected and executed (e.g. check mirrors, set indicator, accelerate, pass).

Knowledge-based In situations where no known rules can be applied, an action must be consciously chosen. Often there are a number of alternative options to choose from and to weigh against each other. On this level the highest mental activity is necessary. The execution, however, is usually a sequence of rules applied to this unknown situation.

A descriptive example for Rasmussen's model is driving in a country where the traffic drives on the opposite road side with a car having the steering wheel on the other side as usual. Then skills and rules can often be not applied anymore and driving takes place on the knowledge-based level. Even experienced drivers must then carefully think about every action, e.g. what lane to take after turning. The models of Donges [43] and Rasmussen [132] are closely related, so that they can be condensed into one. Fig. 2.1

shows the relation of the two models.

The perception of the driving scene and the extraction of relevant information is a crucial point in all presented models. The primary perception channel hereby is undoubtedly the visual channel [23]. Through the visual channel, information about the position, velocity and heading direction of the ego as well as other road users can be perceived which is most important for safe driving. Table 2.1 shows an overview of the most relevant variables [162]. Accordingly, Rockwell [138, 150] attributes 90% of all perceived information during driving to the visual channel. However, multimodal information presentation, in particular in case of warnings, has been shown to be superior to single modal information (e.g. [151]).

Information	Visual	Acoustical	Tactile	Vestibular
Lane deviation	x			
Longitudinal velocity	x	x		
Lateral velocity	x	(x)		
Longitudinal and lateral acceleration			x	x
Heading angle	x			
Yaw rate	x			
Yaw acceleration				x
Pitch angle	x			x
Steering angle	x		x	
Actuation forces			x	
Road noise		x		

Table 2.1: Driving-related information as perceived by human sensory channels (translated from [162]). The visual channel is clearly dominant.

2.1.2 Information Processing

Cherry [30] has found that people were not able to repeat two acoustical messages simultaneously presented one on each ear. They had to direct their attention deliberately to one message and ignore the other. In Broadbent's **Filter Theory** [18] the human perception apparatus is assumed to be a central general-purpose single-channel processor with limited capacity that cannot cope with information exceeding this capacity. After perceiving and storing multiple information in short term memory preattentively, the information is selectively filtered by physical features (e.g. brightness, volume, etc.), so that only one information is passed to processing. Strictly speaking, this means information not passing the filter cannot be processed, which means that "attention controls perception" [89], p. 6. This process is shown in Fig. 2.2, A [89]. Treisman could show that this is not valid in all cases and proposed the **Filter Attenuation Theory** [166]. In contrast to the filter theory, filtered information is not completely blocked but attenuated, and can also be processed if the identification threshold is low enough, e.g. one's name spoken in a mixture of conversations ('cocktail party effect') [88]. Deutsch and Deutsch assume no filtering during perception, but locate the processing bottleneck at **Late Selection** [40], cf. Fig. 2.2, B.

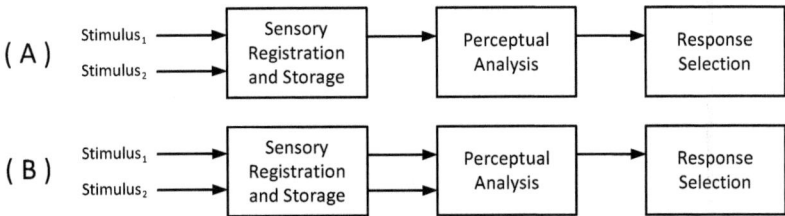

Figure 2.2: Selective attention. A: The bottleneck occurs before perceptual analysis. B: The bottleneck occurs after perceptual analysis (from [89], redrawn).

Later models abandoned the single-channel theories in favour of capacity- and resource-oriented approaches [2]. Kahneman states that "One of the classic dilemmas of psychology concerns the division of attention among concurrent streams of mental activity" [89], p. 5. He sees attention as a single pool of limited capacity that can be allocated to different tasks selectively, depending on task requirements or intentional assignment [89]. Later, Norman introduced the term "resource" for human mental capacity [119].

The dependencies of resources required by two simultaneously performed tasks can be displayed with **Performance Operating Characteristics** (POC) [172]. These graphs show how two tasks that can be accomplished independently to 100%, influence the performance in the respective other. If the tasks require concurrent resources, a performance increase of one task results in a performance decrease of the other task (cf. Fig. 2.3).

Based on the resource approach, one of the most known resource models was developed by Wickens in the **Multiple Resource Model** (MRM) [172]. In his theory, he describes a separation of mental processes in terms of several independent resources. These resources are subdivided in three different dimensions. It is assumed that perception processes access separate resources than information processing and reaction processes (temporal dimension). The information is encoded (verbal or spatial information) and is perceived

2.1 Background on Cognitive Science

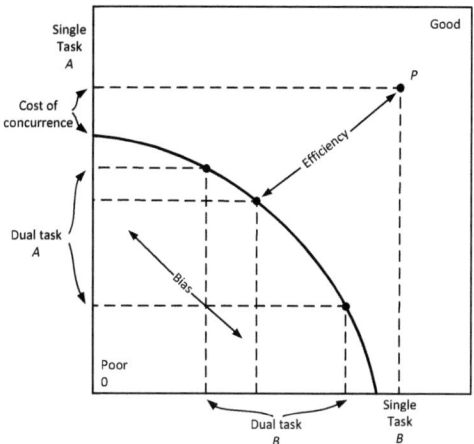

Figure 2.3: Performance Operating Characteristics (POC) showing two tasks performed simultaneously and the cost of concurrence (redrawn from [172]).

through a sensory channel (visually or auditory):

- Temporal stages: Encoding → Central Processing → Responding
- Code: verbal / spatial
- Modality: visual / auditory

Wickens depicts the three dimensions as a cube (cf. Fig. 2.4). Actually there is another dimension, the response, which maps onto the code dimension (verbal → vocal / spatial → manual response). If two tasks access the same resources (i.e rectangles on the cube), a potential conflict occurs. So, "interference will be greater when two tasks demand processing by a single resource rather than distributing their demands across resources" [175], p. 3. Consequently, the performance in these tasks will decrease. To put it another way, the more two task access separate resources, (1) time-sharing between tasks will be more efficient, (2) task difficulty will have less effect, and (3) the POC will take a box-like shape [172]. A reasonable point of criticism at the MRM is that modality is reduced to visual and auditory information. In particular during driving valuable information about the environment can also be perceived through the haptic channel via the steering wheel, the pedals or the seat as well as the vestibular channel. Nonetheless, Wickens' model is central in this work and will also be referred to in 2.1.3 and 3.1.3.

The human information processing mechanism can be summarised using Wickens'

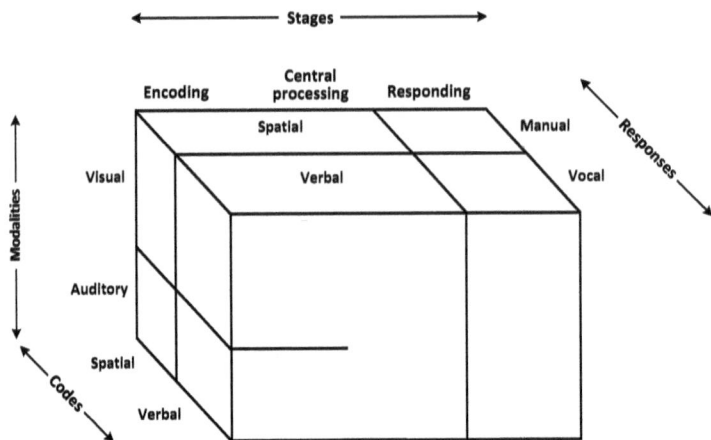

Figure 2.4: Wickens' multiple resource model (MRM), showing the different dimensions. Performance in multiple tasks is typically better when the tasks use different input-output modes (redrawn from [172]).

model for human information processing and memory that integrates components and processes [172], cf. Fig. 2.5. Stimuli enter through a short-term sensory store, are processed and passed on to the working memory (= short-term memory). A complex interaction with the long-term memory allows an interpretation and the selection of a response to the stimuli. The previously mentioned attentional resources influence the quality of perception, processing and consequently, the response.

2.1.3 Secondary Tasks and Driver Distraction

For a long time, research investigating the influence of secondary tasks during driving focused on the use of cell phones, since this was the first widespread secondary activity in cars before the existence of driver in-vehicle information systems (IVIS) or new in-vehicle technologies (IVT). IVIS comprise all technically supported forms of information (traffic, navigation, etc.), entertainment (music, TV, etc.), communication (telephone, e-mail, etc.) and comfort. Usually, IVIS are operated by a centrally mounted control element, an array of buttons or via touchscreen. Moreover, many cars provide interfaces for nomadic devices like smart phones or mp3-players for passengers to bring their own content into their cars and consume it via the in-car displays or audio system.

Lansdown et al. [95] showed that the operation of secondary tasks while driving always leads to a performance decrease in the driving task and to a higher perceived

2.1 Background on Cognitive Science

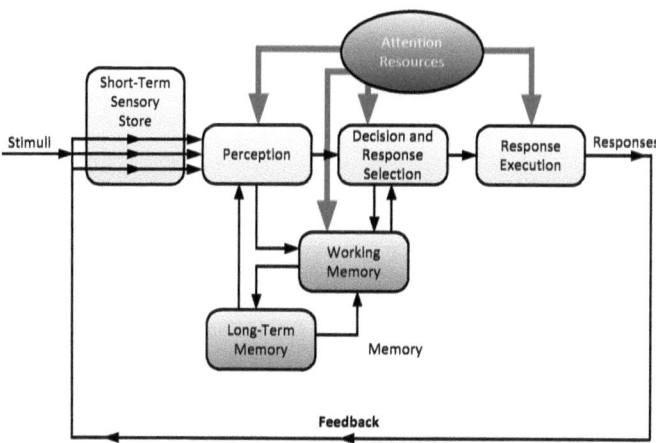

Figure 2.5: Human information processing loop (redrawn from [172]).

workload. Cognitive interference changes driving behaviour in different aspects of vehicle control [78]. Young et al. present a comprehensive literature review on driver distraction [182]. As mentioned, there are plenty of studies regarding the impact of cell phone use on driving performance. The following section can only name few exemplary works.

Hancock conducted a lot of experiments in this field (e.g. [70]), investigating how the operation of a mobile phone influences reaction times, braking distance and driving accuracy. The handling of a mobile phone while driving increased response times up to 30% and led to 15% worse driving accuracy. Interestingly, the braking distance did not increase despite a later reaction. Assumingly the participants were aware of the distraction and braked harder when they recognised the need of an action. Salvucci et al. [139] found consistent results in their study comparing different ways of dialling a phone number while driving. Manual dialling resulted in the worst performance compared to voice, menu and speed dialling. Since the hand-held use of mobile phones is not permitted in many countries in the world because of the potential distraction, later research concentrated on mental distraction imposed by speaking on the phone while driving. Cooper et al. observed that drivers conversing on a hands-free phone had lower mean velocity, made fewer lane changes and were more likely to remain behind a slower vehicle [32]. Iqbal et al. assessed the interference of cognitive load of conversational dialogue with driving scenarios differing in difficulty [82]. They found that both driving performance and conversation performance (response time to call, information recall, quality of speech) suffered from the dual-task situation, in particular in complex driving scenarios.

Popken et al. investigated drivers' reliance on a lane keeping system with different degrees of automation [131] in a dual-task driving simulator setup. They did not introduce automation errors, but confronted the test subjects with situations that exceeded the system's functional scope. They could show that in a critical situation drivers were able to shift their attention away from the secondary towards the primary task.

Very general investigations about "The Role of Driver Distraction in Traffic Crashes" have been conducted by Stutts et al. in the course of same-titled project funded by the AAA Foundation for Traffic Safety [159]. They assessed the coherence between driver distraction and road accidents based on around 17,500 police reports. They did not only consider distractions imposed by IVIS, but also by co-driver or eating and drinking while driving. They found a remarkable low number of accidents where the driver was distracted (8.3%). When distracted, almost 30% of the drivers named a cause from outside the vehicle, and 1.5% distraction through cell phone use. Since those numbers are based on the testimony of the drivers themselves, it is very likely that the majority did not admit the actual cause of the accident out of self-protection. This makes it difficult to obtain reliable numbers.

To be fair, one must mention that drivers do usually not engage in secondary tasks without respect to the surrounding traffic situation. They are normally well aware of the distraction imposed by side activities and wait for a adequate point of time when initiating secondary actions. During an ongoing activity, drivers usually apply certain strategies to compensate for this. It has been shown that during a conversion on the phone drivers reduce their speed and increase the distance to the vehicle ahead (e.g. [156]).

There are efforts to support drivers with managing their workload during driving regarding secondary tasks. This has been done most notably in the AIDE [1] project (Adaptive Integrated Driver-vehicle InterfacE). In difficult traffic situations incoming phone calls have been delayed until the situations were resolved.

---

[1] http://www.aide-eu.org

2.1 Background on Cognitive Science

Common Methodologies for Driver Distraction Assessment

Primary Task Methods

Lane Change Task In the ADAM project (Advanced Driver Attention Metrics), the influence of performing secondary tasks on driving performance were assessed and appropriate measurement techniques were evaluated. A new evaluation methodology was developed, the **Lane Change Task** (LCT), a standardised simulated driving task involving exact lane keeping and lane change manoeuvres [106]. The LCT is the basis for the work presented in chapter 4. More details on the LCT are presented in section 3.2.2.

Peripheral Detection Task Another common methodology is the Peripheral Detection Task (PDT) [105]. In a simulated driving task or a video image of a real driving scene five coloured dots are randomly displayed on a horizontal line at positions $-23°$, $-11.5°$, $0°$, $11.5°$ and $23°$. One dot is visible for 2.0 seconds and must be acknowledged by pressing a button on the steering wheel or a separate key pad. The current workload is derived from the reaction time until a displayed dot is acknowledged. With high workload, test subjects are likely to miss dots displayed in their peripheral field of view, a phenomenon called **visual tunneling** (e.g. [84]).

Secondary Task Methods

Surrogate Reference Task Because of the diversity and variety of potential secondary tasks, another methodology was developed in the course of the ADAM project. The Surrogate Reference Task (SuRT) is a visual search task, in which test subjects must identify the position of a target on a display. The display shows a varying number of circles (distractors) and one target which is also a circle but with a different diameter. Test subjects must indicate if the target is positioned on the left or on the right side of the screen.

Critical Tracking Task In contrast to the easily interruptible SuRT, the Critical Tracking Task (CTT) is very hard to interrupt. The CTT has been reported the first time by Jex [86] and consists of a display and a control element. On the display, a vertically moving bar is shown that must be kept as close as possible in the centre of the screen using a joystick or a key pad. The further away the bar gets from the centre, the faster it moves towards the edge. So permanent visual attention and control is necessary.

How to Design IVIS

One of the most important goals in designing IVIS is to keep distraction as low as possible. Several international authorities have published guidelines, recommendations and "best practices" how design, installation, display, interaction, behaviour and documentation of IVIS is to be implemented in order to achieve this goal. The University of Michigan Transportation Research Institute (UMTRI) has compiled an overview[2] on the major telematics guidelines. Most notably the European Statement of Principles (ESOP) of the European Commission [31], the guidelines of the Alliance of Automobile Manufacturers[3] (AAM) [1] and Japan Automobile Manufacturers Association[4] (JAMA) [85] should be mentioned. All guidelines focus on clear and well-readable information presentation, easy and interruptible interaction, predictable behaviour and the non-entertaining character. In short, any impairment of the driving task must be avoided. A comprehensive overview of the existing documents is given in [136].

There is a lot of research work on the distribution of information inside vehicles and where to present what and how much information, so we can only name a few exemplary works here. Horrey and Wickens [79] examined different types of displays with varying locations and forms of presentations, and found that attention to head-down displays (HDDs) resulted in the longest response times as compared to all other conditions. Nowakowski et al. tried to reduce driver distraction by a head-up display (HUD) while answering a cell phone call and found the HUD an effective means [120]. Also Milicic dedicated her work to HUDs, investigating in what way different kinds of information can be presented and operated in the HUD [110]. More general work on multiple displays is presented by Grudin [65]. We did some work on search-based approaches known from the Desktop or the Internet incorporated as an in-car search engine [62] in order to avoid visual distraction. Handwritten characters via touchpad clearly generated faster operation times and less distraction than input with a traditional control element, since this method allows for blind interaction.

2.2 The Basics on Automation

The following section describes the basic terms of automation in general, and of automated driving in particular. We present established taxonomies, application areas and implications of automation.

---

[2] http://www.umich.edu/~driving/safety/guidelines.html
[3] http://www.autoalliance.org/
[4] http://jama.org/

2.2.1 Definitions

First we want to stipulate a common understanding of the meaning of *automation*. In this step we do not yet aim at *automotive automation*, but at automation in a very general sense. Since automation is principally an abstract term, there is a number of established definitions, often with slightly different emphasis:

- Definition of automation in the Oxford English Dictionary: "Automatic control of a manufacturing or other process through a number of successive stages; the use of automatic devices to save mental and manual labour; the introduction of automatic methods or equipment" [21].

- Parasuraman et al. understand by automation "the execution by a machine agent (usually a computer) of a function that was previously carried out by a human" [125], p. 2.

- Moray et al. see automation as "any sensing, detection, information processing, decision-making, or control action that could be performed by humans but is actually performed by machine" [112], p. 1.

- Billings refers to "a system or method in which many of the processes of production are automatically performed or controlled by self-operating machines", [11], p. 14. He additionally emphasises the human-centred aspect: "automation [is] designed to work cooperatively with human operators in the pursuit of stated objectives", [11], p. 14.

The human-centred aspect of automation is central in this work. Automation must be designed to work with humans interacting, because "to engineer the automation and expect the human to accommodate to it can be a recipe for disaster" [148], p. 6.

2.2.2 Taxonomies of Human-Centred Automation

Automation and non-automation is usually not binary, there is a spectrum between *automated* and *manual* execution of a task specifying the degree to which a task can be automated. In 1978 Sheridan et al. have been the first to present a taxonomy of *Levels of Automation* (LOAs). The main application in mind at that time was the automation of aircraft control. They used a human-centred feedback-oriented approach, i.e. they determined the LOAs according to how far the automated system keeps the human operator in the feedback loop. The taxonomy comprises ten levels from (1) complete manual operation to (10) complete automation, with the term "computer" being synonymous for "automated system" [149] (cited in [50]):

1. Human does the whole job up to the point of turning it over to the computer to implement.
2. Computer helps by determining the options.
3. Computer helps to determine options and suggests one, which human need not follow.
4. Computer selects action and human may or may not do it.
5. Computer selects action and implements it if human approves.
6. Computer selects action, informs human in plenty of time to stop it.
7. Computer does whole job and necessarily tells human what it did.
8. Computer does whole job and tells human what it did only if human explicitly asks.
9. Computer does whole job and decides what the human should be told.
10. Computer does the whole job if it decides it should be done, and if so, tells human, if it decides that the human should be told.

Below level five, humans are responsible for decision making and above level seven the computer is. Between levels five and seven there is genuine collaboration between human and computer at the price of considerable mental or computational workload. In aircrafts and nuclear power plants some operational or control functions already are at level seven [112]. This is also true for unmanned aircraft systems (UAS, also called "drones"). Mainly for military purposes UAS are able to surveil, reconnoitre, transport, or even attack highly autonomously[5].

Endsley focused on the use of expert systems (also with respect to aircraft cockpit automation) designed to supplement human decision making and developed a LOA hierarchy with condensed automation forms [48]:

- **Manual Control** with no assistance from the system.
- **Decision Support** by the operator with input in the form of recommendations provided by the system.
- **Consensual Artificial Intelligence** (AI) by the system with the consent of the operator required to carry out actions.

---
[5]http://www-rucker.army.mil/usaace/uas/US%20Army%20UAS%20RoadMap%202010%202035.pdf

2.2 The Basics on Automation

- **Monitored AI** by the system to be automatically implemented unless vetoed by the operator.
- **Full Automation** with no operator interaction.

Several years later Endsley et al. [50] refined their taxonomy and presented a 10-level hierarchy with the intent to apply to air traffic control [173], piloting of aircrafts, advanced manufacturing and teleoperations. Most notably they introduced four generic functions (also called *roles*) intrinsic to each LOA: *monitoring* (obtain system status by accessing available information), *generating* (gathering possible options or strategies for achieving a formulated goal), *selecting* (deciding on a particular option or strategy), and *implementing* (executing the selected option). Table 2.2 shows the LOAs with respect to the mentioned functions and who fulfils the function on the corresponding level, human (H) or automation/computer (C) [50].

	Level of Automation	Roles			
		Monitoring	Generating	Selecting	Implementing
1	Manual Control (MC)	H	H	H	H
2	Action Support (AS)	H / C	H	H	H / C
3	Batch Processing (BP)	H / C	H	H	C
4	Shared Control (SHC)	H / C	H / C	H	H / C
5	Decision Support (DS)	H / C	H / C	H	C
6	Blended Decision Making (BDM)	H / C	H / C	H / C	C
7	Rigid System (RS)	H / C	C	H	C
8	Automated Decision Making (ADM)	H / C	H / C	C	C
9	Supervisory Control (SC)	H / C	C	C	C
10	Full Automation (FA)	C	C	C	C

Table 2.2: Endsley's hierarchy of levels of automation with intrinsic functions [50] (H = Human, C = Computer).

A very similar approach has been presented by Parasuraman et al. [126]. They based their taxonomy on the mentioned model of Sheridan et al. [149] and added four phases that have to be run through on each level. The phases follow the common stages of human information processing: *Perception, Analysis, Decision Making* and *Execution*. These stages basically match Endsley's intrinsic functions [50].

Also referring to the automated control of aircrafts, Billings shows a series of levels categorised by the degree of direct or immediate involvement of the pilot (cf. Fig. 2.6, [11], p. 15). He displays a control and management continuum as a graph with

24   2. Background and Related Work

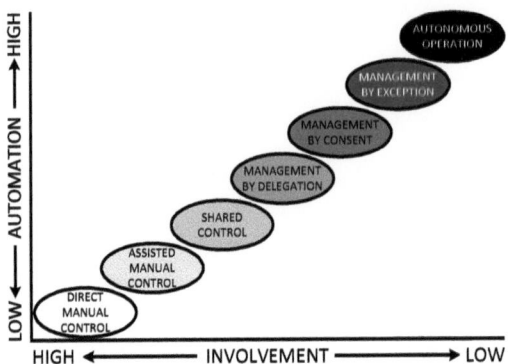

Figure 2.6: Pilot control and management continuum (from [11], redrawn.)

automation as one axis and involvement with the control task as another.

A transition-based approach is proposed by Flemisch with the so-called *H-Mode* based on the *H-Metaphor* (Horse-Metaphor) [55]. He describes a control-sharing-relationship between rider and horse as a metaphor for human-automation interaction, already targeting vehicle automation. A horse as an intelligent animal is capable of making reasonable decisions of its own, it doesn't walk against walls, for instance, because it is aware of the consequences (pain, injury). Together with a rider the control is shared. The horse can be ridden with tight reins (more human control) or loose reins (more horse control). This concept applied to human-automation interaction means a seamless transition between stages of higher and lower automation (cf. Fig. 2.7, top), that can be applied in a parallel or serial manner [67]. In particular, it allows for separate automation levels of longitudinal and lateral control, which is often not the case with previously mentioned approaches. Since this metaphor is not trivial to implement with current control elements in cars (pedals, steering wheel), as a first step, the seamlessly varying control concept has been mapped to active control sticks as they are used in aviation. Eckstein was the first to show how a car can be driven by active side sticks [45]. Kienle et al. implemented the concept of the H-Mode also by using an active side stick [91], cf. Fig. 2.7, bottom. The transition between higher and lower levels of automation can be seamlessly controlled by grasping the side stick firmer or looser with one's hand [35]. Yet, there haven't been promising approaches involving a standard steering wheel so far.

A higher level of automation is not more desirable per se. Automation should not

2.2 The Basics on Automation

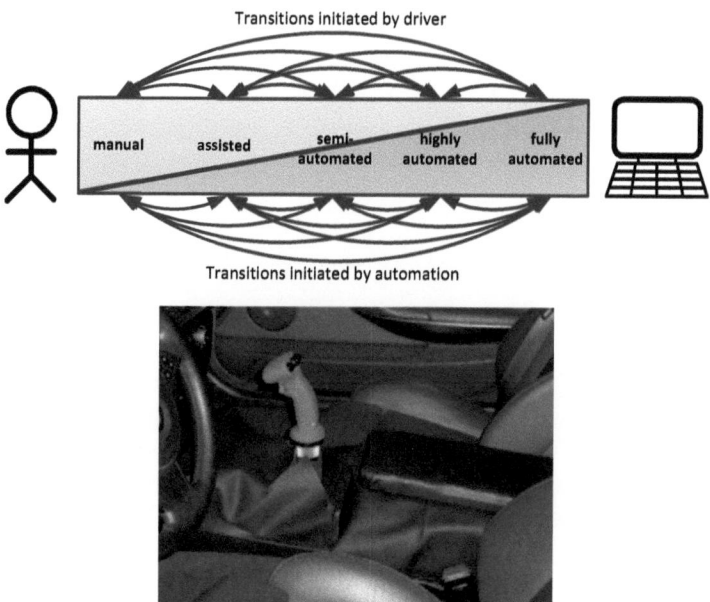

Figure 2.7: Top: H-Mode automation spectrum and seamless transitions between different LOAs (translated from [55], redrawn). Bottom: Mockup car augmented with active side stick (from [91]).

be used for the sake of automation. Fitts argues in favour of intelligent sharing of control by the MABA-MABA principle (*men are best at - machines are best at*) ([53], cited in [75]), so a task should be done by the more suitable part. However, a higher level of automation does always imply higher technization and higher technical complexity necessary to provide the desired functionality. This again means higher costs and efforts for development and testing of automated systems.

Note: We will use Flemisch's taxonomy of automation in the course of this work, since it is compact and well apt for describing automated driving. However, when we speak of automated or highly automated driving, we imply automated longitudinal control and automated lane keeping, and also automated manoeuvres, if not stated otherwise.

2.2.3 Application Areas and Benefits of Automation

Automation in a modern sense is often attributed to the developments that took place in the age of industrialization beginning in the 18th century. With the emergence of factories, human labour has been increasingly replaced by (at that time) huge mechanical machines, capable to do work faster and more efficiently. Today we have automation in almost every part of our lives, e.g. industrial production, power plants, exploitation of natural resources, maintenance, quality control, computer software generation and tests, medical care, home automation, etc., to name but a few. Moreover, another very important field is transportation:

- In the last century, a lot of effort has gone into **aviation** automation. This comprises the aircraft on the one hand and air traffic flow management (ATFM, e.g. runway allocation) from the ground on the other hand. The first automated systems in aircrafts were stabiliser systems (e.g. stall avoidance). Autopilots became available in the 1930/1940's, coupled navigation in the 1950's, automatic landing in the 1970's (cf. [11]). Latest developments with airplane automation go that far that even the co-pilot is considered not necessary anymore [165].

- Also in **ships** many tasks have been automated. Modern ships make use of automatic route following, aids for position fixing, collision avoidance, etc., as well as non-manoeuvring systems as automatic data logging, cargo planning, maintenance diagnostic, etc. (cf. [97]).

- Automated **trains** find their primary application in driver-less underground transportation. In Europe there are several underground lines in operation without a train driver, e.g. in Paris, Lyon, Lille (France), Turin (Italy) and since 2008 in Nuremberg, Germany, developed in the RUBIN project[6]. While the French and Italian driver-less trains operate on a separate part of the underground, in Nuremberg all trains share the same network with regularly driven trains.

- **Vehicle** automation targets the automated or autonomous driving of vehicles, in particular cars.

The reasons for automation are numerous. Wickens and Holland [174] name four categories why a task may be automated:

- there are inherent limitations why humans cannot perform the task,

- humans may be able to perform the task, but their performance is poor or involves high workload,

---
[6]http://www.rubin-nuernberg.de/

2.2 The Basics on Automation

- human performance can be improved by augmentation or assistance through automation,

- it is more economical for a machine to perform the task.

These categories can be summarised again: *Facilitation* and *efficiency* are the two primary benefits that are to be achieved by transferring tasks, formerly performed by humans, to machines. Humans shall be relieved from hard, strenuous, dangerous or monotonous manual work. Machines are often able to perform routine tasks many times faster than humans, and often with a more uniform, reliable and qualitatively better output. For enterprises, replacing humans by machines often means saving expenses by rationalising workplaces.

These benefits can be specifically applied to the domain of automotive automation. The main motivations for automation in vehicles are *safety* and *comfort* aspects. The major share of accidents is caused by human failure [137]. Automatic control systems can contribute to reduce the risk of accidents by driver inattention or driving errors, because these systems are able to react significantly faster and more accurately than a human driver. Thus, driving becomes safer for all traffic participants. Although giving up manual control can affect driving pleasure, letting a system take over control in monotonous and unpleasant driving situations (e.g. stop-and-go traffic) is a tempting thought [93]. In stressful control tasks automated systems can substantially contribute to reducing stress [99, 184], and can outweigh the hedonic quality of manual driving [174]. Moreover, with perfectly working automation without the need to supervise, the driver could potentially use the time in the car for relaxing, entertainment or even work.

Through automated vehicles, the efficiency of the whole traffic could be increased [3]. In theory, by automation of all vehicles it would be possible to minimise the space between vehicles and maximise the speed, and thus increase the overall road capacity and throughput of vehicles by time. Through better usage of road space and predictability of vehicle behaviour traffic congestions can be avoided or, if already existing, quickly resolved. According to Goldbole et al. more than 50% of traffic congestions are due to adverse driving behaviour (fatigue, inattentiveness or aggressiveness), rather than insufficient road capacity [59]. Enhanced traffic flow can lead to more predictable trip times [99] and reduce fuel consumption by decreasing necessary braking/accelerating actions which therefore has a positive effect on the environment. So automated vehicles could also have a significant impact on *economy* and *efficiency* of the whole road traffic system. Of course, those reflections contradict traditional traffic safety policies, that postulate a reduction of speed and traffic density and an increase of safety margins between vehicles (cf. [47]).

2.2.4 From Driver Assistance to Automation

Section 2.2.2 explained different levels of automation in a very general sense. In this section we want to apply these concepts specifically to the automotive domain. Automation that is present in cars already today, found its way into the automobile via driver assistance systems. These systems, integrated with the vehicle, support the driver particularly in safety-critical situations, and provide comfort functions as well and relief the driver from routine tasks (cf. [41]). As opposed to driver information systems, driver assistance systems are able and designed to intervene actively with the control of the vehicle. Complex and sophisticated assistance systems are usually called **advanced driver assistance systems** (ADAS). ADAS are defined by all of the following characteristics [33], p. 4:

- ADAS support the driver in the primary driving task
- ADAS provide active support for lateral and/or longitudinal control with or without warnings
- ADAS detect and evaluate the vehicle environment
- ADAS use complex signal processing
- direct interaction between the driver and the system

The mapping of existing driver assistance systems onto the described levels of automation (cf. 2.2.2) is not entirely possible. Most driver assistance systems act only in very specific situations, e.g. warning against a certain danger (e.g. forward collision). Only a few are performing a permanent control task (e.g. cruise control). Therefore, in the automotive domain, the taxonomies choose a more use-case-related approach for expressing the degree of intervention with the driving task. Usually we distinguish between five degrees of assistance (cf. e.g. [115]):

- **Information**: The system presents the driver additional, uninterpreted information (e.g. current position on a map).

- **Recommendation**: Presenting information to the driver suggesting an action (e.g. low temperature information or speed limit information implying to adapt speed if too fast).

- **Warning**: Signals the driver an immediate action is strongly advised in order to avoid a potentially dangerous situation or collision (e.g. lane departure, forward collision warning).

2.2 The Basics on Automation

- **Active intervention**: The system proactively intervenes in a safety-critical situation with the vehicle control (e.g. steering to support lane keeping, braking to avoid forward collision).

- **Automated control**: Long-term activity of the system, it takes over a part of the driving task completely (e.g. ACC longitudinal control).

Primary driving task	Driver Assistance System	Degree of Assistance
Stabilisation	Anti-lock Braking System (ABS)	Active intervention
	Traction Control System	Active intervention
	Electronic Stability Program (ESP)	Active intervention
Manoeuvring	Speed Limit Information	Information / Recommendation
	Cruise Control	Automated control
	Adaptive Cruise Control (ACC)	Automated control
	Forward Collision Warning (FCW) / Forward Collision Avoidance (FCA)	Warning / Active intervention
	Lane Departure Warning	Warning
	Lane Keeping Assist / Support	Warning / Active intervention
	Park Distance Control (PDC)	Information / Warning
	Park Manoeuvre Assist (PMA)	Automated control
	Night Vision System	Information / Warning
Navigation	Navigation System	Information / Recommendation
	Traffic Message Channel (TMC)	Information / Recommendation

Table 2.3: Selection of common driver assistance systems currently available in modern cars and the provided degree of assistance.

Table 2.3 shows an overview of common driver assistance systems currently available in modern cars together with their corresponding degree of assistance (also cf. [68]). All degrees but automated control become active selectively and short-term. In Flemisch's definition (cf. Fig. 2.7, left) degree 1–4 would be subsumed as *assisted*. Only with permanent control for a longer period of time (degree 5) it is legitimate to speak of automated driving. Usually only a part of the driving task is automated (longitudinal or lateral control), which is then described as *semi-automated* driving. Combined longitudinal and lateral control (speed and heading) is *highly-automated*. *Fully automated* is synonymous to *autonomous driving* including all parts of the driving task (stabilisation, manoeuvring and navigation) are completely taken over by automation (cf. 2.2.2). To fulfil this, a car must be able to drive to a pre-set destination using unmodified infrastructure. The paradigm of Conduct-by-Wire [178] automates stabilisation and manoeuvring. The driver issues a manoeuvre request and the automated system performs it. Automated driving involves necessarily the control of the vehicle's movement. Although there are many automated functions inside the car (automatic windscreen wipers, adaptive headlights, automatically closing the hood of a convertible car in case of rain, etc.), the term 'automated driving' requires locomotion.

It is important to mention that automated driving cannot be seen without constraints. Even if driving (semi-/highly) automatically, the driver still has the responsibility for his vehicle. This has been stipulated in the **Vienna Convention on Road Traffic**[7], a UN treaty signed 1968 in Vienna in order to standardise traffic rules. The Vienna Convention (VC) states in Article 8, paragraph 5:

> "Every driver shall at all times be able to control his vehicle or to guide his animals."

This is further specified in Article 13, paragraph 1:

> "Every driver of a vehicle shall in all circumstances have his vehicle under control so as to be able to exercise due and proper care and to be at all times in a position to perform all manoeuvres required of him."

Based on today's legal situation in most countries in the world as stated in the VC, complete automated driving without involving the driver at all would therefore not be permissible on a large scale. The crucial question is, who is responsible in case of an accident: the driver, the car, the car manufacturer, the sensor manufacturer, the programmer? The VC clearly identifies the driver still as the single responsible instance. But there are already efforts undertaken to bring the probably outdated phrasing in the VC up to date for future forms of driving.

2.2.5 Research Programmes on Automated Vehicles

There is a number of notable research projects targeting fully automated driving. An overview of worldwide activities until 2005 is presented by Bishop [12].

- The project **PROMETHEUS** (PROgraMme for a European Traffic of Highest Efficiency and Unprecedented Safety) running from 1987 to 1995 within the frame of the research initiative EUREKA was the pioneer project on driverless cars [16].

---
[7]http://live.unece.org/fileadmin/DAM/trans/conventn/Conv_road_traffic_EN.pdf

2.2 The Basics on Automation

They demonstrated autonomous driving on regular roads solely based on computer vision. As a remarkable milestone, in 1994 they drove more than 1,000 km at a maximum speed of 130 km/h on a three-lane highway near Paris including lane changes and passing of other cars. In 1995 Ernst Dickmanns and his team at the Bundeswehr University of Munich had their autonomous vehicle drive the 1,000 km from Munich to Copenhagen, Denmark, and back in regular traffic and at a maximum speed of 180 km/h [42]. For safety reasons, a driver was in the car to intervene if necessary, which was the case in construction sites or other unclear traffic situations.

- **PATH**[8] (Partners for Advanced Transit and Highways), founded in 1986, has been established by the Institute of Transportation Studies of the University of California, Berkeley, in order to tackle California road traffic problems. They make use of the Automated Highway System (AHS) with magnetised steel spikes integrated with the road surface as positioning aid for automated vehicles. They realised a number of advanced functions most notably car, bus and truck platooning. A number of automatically controlled vehicles drove behind each other with few meters distance, in order to maximise road capacity and minimise congestion (cf. 2.2.3, [59]). Moreover, they demonstrated collision warning, automated bus lane change and docking, lane merge, smart parking, crosswalk and intersection assistance, etc. Truck platooning activities have also been addressed in the German project **KONVOI** [94].

Figure 2.8: Car platooning using the Automated Highway System (from [93]).

- In 2002 the DARPA (Defense Advanced Research Projects Agency), a technology

---
[8]http://www.path.berkeley.edu/

agency of the US Department of Defense, originated a competition called **DARPA Grand Challenge**[9]. Driverless vehicles had to autonomously navigate and reach a destination 150 miles away in the Mojave desert, USA. The first Grand Challenge took place in 2004, where none of the started vehicles reached the destination. 2005 five of 23 participating teams could finish the challenge, the fastest vehicle in a time of less than seven hours. The last competition so far was the **Urban Challenge** in 2007. The setting had been changed from a desert to an urban area, an abandoned Air Force base. The autonomous cars had to navigate through a given 60-mile course following traffic regulations and without hitting obstacles or other (also manned) vehicles. Six teams were able to accomplish this task within the time limit of six hours [29].

- A different application field of automated driving is taken by the **TrackTrainer**, developed by BMW in 2006 [169]. The TrackTrainer is a system designed to support drivers in finding the ideal line on a race track and is used in BMW's driver training programme. The system works in three phases: first, the car drives the previously recorded ideal line on the track autonomously. The driver behind the steering wheel memorises the driven path and tries to follow it as closely as possible in the next round when driving manually. This is supported using a feedback mechanism that indicates the deviation from the ideal line. After the drive, the driver can analyse the recorded data offline, compare the manual driven path to the ideal line and discover potential improvements.

- The European **HAVEit**[10] (Highly Automated Vehicles for Intelligent Transport) project was launched in 2008. A consortium of automobile manufacturers, first tier suppliers and universities develop a virtual co-system supporting the driver in order to drive safe, energy-efficient and comfortable. The relevant use cases are automated merging into traffic flow, automated queue assistance, temporary autopilot, and active green (energy-efficient) driving.

- In 2010, Alberto Broggi and his group from the Vislab, University of Parma, Italy, originated the **Vislab Intercontinental Autonomous Challenge**[11], the longest distance driven autonomously by then. Their automated vehicle followed a leading car along 13,000 km from Parma in Italy to Shanghai in China from July to October. The vehicle was electrically powered and equipped with an array of cameras, laser scanners and solar panels. Broggi is also known for his activities in

---

[9]http://www.darpa.mil/grandchallenge/
[10]http://www.haveit-eu.org/
[11]http://viac.vislab.it/

the earlier **ARGO**[12] project (1996-2001), where the ARGO autonomous car drove 2,000 km automatically within one week, only equipped with two black/white cameras [10, 19, 20].

- In the project **Stadtpilot** of the Technical University of Braunschweig, Germany, an intelligent vehicle called 'Leonie' has been shown to drive autonomously in an urban environment in dense traffic [177]. Based on experience gained in the mentioned DARPA challenge, Leonie was enabled to drive on Braunschweig's Inner Ring Road by itself.

Also the US internet company Google engages in developing autonomously driving cars, supposedly out of interest in challenges in artificial intelligence[13]. General Motors presented the **EN_V**[14] in 2010, an electricity-powered drive-by-wire concept vehicle for two passengers, able to operate autonomously.

The named projects mainly deal with the technical realisation of automated driving, the interaction with the driver in case of automation errors has not yet been addressed sufficiently. Despite all those and many more activities in the area of automated driving research, there is still a long way to go, until safe autonomous door-to-door transportation in an arbitrary environment can be reached.

2.3 Implications of Human-Automation Interaction

This section discusses potential risks and pitfalls of human-automation interaction. It is important to understand that perfectly working automation that works exactly as supposed to and never fails or misinterprets a situation is not the source of problems with automation that is discussed below. We assume **imperfect automation** that will not act all the time objectively correctly. Very similar to human information processing (cf. Fig. 2.5), automated control systems also *sense*, *interpret* and *act*, which is called a **closed control loop** (cf. Fig. 2.9).

Unfortunately, each of those steps is subject to potential errors. Sensory measurements of the environment can be noisy, inaccurate or even incorrect. This can lead to performing an inappropriate action or not performing an appropriate action. As a technical system consisting of hardware and software, it is probably not possible to

---
[12] http://www.argo.ce.unipr.it/ARGO/english/
[13] http://www.nytimes.com/2010/10/10/science/10google.html
[14] http://media.gm.com/content/media/us/en/news/news_detail.html/content/Pages/news/us/en/2010/Mar/0324_env

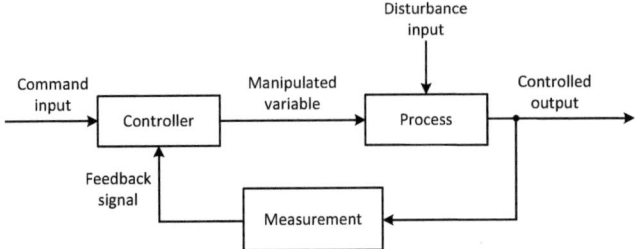

Figure 2.9: A closed control loop consisting of the controller (act), processor (interpret) and measurement device (sense). Redrawn from [61].

guarantee 100% perfection. Sensor measurement errors, actuation failure, undefined system states, hardware defects, incorrect or outdated digital maps, locating inaccuracies, etc. can be minimised at most, but not entirely avoided. We use the term *automation failure* for any incorrect system behaviour in consequence of any errors occurring in the information processing chain.

Delegating a previously manually executed task to an automated system changes the role of the operator and the nature of work from active control to passive **supervisory control** [125]. The operator is no longer part of the control loop, is **out-of-the-loop**, but monitors the actions executed by automation. If the automated control does not work as supposed to, the operator must take over control and correct the automated system. Nearly all automation involves humans supervising [125, 144, 148]. This shift of roles can lead to a number of risks, manifesting itself in lower operation performance. Many authors have documented those out-of-the-loop performance problems (e.g. [11, 172, 176]). Endsley and Kiris identified the **loss of situational awareness** of the state and processes of the system as one of the major issues associated with automation [51]. Situational Awareness (SA) means "the perception of elements in the environment within a volume of time and space, the comprehension of their meaning, and the projection of their status in the future" ([51], p. 2). This particularly involves the perception, understanding and anticipation of system state variables. Degraded to a passive observer, the situational awareness of the operator is likely to decrease due to (1) insufficient supervision, (2) a change of feedback type, (3) insufficient automation transparency, and (4) complexity [104]. With correctly working automation this is not too problematic. But it can be as soon as manual intervention becomes necessary and when the operator does not possess a complete mental model of the situation and does not know the state of the system. With those fears in mind the expected reduction of

2.3 Implications of Human-Automation Interaction 35

workload can be foiled. Billings refers to observations that automation may decrease workload when it is already on comparatively low level, and that workload may increase by automation when it is high anyway [11].

Another potential problem with automation is the **loss of manual skills**. With a task automated, motor or cognitive skills are likely to deteriorate through the lack of continuous manual training *(deskilling)*. At the same time, the operator is expected to take over control in case of automation failure and be able to perform the task perfectly to the full extent. Wiener and Curry report the fear of aircraft personnel to lose their skills through extensive use of automation and to be inefficient and inaccurate in case of need [176]. Applied to automated driving, the use of automated longitudinal or lateral control systems over a long time may lead to potentially inaccurate control actions in the first moments, when the control is taken over by the driver. However, theories say that the better the operator mentally reproduces the actions executed by the supervised automated system, the lower is the effect of deskilling [104].

The most decisive factor in human-automation interaction congruently is the **trust in the automation**. Trust is tightly tied to the *reliability* of an automated system. A system that often fails will lead to less trust than a system that very rarely fails. Parasuraman and Riley [125] describe the influence of attitude towards automation in terms of different *uses*. Low trust in automation will probably lead to underutilization of an automation system *(disuse)*. In contrast to that, overreliance on the automation can lead to less supervision *(misuse)*. Using an automated system for a different purpose than it was built for is *abuse*.

Errors resulting from inappropriate reliance on automation can be expressed in two types of errors: following an incorrect decision directive of an automated system is called **commission error**, whereas not noticing a problem that is also not detected by an automated system is an **omission error**, cf. [77, 113]). To be precise, the error is always made by the human by relying on the imperfect automated system. In this work, we will use the terms commission and omission errors more liberally also for the description of the errors made by automation itself (cf. chapter 4).

The establishment of trust in an automated system is mainly influenced by frequency, characteristics and comprehensibility of automation failure [104]. If it is obvious to the operator, why the automation failed in a certain situation, the operator rather accepts it, which thus does not necessarily lead to a decrease of automation trust. However, if a system frequently fails without the cause becoming apparent, the trust in this system is very likely to be low. Acceptance of automation failure also depends on the usefulness of the system. Whereas underreliance on automated systems (and therefore more manual work) only misses the desired effects of workload reduction and increase of efficiency, overreliance (also referred to as *complacency*, cf. [37, 112]) can result in serious safety issues. Complacency usually involves an insufficient supervision behaviour which potentially results in overlooking an automation failure. Oakley et al. point out an inverse relationship between reliability and detection rate of automation failures [121]. The more performant, reliable and "better" the automation, the more undesired effects like overreliance and complacency are likely to occur. Ironically, the better the automation (still less than 100% reliable), i.e. the less likely an automation failure, the less likely an automation failure will be noticed [5]. In other words, automation will fail, when it is most needed [118]. Wiener and Curry state that "the question is no longer whether one or another function can be automated, but, rather, whether it should be, due to the various human factor questions that are raised" [176], p. 1. So, human error follows automation error [117, 135].

Repeatedly there are reports on aircraft pilots so confiding in their autopilot system that they neglect their monitoring duties [114]. Deviating hundreds of miles off course and even not noticing warning messages from air traffic control [163, 164], the impact of inappropriate automation trust becomes clear. Disregarding supervision can also result from a **lack of vigilance**. "Vigilance refers to the ability of organisms to maintain their focus of attention and to remain alert to stimuli over prolonged periods of time" ([171], p. 1, from [36]). A lack of stimuli in a task can lead to monotony and boredom [63], and eventually to fatigue [39]. In order to avoid hypovigilance, tasks must be activating. Yerkes and Dodson were the first to describe the relationship between arousal (or activation) and performance [181]. According to their theory, performance increases with arousal, but only to a certain point. With even more arousal, performance decreases again. This relationship can be depicted in an inverted parabola (cf. Fig. 2.10). Galley [57] takes the view that there is not a single optimal point where performance is best, but there is a broader range of good performance, if the arousal level is not too low and not too high. They agree that too low activation (monotony, fatigue) and too high activation (stress, overload) affect performance negatively.

Wiener and Curry [176] come to a similar relationship (cf. Fig. 2.11) and point out the independence of automation control and monitoring functions. They also locate fatigue at the other end of the scale, resulting from long-term high workload.

2.3 Implications of Human-Automation Interaction   37

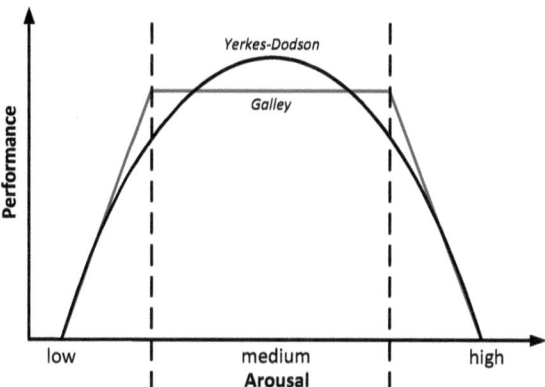

Figure 2.10: Relationship between arousal and performance. Graphs according to Yerkes and Dodson [181] and Galley [57].

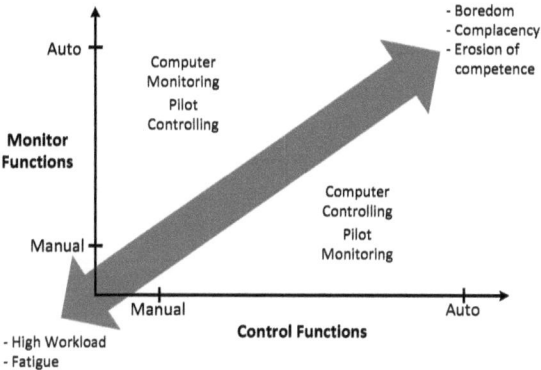

Figure 2.11: Relationship between control and monitoring functions and the corresponding implications for the human operator (redrawn from [176]).

There seems to be consensus in the whole research community that the level of automation should be intermediate, in order to mitigate side effects. In the context of automated driving, Hancock et al. argue in favour of a driver-in-the-loop architecture, that should be flexible enough to match the wide range of abilities and skills of drivers [69]. But even in a shared control setting, perhaps with dynamically changing LOAs, confusion over authority, i.e. who is responsible for what, is likely to happen [147]. Sheridan and Parasuraman [145] propose a formalised methodology based on expected-value analysis in order to decide whether a human or the machine is most suitable for responding to failures. Another issue potentially resulting from shared control with changing levels of control is **mode confusion** [140, 141]. Due to a lack of **mode awareness**, the operator is not clearly aware of the system mode and the tasks this mode implies for him to execute, or the operator assumes the system to be in a different mode it actually is. This problem could also be shown by Petermann [129] in an experiment with changing automation modes in an automated driving scenario.

Norman sees the main source of many problems with automation in inappropriate feedback rather than over-automation [118]. However, Woods warns against *clumsy* automation, that prompts the human operator with system feedback during a high workload situation [179]. Gao et al. promote the sharing of automation- related information, which may improve reliance and promote the cooperation between human and machine. Also the sharing of reliance information based on the current context could contribute to a working human-automation interaction [4].

2.4 Summary

This section presented an introduction to basic principles, terms and theories relevant to this work. It is important to know the different dimensions of the driving task and the processing of information, in order to be able to understand the issues automated driving implies. Automation and the ramifications on humans is a topic that has been researched on for decades, with a clear focus on aviation as the main application area with actually deployed and productively working systems in place. But automated driving is only just becoming a concrete research field, since technological advances make it appear more than a distant vision.

More related work specifically targeting the solutions that have been developed and evaluated in this work, is presented in chapter 3.

Chapter 3

Methodology and Procedure

This chapter describes the methodological basis for the central parts of this thesis based on the research questions stated in 1.2. We present the procedure, relevant related work as basis for specific decisions and an argumentation for the chosen solutions that were implemented and assessed in chapters 4 and 5.

In section 3.1 we establish a formal categorisation of secondary in-car tasks in terms of different dimensions. Thus we are able to identify precisely what kind of tasks have a measurable effect. From this categorisation a certain collection of tasks has been derived, which was used in all studies presented in this work. Chapter 3.2 describes the process of deriving an adequate methodology to assess the recognition of errors made by an automated vehicle control system. In section 3.3 we discuss the next logical step after measuring error recognition, namely how the recognition of automation errors can be supported. In this respect, one specific measure – a prospective display of the future driving path – has been identified as the most promising approach. Parts of this chapter have been published in [153, 154] and parts have also been described in a diploma thesis prepared by Marion Mangold under the supervision of the author [103].

3.1 Formal Categorisation of Secondary In-car Tasks

For a meaningful assessment of secondary tasks and their influence on automation error recognition there is the necessity to find a formal categorisation. Since testing every single possible task is neither reasonable nor feasible, we reduce the magnitude of all tasks to a group of representatives. Those stand for certain qualities common to all tasks included within a category. Furthermore, similar tasks that only differ in one specific aspect can thus be directly compared. So the categorisation will serve mainly as a basis for the selection of tasks in the upcoming studies. In order to find appropriate categories, we proceed as follows.

- First, we consider previous approaches. During the ADAM project, different tasks have been tested and assessed for their influence on driving performance. We take their tasks as a starting point (3.1.1).

- The next step towards a general, comprehensive categorisation of secondary tasks is the estimation of workload and demands imposed by those tasks. We have conducted a Delphi study with the focus on tasks performed during manual driving and report on its results (3.1.2).

- Based on the previous steps and related work we create an abstract secondary task categorisation (3.1.3).

- This categorisation is used in the studies in chapters 4 and 5 in the form of specific tasks that have been derived from it.

3.1.1 Secondary Task Analysis in ADAM

The **ADAM** (Advanced Driver Attention Metrics, 2001 – 2004) project [17] was originated with the goals to assess driver distraction due to secondary tasks and to verify the guidelines on *Driver Interactions with In-vehicle Information and Communication Systems* drafted by the European Commission in 2000 [31]. In the course of the cooperative project with Daimler-Chrysler and BMW a number of simple assessment methods were developed and evaluated, including the Lane Change Task (cf. 3.2.2).

They chose tasks that cover a wide range of (assumed) task difficulty, represent the control of in-vehicle systems, but also other activities people do while driving, and impose visual, auditory, motoric, and cognitive demand [17]. Table 3.1 shows the final selection of tasks. A classification scheme was established in terms of different demands: visual, visual-motoric, auditory, verbal, motoric left hand, motoric right hand, central processing and memory.

All the named tasks have been evaluated in studies using different methods. Mattes used a newly developed method, the Lane Change Task (cf. 2.1.3, 3.2.2), for evaluation [106]. In the telephone task (TT) the test subjects showed the best dual-task performance, taking coins out of a purse (CO) resulted in the worst performance [106]. Bengler et al. found widely consistent results and a clear main effect of secondary tasks in a driving simulator study analysing the same task set which was mainly caused by

3.1 Formal Categorisation of Secondary In-car Tasks

Category	Name	Abbr.	Task
Integrated System "CARIN"	Radio tuning	RT	Set radio to a certain frequency
	Sound adjustment	SA	Set treble to maximum
	Change Cassette	CC	Change audio cassette and put in case
	Navigation speller	NS	Enter street name with rotary push button
	Navigation map	NM	Set target cross of navigation system to a certain point on map
Other Tasks	Cell phone	CP	Enter 4-digit PIN in cellular phone
	Sweets	SW	Unwrap a sweet and put it into the ashtray
	Talk on telephone	TT	Answer some simple questions in hands free mode
	Kleenex	KX	Unfold a Kleenex and put it onto passenger seat
	Address Book	AB	Lookup phone number in small paper address book
	Map book	MB	Open map book on page X and decide which of two towns Y and Z is further North
	Coins	CO	Get a 20 and a 10 Cent-coin out of a purse, close the purse and place it back onto the passenger seat

Table 3.1: Secondary tasks selection used in the ADAM project (from [17]).

manual or manual/visual tasks [7]. However, a real-life field trial which again comprises the tasks listed above could not reproduce these results with the chosen metrics [46]. Yet it could be shown that the test subjects increased their minimum headway when engaging in a secondary task.

3.1.2 Delphi Study on Secondary Task Demands

Since the ADAM tasks do not capture adequately enough the contemporary driver needs and partially covers obsolete tasks (e.g. change cassette), we decided to conduct a study judging task demands by a standardised scale for subjective workload estimation. As an evaluation procedure we decided to use the **Delphi** method (cf. [76, 101]) that is known for its decisive character. Delphi studies comprise two survey rounds. In the first round, the participants fill out a questionnaire containing questions concerning the object of study. In the second round, the participants have to answer the same questions, but only those that did not produce an unambiguous result. Additionally, they are shown the aggregated results of the first round. Thus, they are able to rethink their answer to each question and either confirm or thoughtfully revise it.

In our study, we had a sample of 19 participants familiar with in-car interaction involving secondary tasks. We had 13 male and six female test subjects with an average age of 29.47 years ($SD = 4.94$). We created a digital questionnaire with 21 tasks that the participants are to perform during an imaginary, relaxed drive on the motorway. We adopted some of the ADAM tasks, and also added some more. Consistent to the selection in the ADAM project, we chose tasks that are likely to occur while driving, but only those that use in-car technology, e.g. a navigation system. The participants had detailed instructions how to perform each task. An example of a used question is shown in Appendix Fig. A.1, the complete list of tasks is shown in Table 3.2.

1	Destination entry controller	12	Destination entry controller - complex
2	Destination entry speech	13	Activate rear window heating
3	Find target on digital map	14	Climate control
4	Adjust bass settings	15	Watch TV
5	Select mp3 with controller	16	Calculation task
6	Volume control steering wheel	17	Insert CD
7	Select phonebook contact	18	Read e-mail
8	Talk on the phone	19	Texting on mobile phone
9	Volume control	20	Select contact from mobile phone
10	Radio tuning	21	Select mp3 on iPod
11	Adjust bass settings - complex		

Table 3.2: List of tasks rating in the Delphi study.

For each task they had to give a rating regarding the demands imposed by this task. As a rating scale we used the approved **Driver Activity Load Index** (DALI, [128], [127]) that has been derived from the more general workload questionnaire NASA-TLX (**Task Load Index**, [74]). The NASA-TLX follows the assumption that workload is influenced by mental demand, physical demand, temporal demand, performance, frustration level and effort. The DALI assesses seven dimensions of subjective workload during a dual-activity setup (cf. [87]):

1. *Effort of attention*: Attention required by the activity (think about, decide, choose, look for...)

3.1 Formal Categorisation of Secondary In-car Tasks

2. *Visual demand*: Attention of the visual channel required for the activity

3. *Auditory demand*: Attention of the auditory channel required for the activity

4. *Tactile demand*: Attention of the tactile channel required for the activity

5. *Temporal demand*: Specific constraint due to timing demand when running the activity

6. *Interference*: Possible disturbance when performing the driving activity simultaneously with another task

7. *Situational stress*: Level of constraints while conducting the activity, such as fatigue, irritation, discouragement, feeling of overload, etc.

The global attention demand results from $\frac{\sum_{n=1}^{7} d_i \times 20}{7}$ with $d \in \{0,...,5\}$, which means that all dimensions d are rated on a $0 - 5$ scale. For the Delphi study we adapted the DALI range to $1 - 5$ in order to obtain a balanced scale. The DALI score translates to demand, so a lower rating indicated less demand and is therefore a better result.

Results Texting on a mobile phone resulted in highest cumulated mean score ($M = 2.30$), adjusting the volume on the steering wheel in the lowest ($M = .61$, cf. Fig. 3.1). The highest attentional demand was imposed by the mental calculation task (M=3.58) and the lowest by manual volume control ($M = .53$). Watching TV resulted in the highest estimated visual demand ($M = 3.58$), talking on the phone in the lowest ($M = .32$). The TV task was also judged as the task with the most interference with the driving task ($M = 3.42$), adjusting the volume on the steering wheel with the lowest ($M = .47$).

3.1.3 Final Task Categorisation

For a final categorisation we took the previously reported work into account. Wickens' model of multiple resources ([172], as described in 2.1.2) turned out to be most helpful. Wickens categorises the available resources into modality (visual and auditory information) and encoding (verbal and spatial). Also in ADAM tasks were judged by visual and auditory information. For supervising an automated control system, mainly visual resources are needed. In case of a secondary task also requiring visual resources, the resource conflict will cause interference resulting in a performance decrease in the primary task [151]. Verbal information can be conveyed in writing or orally, whereas spatial information in our definition means information that requires visual thinking and the capacity of thinking in two or three dimensions, independent from a vocal or manual

3. Methodology and Procedure

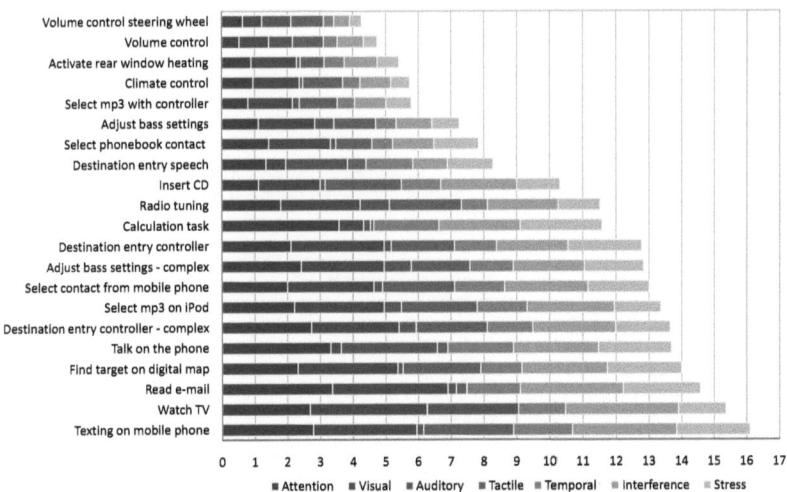

Figure 3.1: Mean results of the final Delphi rating comprising the DALI dimensions for each of the 21 tasks (standard deviation not displayed).

response.

We adopted Wickens' resource dimensions **modality** and **information encoding** for the categorisation of arbitrary secondary tasks that are likely to be performed during driving in a car. We decided not to include 'haptic' or 'kinaesthetic' as modality dimension, because we could not find a common secondary in-car task that solely conveys information through a haptic or kinaesthetic channel. Since modality and information encoding did not suffice for a distinct categorisation, we included another dimension regarding the **degree of interaction** necessary to perform a task. Studies indicate that the degree of interaction plays an important role in driver distraction (e.g. [157]). ADAM additionally distinguished motoric and cognitive demand. Since our focus is on tasks that require technical means, and therefore could potentially be controlled by the car manufacturer, those demands often go hand in hand. So we decided to subsume these to *active* and *passive* tasks. If an active engagement is necessary, such as operating a character input device or talking on the phone, we term this as an active task, whereas a task with a more consuming character, such as reading or listening, is categorised as passive. An active task can probably also be described as a task that induces high mental workload.

We also tried to account for guidelines issued by official authorities. As mentioned, the AAM for instance demands easy **interruptibility** of in-vehicle systems. This means that

3.1 Formal Categorisation of Secondary In-car Tasks

the perceived cost to interrupt and resume an ongoing task must be as low as possible. This includes visual processing, visual search, absence of external memory aids, temporal pressure, loss of coherence, and motivation [1]. The criterion of interruptibility was judged by a number of experts by the duration of a minimal subtask (operating action, written or spoken sentence, etc.). For instance, reading a news headline consisting of a few words is rated as better interruptible than reading a fully spelled sentence. The final categorisation scheme consists of the dimensions:

- **Modality**: visual – auditory,
- **Degree of Interaction**: active – passive,
- **Interruptibility**: good interruptibility – bad interruptibility,
- **Information Encoding**: verbal – spatial.

Out of consistency reasons, we chose a dichotomous (two-part) scale for each dimension, in particular for the degree of interaction and interruptibility, i.e. each dimension has only two extreme factor steps. It would have been easy to introduce more than the two levels in each dimension, but since the dimensions adopted from Wickens (modality and information encoding) only have two possible levels, we chose a dichotomous scale for all dimensions. According to our definition, the driving task can be categorised as follows:

- **Modality: Visual**. As mentioned in section 2.1.1, driving-related information is conveyed visually for the most part. Driving without the sense of hearing is probably less dangerous than driving without sight.

- **Degree of Interaction: Active**. The driver is actively in the control loop, must take care of stabilisation, manoeuvring, and navigation.

- **Interruptibility: Bad interruptibility**. Permanent action is necessary.

- **Information Encoding: Spatial**. The vehicle moves in a three-dimensional environment.

This is true for both manual and automated driving. Although automated driving may convey the impression of being a passive activity since stabilisation and manoeuvring is carried out by the automated system, with imperfect automation active and permanent supervising is necessary, and is therefore categorised as *active* and with *bad interruptibility*. So one of the two tasks simultaneously performed is always the driving task, respectively the task of supervising the automated driving system.

Category	Modality	Degree of Interaction	Interruptibility	Information encoding
1	visual	active	good	verbal
2	visual	active	good	spatial
3	visual	active	bad	verbal
4	visual	active	bad	spatial
5	visual	passive	good	verbal
6	visual	passive	good	spatial
7	visual	passive	bad	verbal
8	visual	passive	bad	spatial
9	auditory	active	good	verbal
10	auditory	active	bad	verbal
11	auditory	passive	good	verbal
12	auditory	passive	bad	verbal
Driving Task	visual	active	bad	spatial

Table 3.3: Categorisation of secondary tasks according to the dimensions modality, degree of interaction, interruptibility and information encoding.

Table 3.3 shows a number of exemplary side-tasks that are popular, likely or even designed to be performed during driving, sorted into the classification scheme by their corresponding dimensions. Secondary tasks demanding resources which interfere with the driving task are depicted with a dark background; complementary, i.e., non-overlapping resources are shown with a light background. We assume that the more interfering dimensions a secondary task covers, the more the error recognition performance will decrease. Categories 1 to 8 describe tasks that need visual attention. Category 1 covers a classic example, the input of a destination in an integrated navigation system, that can be described as [visual – active – good interruptibility – verbal]. Good interruptibility is a key demand for those systems (cf. [1]) that are to be operated while driving, even if it is explicitly not recommended for safety reasons, and they are explicitly designed as unambiguously interruptible. This category also covers a lot of similar tasks provided by an IVIS that requires the input of characters (search for contact in the phonebook, selection of mp3, etc.). Category 2 represents the same class of tasks, but uses spatial information encoding. In-car tasks with mainly spatial information conveyance are actually rare, examples are navigation hints and interactive maps, offering the user a paper-map-like option to select a destination directly by pointing at it on a

3.1 Formal Categorisation of Secondary In-car Tasks

schematic depiction of the target area. Not every category has an example task assigned (cf. category 3, 4 and 8), since in some cases there were no common in-car tasks covering the corresponding dimensions. Category 5 comprises well interruptible reading tasks, such as news headlines or short text messages, as opposed to category 7 that covers less interruptible reading tasks, e.g. a long news article. Tasks in the categories 9 to 12 use the auditory channel involving active speaking (speech commands, talking on the phone) or passive listening (music, news) that also comprise different interruptibility. Auditory tasks use only verbal information encoding.

3.1.4 Selection of Secondary Tasks for Experiments

An important step in the design of the user studies reported in this work is the final selection and implementation of specific tasks that the test subjects have to perform during the test runs. Despite the thoughtful categorisation, there is still a wide scope of potential tasks to be performed. As a basis for decision, we considered the tasks chosen in the ADAM project and the Delphi study. Yet, all those tasks have been judged in a manual driving context, so an adaptation is necessary for dealing with automated driving situations.

Interview on Drivers' Wishes during Automated Driving

Since there is a fundamental difference between manual and automated driving, we decided to conduct a brief interview ascertaining driver wishes for secondary tasks during an automated drive. We interviewed 33 drivers with an average age of 35.2 years ($SD = 7.13$). The participants were asked to project their thoughts into a situation in which they drive in heavy, slow traffic. They were told that they had a novel assistance system in their car that would be able to take over accelerating, braking and steering at low speeds. Set in this situation, the participants were asked to indicate how much they would like to perform certain tasks on a five-point Likert scale, from 1 (very much) to 5 (not at all). We deliberately chose tasks that could not be performed easily or were not allowed during a manual drive. Furthermore, as a reference item, we also included 'Listen to the radio'. We asked for their estimation on the following tasks:

- Watch TV
- Read online news articles
- Perform work tasks, e.g. read e-mails, manage appointments, etc.
- Listen to the radio (reference)

The reference item 'Listen to the radio' was rated as the most desired activity which drivers would perform during an automated drive, with 32 of 33 subjects choosing 1 or 2 ($M = 1.21$, $SD = .48$, cf. Fig. 3.2). The other items showed polarizing results. Whereas approximately half of the participants would like to do those tasks during an automated drive (answering with 1 or 2), the rest of the participants rejects such activities (answering with 4 or 5) or is undecided (answering with 3). 'TV' was named by 18 participants as desired activity ($M = 2.67$, $SD = 1.49$), 'News' by 22 ($M = 2.33$, $SD = 1.51$) and 'E-Mail' by 17 ($M = 2.88$, $SD = 1.47$). These results were taken into account for the final selection of tasks to be implemented and used in the studies presented in chapter 4 and 5.

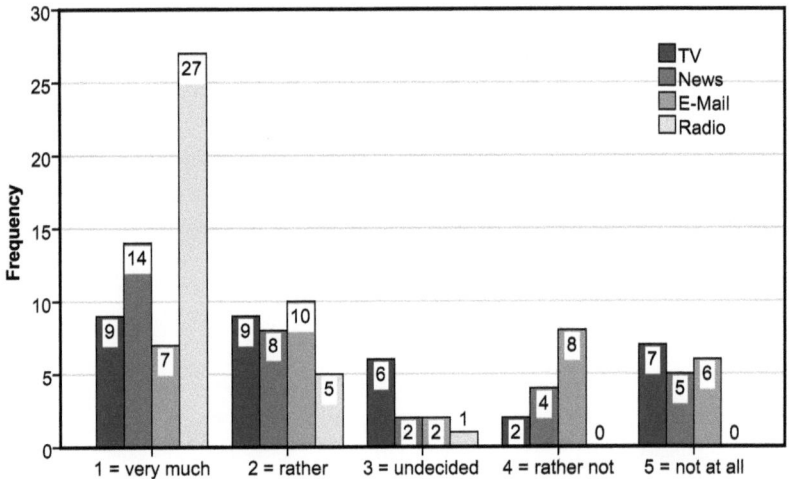

Figure 3.2: Results from the survey on desired tasks during automated driving.

Final Task Decision

The final decision comprised six tasks: Entering a destination into the navigation system (**navigation**), finding a target on an interactive map (**interactive map**), reading short lines of text (**short text**), reading long paragraphs of text (**long text**), having a conversation on the phone (**phone call**), listening to an audio book (**audio book**).

Our goal was to select tasks that are common, likely to be performed during an automated drive, and cover a broad range of the established categorisation, i.e. all tasks must be different from all others in at least one dimension (cf. Table 3.3). Furthermore, we follow the assumption that the tasks require technical means, so we restricted the

3.1 Formal Categorisation of Secondary In-car Tasks   49

choice to tasks that exist in modern in-car information systems or are likely to be available soon. Within the boundaries of the dimensions, we derived more abstract tasks (reading long and short pieces of text) from specific tasks (reading news, e-mails, SMS) and tried to make the tasks also interesting for the participants (audio book instead of random radio content). We also decided not to use surrogate or reference tasks, such as SuRT or CTT (cf. 2.1.3). The definition of the SuRT task was too artificial for our purpose. The CTT can be categorised as [visual – active – bad interruptibility – spatial] which has the maximum overlap with the driving task. This means that the CTT is most distracting, but it does not map onto a realistic in-car task that is performed during driving.

We excluded tasks that are legally not allowed. Even if some tasks were rated as demanding and explicitly desired, we decided not to include those tasks in our study. So we discarded all tasks involving interaction with handheld devices, since this is forbidden in many countries in the world. This is also true for watching TV while driving. If a TV or DVD function is available, car manufacturers must disable the video image when the vehicle is in motion. Video is also not unambiguously categorisable in our secondary task scheme, since it addresses the visual as well as the auditory channel. Moreover, in an informal pre-test we found that the video task is heavily dependent on the content and therefore interruptibility is not clearly classifiable. The response of the test subjects was very different when watching a narrative science show, a cartoon, and a boxing fight. The content variably claims attention and does naturally not respect the current demands of the driving respectively the supervision task. On these grounds, we did not select watching TV as a secondary task for our study.

Task Implementation

We briefly describe the characteristics, categorisation and implementation of each task chosen for an experimental setup:

Navigation (Category 1: *visual – active – good interruptibility – verbal*): Test persons have to enter a destination in a simulation of the BMW navigation system shown on a central information display and using a central input device (iDrive controller, cf. Fig. 3.4). One destination consists of city, street and house number. This is a very common task drivers perform in the car. Information in this task is presented visually and verbally, active input is necessary and the task can be interrupted at any time (cf. Fig. 3.3, left), which is also a clear demand of the AAM amongst others for built-in navigation devices (cf. 2.1.3).

Interactive map (Category 2: *visual – active – bad interruptibility – spatial*): A different way of entering a navigation destination is the interactive map. Destinations are not entered character-wise but via selecting a target city directly on a digital map. This function can also be found in many existing navigation systems in the market, although it is not as known as the traditional way. This task could be abstracted to an arbitrary x-y-positioning task which would probably also apply to browsing web pages. Using again the iDrive controller test persons can navigate on the map by tilting the controller in four cardinal directions which results the map to scroll up, down, left and right. Rotating the controller zooms the map. We implemented a simplified map of Germany as a destination source where we put 80 of the biggest German cities. The goal was to navigate a red rectangle placed in the centre of the screen over the given city on the map (cf. Fig. 3.3, right). On the lowest possible zoom stage only the names of the 16 Federal states and the locations of the cities were shown, but not their names. The names of the cities were only visible in the highest zoom stage. Thus continuous visual attention was necessary using spatial information encoding, as well as heavy controller activity.

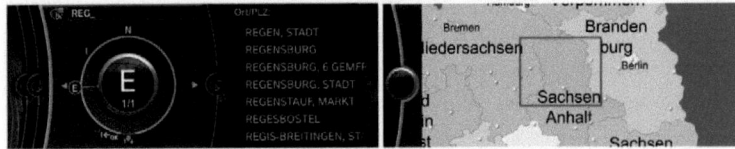

Figure 3.3: Left: Navigation destination entry; right: Interactive map.

Figure 3.4: BMW iDrive controller. Push, tilt and rotate a central knob, mounted in the centre console.

Short text (Category 5: *visual – passive – good interruptibility – verbal*): Another visual-verbal task was a reading task. Test persons had to (silently) read single lines of text from the central information display (cf. Fig. 4.6). In reality these short chunks of

3.1 Formal Categorisation of Secondary In-car Tasks

information can correspond to news headlines, traffic information, short messages, e-mail subject lines, etc., which are upcoming and therefore not unrealistic information use cases in cars. In order to ensure appropriate attention towards the secondary task, test persons had to answer questions about the content after the test run. The participants had to state if a certain item had been among the read lines. As content we used news headlines from the categories politics, economy, sports, entertainment, weather and traffic information. Test persons were able to self-control the presentation of the text lines by tilting the iDrive controller to the right. Although this requires activity, this task is categorised as passive because of the very low complexity of interaction. This task is easily interruptible.

Long text (Category 7: *visual – passive – bad interruptibility – verbal*): As contrast to the short text lines another task consisted of long, unstructured text reading. Text content was presented as a block-aligned paragraph without any line feeds, markup or other visual cues that facilitate reading. This task was again visually presented on the central display and required minimal activity using the iDrive controller to flip to next page of text (cf. Fig. 4.6, right)). After the test run participants had again to answer questions about the short story we used as content, which could also be the body of an e-mail or a news article. The long text task is categorised as hard to interrupt as it is much harder to interrupt than the short text task. Shifting gaze contact from the display towards the driving scene each time results in a search in the text for the last position or even makes it necessary to read the whole phrase over again.

Figure 3.5: Left: Short text reading task, single lines of text; right: long text reading task, unstructured block of text, crime short story.

Phone call (Category 10: *auditory – active – bad interruptibility – verbal*): Probably the most common and best researched secondary task in the car is talking on the phone (e.g. [32, 139, 157]). Surprisingly there is no established methodology for simulating a phone call in an experiment. Despite the legal restriction of hand-held phoning in the car in many countries, the critical factor is the cognitive distraction induced by the conversation itself. Phoning is an active verbal task with auditory information conveyance that is difficult to interrupt because of the character of speech. We realised the telephone task as a quiz game. Test persons were asked questions (medium difficulty) with four possible answer options which were only presented orally. They had to choose the answer and to explain why they chose this and why they did not choose the other options. They were also allowed to report from their personal experience. The main focus was on creating mental effort by establishing a real conversation with another person that is not present in the same location.

Audio book (Category 12: *auditory – passive – bad interruptibility – verbal*): As a passive, auditory task there is an audio book to listen to. This is also a common task drivers do in the car. After the run, the test persons had to answer content-related questions. During the drive, no interaction was required. We used a short crime story that matched the length of one test run. The test subjects could not interrupt the playing of the audio book. When mentally distracted from listening, the participants were likely to miss important parts of the story.

3.2 Towards an Assessment Methodology for Error Recognition in Automated Driving

3.2.1 Need for a Methodology

One of the main research questions we are pursuing in this work is how human error recognition can be assessed in the context of automated driving in a feasible, safe and cost-effective way. The challenge is to find an adequate representation of the situation of a failing automated vehicle control system on a real road with a real car in real traffic. The real situation itself is ineligible as a test method, because it is hard to establish reproducible experimental conditions, dangerous to the driver and the surrounding traffic, and expensive.

Currently there is no dedicated methodology known which provides appropriate means to do this or which has been particularly designed for this purpose. However, there have been made some approaches to explore the response of test subjects to failing (partially) automated systems. De Waard et al. [37] confronted test subjects in a driving simulator experiment during a drive with an Automated Highways System (AHS, cf. 2.2.5) with a single automation failure event (not braking to a closely merging vehicle) and observed their reaction. Half of the participants did not react at all. Flemisch et al. [54] explored in a driving simulation experiment different levels of automation using a driving stick. When driving with full automation and approaching a road bend, in the case of a sudden failure (indicated by an acoustical signal) none of the five participants

3.2 Towards an Assessment Methodology for Error Recognition in Automated Driving

was able to regain manual control before the vehicle left the road. It is not clear, however, how the participants were instructed before the test drive, if they were aware of possible failures and if they were busy with secondary tasks at the time of failure. In both works the recognition of automation errors is addressed. Yet, none had the focus on the design of a reproducible methodology, but only introduced a single failure event in a specific driving situation.

An interesting methodological approach of event detection is reported by Greenberg et al. [64]. During a manual drive also set in a simulated driving environment, the driver must detect outside events in the form of swerving vehicles in front or behind the driver. When detected, the driver must use the turn signals in the direction of the lane violation to indicate the recognition of the event. Popken et al. investigated drivers' reliance on a lane keeping system with different degrees of automation [131]. Gugerty and Falzetta [66] present a similar study based on Greenberg's work and extend possible events to swerving or deceleration, ahead, behind or on the oncoming lane. They state the event-detection measure would be superior to other techniques, for instance Endsley's SAGAT (Situation Awareness Global Assessment Technique, [49]), which blanks the simulated driving scene at some point and the test subject must answer scenario-related questions about the current situation before the simulation was stopped.

A more abstract method concerning automation supervision is presented by Buld et al. [26] in the form of a virtual ball sorting machine. The 'Ballomat' automatically sorts coloured circles into buckets with the same colour (cf. Fig. 3.6). If a ball is assigned incorrectly, one must intervene and put the ball manually in the correct bucket. The setting is PC-based and users interact via the cursor keys on a regular keyboard. The Ballomat represents a choice-reaction task that can also be combined with secondary tasks. During the project EMPHASIS the Ballomat was used to test different error rates, respectively reliability, and the corresponding reaction times. The authors showed that the lower the error rates, the longer the reaction times. They point out that 90% reliability produce the longest reaction times [26]. We will take this into consideration for the design of our methodology. Although combining automation supervision and event-detection, this approach is not suitable for testing failure in automated driving, because it does not reproduce adequately the overall situation of a moving vehicle in two dimensions.

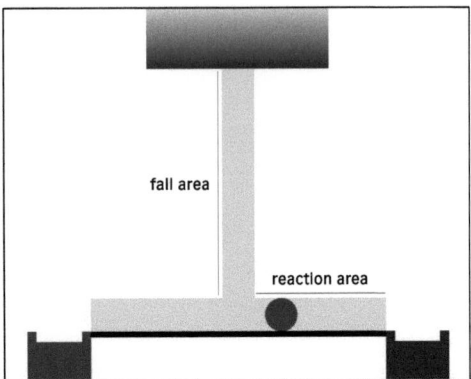

Figure 3.6: Ballomat. A neutral-coloured ball drops to the ground. The ball then is randomly shaded with red or blue colour and starts moving towards a bucket. If the colour of the ball and the bucket do not match, the user must intervene.

3.2.2 Lane Change Task as Methodological Basis

Learning from the described approaches, we decided to model the situation of automated driving in a way as realistic as possible and as abstract as necessary. As a basis for this, we used the Lane Change Task (LCT, also Lane Change Test, [106, 107]), which has recently completed the process of standardization by the ISO as a tool for driver distraction assessment (cf. section 2.1.3, [81]). The LCT is set in a clear, simplified, highly structured virtual driving environment with low complexity and is therefore very apt for eliminating possibly interfering influences. It has also been developed during the ADAM project. During a simulated driving task human performance degradation is measured. The LCT can be applied to various interaction forms with in-vehicle information, entertainment and communication systems that are operated while driving.

System Setup und Functionality

The original LCT setup consists of a standard desktop PC with a monitor and a gaming steering wheel attached to a table and foot pedals (cf. Fig. 3.7). The driving task is implemented as Microsoft Windows-based racing simulation.

Test subjects drive a virtual car at a constant speed of 60 km/h on a straight three-lane-track with a virtual lane width of 3.85 m and a total length of 3,000 m ($\hat{=}$ three minutes). Road signs along the track showing an arrow next to two X symbols indicate which lane the driver is supposed to change to. Signs are always visible; sign contents are invisible by default and become visible when the car is within a distance of 40 m. Only after the

3.2 Towards an Assessment Methodology for Error Recognition in Automated Driving

Figure 3.7: Lane Change Task. Left: Original setup with PC and gaming wheel (from [122]). Right: Virtual LCT driving scene.

sign contents have been revealed the driver is able to see the next supposed lane.

A change can be necessary from one lane to the next or across two lanes. Each possible change (e.g. lane 1 to lane 2, lane 3 to lane 1, etc.) occurs three times which results in 18 lanes changes in one run. The driver is instructed to change lanes as fast and as accurately as possible, as well as to keep the car in the lane between lane changes with the least possible deviation from the middle.

The ideal 'racing line' is based on a normative model that assumes a reaction time of 0.6 s after the sign symbols become visible as well as 0.6 s time for the lane change which means a way of 10 m at a speed of 60 km/h. According to this, the lane change should ideally be completed 20 m before passing the road signs (cf. Fig. 3.8). This is valid for a change across one and two lanes [122]. To achieve this, a thrustful steering wheel movement is necessary, which could be compared to an emergency turn when applied in a real car. If a sign is overlooked or incorrectly interpreted, the consequence is a massive deviation from the normative model.

The mean deviation (MDEV) of the manually driven path from this normative model is the main measurement of the LCT and is calculated as follows [81]:

$$MDEV = \bar{x}_{deviation} = \frac{1}{S} \sum \left(x_{deviation,i} \left(\frac{y_{i+1} - y_{i-1}}{2} \right) \right)$$

$$x_{deviation} = | x_{position,i} - x_{reference,i} |$$

with

$\bar{x}_{deviation}$ as the mean deviation between the normative model and the actual course,

$x_{deviation,i}$ as the lateral deviation at position i,

S as the length of the analysed segment,

y as the longitudinal position of the vehicle on the track,

$x_{position,i}$ as the current lateral position of the vehicle on the track,

$x_{reference,i}$ as the current lateral reference position on the normative model path.

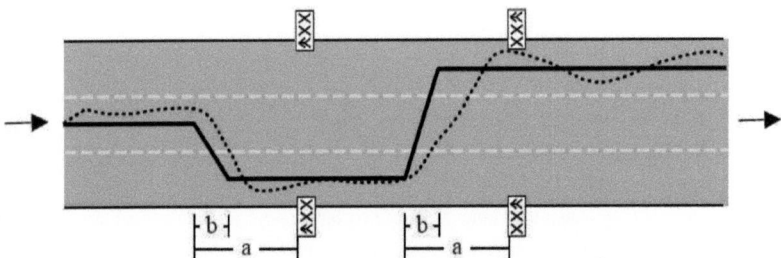

Figure 3.8: LCT normative path model (solid line), realistic manually driven path (dotted line), and sign distances. The lane change manoeuvre should ideally start 30 m (a) before passing the sign and completed within 10 m (b), regardless of a change across one or two lanes (from [122]).

The ISO document requires a baseline training phase prior to the actual test drive. As an acceptability criterion for the driving performance in the baseline condition, an MDEV value of less than 1.2 m using the basic model, or less than 0.7 m with an adaptive model is considered [81]. The adaptive model does not use a rigid reference path, but a trajectory adapted to each participant.

Discussion on the LCT

Since its initial deployment and undergoing ISO standardization, the LCT method has been widely used in a large number of studies assessing different driving conditions (e.g. [28, 52, 72, 73, 111, 167]). The measurement of the mean deviation from the normative model has proven sensitive regarding the execution of secondary activities simultaneously with the primary driving task [106]. It has been shown that the mean deviation from the normative model increases with the level of distraction imposed by the secondary task. However, the validity of this method is not undoubted and various aspects of it are sceptically discussed:

3.2 Towards an Assessment Methodology for Error Recognition in Automated Driving

- **Driving behaviour**: In order to achieve a good result, the gaming steering wheel needs to be turned very quickly to an angle of more than 100° in order to be able to follow the ideal course closely. This steering behaviour applied in reality would probably destabilise the car.

- **Training**: As mentioned, the LCT ISO standard stipulates training on the primary task [81]. It takes a lot of practise to get used to the steering wheel and the vehicle dynamics. It is often necessary to complete several practice runs until an acceptable performance is reached. This has the consequence that the baseline MDEV varies between .64 to 1.6 in different studies [130], and is therefore hardly comparable.

- **Metrics**: The MDEV obtained from the deviation from the normative model as the only metric is often criticised (e.g. [28, 72, 167]). Harbluk et al. state that it does not adequately allow for lengthy tasks [73]. They propose the inclusion of the mean deviation per task ($MDEV_{task}$) to better match the interaction demands of various navigation tasks. Furthermore, Harbluk et al. point out that the overall LCT performance depends to a great extent on the point of time when a lane change is initiated [72]. This can be delayed when performing secondary tasks. They propose the inclusion of the lane change initiation (LCI) metric as an event detection measurement, which incorporates the distance between the ideal and the actual point of lane change initiation. Vöhringer-Kuhnt points at the often insufficient power of discrimination between different experimental conditions of the MDEV [167]. He proposes the inclusion of a measurement of correlation that is more suitable to reveal differences between similar tasks.

- **Gender effects**: The ISO document does not require an LCT experiment to be balanced for gender. However, it appears that the measurement of the MDEV is subject to the gender of the test participants. Petzold et al. analysed the data obtained by three LCT experiments and found that male subjects consistently produced better MDEV results and better secondary task performance [130]. For comparability reasons they recommend the balancing of the test sample for gender when applying the LCT.

- **Environment**: The LCT can also be set in a driving simulation environment for better matching the ergonomic situation in a real car. Bruyas et al. show in a study that in the driving simulator the MDEV value is significantly smaller than in the original PC setup [22]. They ascribe this to a deeper feeling of immersion in a more realistic environment compared to the artificial PC setup.

Nonetheless, the LCT served as a technical and semantic basis for our intended laboratory methodology for error recognition assessment during automated driving. In chapter 4 the development of our method is described in detail.

3.3 Towards Driver Support for Error Recognition in Automated Driving

The second main research question is about how can the driver be supported when he/she is driving automatically and an automation error occurs, particularly in lateral control. The crucial point in this question is that a complete failure of an automated system is not the worst case, because there is a good chance that this can be detected and the driver can be warned and prompted to take over. The most difficult case is when the automation seemingly works fine, but actually does not perform as supposed to. For instance, erroneous sensor or camera data can lead an automated lane keeping system to believe that the vehicle is right on course, when it actually is not, which can result in unintentional lane departure. This is technically hard to detect and the driver cannot be warned. A warning system has to rely on the available information, but if this information is flawed, the warning will not be issued, even when necessary (cf. [113]).

So from an HCI point of view, it is crucial to support the driver in the supervision of an automated control system and make it easier for the driver to detect malfunctions and erroneous behaviour that is not detected by the system itself.

3.3.1 Related Work

On the one hand, supporting the driver in detecting incorrect automation behaviour can be achieved in various ways, on the other hand, it is not clear how effective potential countermeasures are. Regarding this topic, there is little published related work available. For automated systems in general, Parasuraman et al. suggest the integration of elements within a display to an emergent feature in order to reduce the attentional demands of fault detection [124]. This idea is taken up in chapter 5. In a manual driving context, Lee names a few general techniques how to direct the driver's attention back to the road when distracted, such as sharing information with the driver on gaze time away from the road or gadget usage [96]. Coughlin et al. propose to provide feedback to the driver about his state in the form of an illuminated orb [34]. The colour of the orb displays ambiently the driver's current state (health, attention, etc.) and changes if his state changes. These approaches do not allow for automated driving, and are therefore not directly helpful. In

3.3 Towards Driver Support for Error Recognition in Automated Driving

trains for example, there is a safety mechanism, the so-called dead man's switch. If not pushed regularly, an alarm is set off and the brakes apply automatically. This is done to make sure that the human operator is still able to control the train. Variations of this mechanism are also used in power plants, machines, air planes, etc.

3.3.2 Discussion of Potential Support Measures

In several workshops with HCI experts we gathered and discussed a large number of measures that could be used to support the recognition of automation error by means of HCI. Below we present a selection of the discussed approaches and a common judgement by assumed effectiveness, acceptance and feasibility.

One of the simplest, but probably most effective measures, is for the driver to **keep the hands on the steering wheel**. Even with automated longitudinal and lateral control, with no immediate necessity to have the hands on the steering wheel, the haptic feedback from the road through the steering wheel can provide helpful information about the vehicle dynamics and therefore a better connection to the driving task (cf. [27]). Some internal studies have been conducted which indicate high effectiveness of this measure. Even with the eyes off the road, the driver is still aware of his or her situation in a moving vehicle on the road. So the supporting role of this measure is achieved by the maintaining of driving-related feedback. Driver acceptance is questionable, though, since a potential gain of comfort might be lost if the driver cannot take the hands from the steering wheel. However, we require "hands-on driving" in all user studies presented in this work.

Another potential measure related to the one named above is the provision of **vestibular feedback**, i.e. addressing the vestibular organ by deliberately changing speed or direction to a noticeable extent. Of course, this is only possible on a very small scale in real traffic and driver acceptance is doubtful. Moreover, sudden acceleration, braking or steering without relation to outside events can be counter-productive and might be interpreted as a system malfunction.

Targeting the engagement in secondary tasks during automated driving, in particular visually distracting tasks presented on an in-car display, discussions about deliberately directing the driver's attention arose. In order to avoid unintentional distraction, in-car displays showing secondary task content could be turned off by default when driving automatically. **Only when a button is pushed**, the display is turned on as long as the driver presses the button down. When the button is released, the display is turned off again. Thus it is always known to the control systems in the car when the driver is likely to watch the display. It is questionable, though, if such a system design is acceptable to the driver.

Based on Lee's proposal to take **operation actions and gaze behaviour** into account [96], there are a number of options to react to driver gaze and input behaviour. In order to motivate the driver to check the road frequently, displays could be accessible only for a limited amount of time. After a while of watching the display, or after a certain time of input operation, it could be turned off or, in a more ambient way, subtly reduced in quality. It is likely that such measures will not find broad acceptance, since they all patronise the driver. Moreover, eye tracking systems inside the car create significant technical expenditure. It is questionable if forcing the driver to look back to the road at certain intervals is really efficient and would contribute to detect automation errors.

With the eyes already from the road, would it be possible to bring the road to where the eyes are? This could be achieved by a **video image of the driving scene** permanently visible in a splitscreen-view or displayed repeatedly in certain intervals could contribute to an increased situation awareness by having the driving scene at least in the peripheral field of view even when the eyes are not on the road (cf. Fig. 3.9). However, this bears the risk of drivers relying on the camera image alone and watching the road and the automated control systems even less. Because of the limited aperture angle of the camera, driver's field of view is smaller than the real road view and objects beyond the field of vision cannot be seen. A variation of this could be an **abstract view of the driving scene** instead of the original camera image in order to reduce the details to be displayed, e.g. in the form of a differential contrast image. The danger is that critical content is lost due to the abstraction.

A promising approach appears to be the augmentation of the driving scene with helpful information, for instance the **projected driving path** that will be taken by the vehicle in the next seconds, based on sensor information and the computed trajectory by the automated control system. Thus the driver even gets more information about the state of the automated control system as he would by watching the road alone. The visualization of an otherwise hidden system state and the future projection of this information might bear the potential of facilitating in a unobtrusive and simple way the recognition of incorrect automated control. This idea is further pursued and elaborated in chapter 5. Different ways of realising such a system are discussed in 5.1.

Figure 3.9: When engaging in a visual task on a display, a video image of the frontal driving scene could be displayed in a splitscreen-view (montage).

3.4 Summary

This chapter presented the methodological and procedural fundament of this work. We introduced a comprehensive formal categorisation of secondary in-car tasks with the dimensions modality, degree of interaction, interruptibility and information encoding. This will serve as a decision aid for the selection of tasks in the following chapters. We argued for the need of a dedicated methodology designed for the assessment of error recognition in an automated driving context and described the process of finding a suitable platform. Since we do not only want to assess the driver's ability to recognise automation errors, but also provide means to improve error recognition, we provided a discussion on potential supporting measures. Displaying the future driving path was identified as the most promising measure to support the driver in recognising automation errors.

Chapter 4

Development of the Automated Lane Change Test

This chapter presents the development of a novel methodology to assess human detection of errors in the context of automated driving. Section 3.2.2 has described the motivation, the background and related method that have led in the end to the proposed methodology, the **Automated Lane Change Test (ALCT)**. In section 4.1 we explain in detail the characteristics and qualities of the ALCT and why they were designed that way, as well as the technical implementation. We conducted two studies using this method assessing the recognition of errors in an automated driving scenarios, and the methodology itself. Parts of this chapter have been published in [153] and [154].

4.1 System Design

As already mentioned, the ALCT method is designed as an instrument to judge the recognition of errors in an automated driving scenario. We assume a semi-automated system as a technical basis that takes over the stabilisation and partially the manoeuvring task, i.e. is able to maintain the speed and keep the vehicle inside its definite lane. Moreover, it is able to perform lane change manoeuvres autonomously.

4.1.1 Functionality

Interaction

The ALCT is set in a virtual driving scene that is identical to the scene in the LCT (straight three-lane track, no traffic, road signs indicate lane changes). However, the driving task has been fully adapted to the paradigm of automated driving, i.e. the virtual car has automated longitudinal and lateral control:

- The virtual vehicle accelerates automatically up to 60 km/h and keeps the speed permanently during the run.

- The vehicle is automatically kept in the middle of the lane.

- When a road sign is approached and the sign contents become visible, the virtual car starts to change to the indicated lane automatically.

As long as the automation works perfectly, no interaction is necessary. But targeting imperfect vehicle guidance, intervention is required in case of automation failure. Automation failure in the ALCT only occur in the lateral direction (cf. 1.2) and is implemented in the form of incorrect lane change manoeuvres. Following the – slightly adapted – principle of commission and omission errors (cf. 2.3), the following errors can occur (cf. Fig. 4.1):

- Lane change when the signs indicate straight driving (error 1), commission error.

- No lane change when the signs indicate a change (error 2), omission error.

- Lane change indicated and carried out, but to the incorrect lane (error 3), commission error.

Figure 4.1: Error categories. Left: Lane change when not supposed to (error 1); middle: no lane change when supposed to (error 2); right: change to the wrong lane (error 3).

Naturally, error 1 can only occur when the road signs indicate to drive straight, i.e. the signs show the same lane the car already drives in. Error 2 is only possible in case of a supposed change, i.e. the signs point to a different lane the car currently drives in. Error 3 is basically a special case of error 1 that can only happen when driving on the centre lane. Errors can only occur at the point of time when the road signs become visible. Table 4.1 shows an overview of all possible manoeuvre and error constellations.

In an ALCT session, the driver is instructed to intervene as fast as possible when

4.1 System Design

ID	Manoeuvre	Target lane in case of			
		Correct behaviour	Error 1	Error 2	Error 3
1	Left to centre	Centre	n/a	Left	n/a
2	Left straight	Left	Centre	n/a	n/a
3	Centre to left	Left	n/a	Centre	Right
4	Centre straight	Centre	Left or Right	n/a	n/a
5	Centre to right	Right	n/a	Centre	Left
6	Right to centre	Centre	n/a	Right	n/a
7	Right straight	Right	Centre	n/a	n/a

Table 4.1: Possible manoeuvres in the ALCT and the corresponding target lanes in case of error category 1, 2 or 3. n/a means that this error is not applicable for this manoeuvre.

an automation error occurs, and to correct the vehicle's incorrect behaviour by turning the steering wheel in the direction of the correct lane, as indicated by the road signs. For instance, if the driver is on the centre lane, the road signs indicate a change to the left and the car changes to the right lane, the driver has to turn the steering wheel to the left, because that is the direction of the indicated (correct) lane. Errors can always be detected directly at sign appearance, as the car will immediately start changing lanes. Changing across two lanes – as is common in the LCT – is not allowed, since then it would not be possible to determine a clear point of time when an error can be recognised as such, e.g. when a change across two lanes is required and the car only changes to the next lane. In terms of the categorisation of the driving task, the recognition of automation errors happens on the knowledge-based level, the intervention with the steering wheel on the rule-based level (cf. section 2.1.1).

The characteristics of the steering wheel have been realised in two versions:

– In the **LO version** (low), the steering wheel serves only as a binary input device. It remains in neutral position during the drive and all lane changes. In case of an error, the driver turns the steering wheel at least 90 degrees in the correct direction and back to the original position as described above. Turning the steering wheel has no influence on the car's driving path. An acoustical signal indicates that the driver's action has been registered. The LO version is examined in the experiments described in 4.2 and 4.3, the implementation is described in 4.1.2.

– In the **HI version** (high), the steering wheel actually controls the car on the track, but the steering action is automated. Hence, the steering wheel moves according to the path of the virtual car, as it would in an actual car with automated lateral control. Due to this direct haptic feedback, the driver receives useful information about the vehicle's trajectory. In case of an error, the driver overrules the steering wheel by applying force greater than 3.0 Nm into the desired direction. By doing so the automation is switched off and the driver must steer the car into the correct lane by himself. After the lane change is completed the automation is faded in again. The HI version is examined in the experiment described in 4.3, the implementation is described in 4.1.2.

Automation Reliability and Error Rate

A crucial question in the design of the ALCT method is in which frequency errors occur. Buld et al. recommend an overall system reliability of at least 90% in order to establish a sufficient level of automation trust [26]. As described in chapter 2.3, lower reliability and higher error rates respectively can lead to less trust in automation and therefore lower attendance to secondary activities along with lower system acceptance. Lower error rates, however, are likely to result in a number of measured values that is insufficient for statistical analysis. Following this, nine out of ten lane changes in the ALCT setup are performed correctly and one out of ten is incorrect. In total, a run comprises 90 lane changes with nine errors. Errors are randomly distributed over the course and can occur at any sign except for the first two and the last sign, as well as for only two consecutive errors in a row. Each error type (cf. Fig. 4.1) occurs exactly three times.

4.1.2 ALCT Implementation

Driving simulation environment

As mentioned above, the ALCT is set in a driving simulation environment. This is done in order to create a deeper feeling of immersion – compared to a PC-based version – and to potentially contribute to establishing better automation trust (cf. [22, 98]). A fast Ethernet network is the backbone of all simulation computers. Each graphical output channel (projector or flatscreen display) is controlled by a dedicated computer that renders the virtual graphical scene displayed via that channel. All graphic computers are orchestrated by the central Linux-based simulation software SPIDER (Software Programming Interface for Distributed Realtime Driving Simulation, [158]). SPIDER supports the definition of static and dynamic content, e.g. the virtual driving environment, behaviour of vehicles, pedestrians, traffic lights, etc. Dynamic behaviour can be specified in an event-based

4.1 System Design

scripting language. Hardware car mockups are connected via a CAN[1] interface to the driving simulation where specialised CAN software (CANoe[2]) emulates physical control units and bus communication.

Parameters

There are a number of parameters that determine the ALCT configuration. The Ballomat method proved useful for finding a suitable parameter configuration concerning number of signs, errors, timing, etc. The most important parameters are listed below.

- $number\_of\_signs = 90$, $number\_of\_errors = 9$
  As argued in 4.1.1, an error rate of 10% is set. Each error category appears three times. All errors occur at random signs.

- $speed\_kmh = 60$
  We decided to use the same speed that is used in the LCT. With 90 signs, one run takes approximately 11 minutes.

- $max\_consecutive\_errors = 2$
  It is not desirable that too many errors occur in a row, in order to avoid that there are no errors left for the rest of the run.

- $number\_of\_correct\_first\_signs = 3$
  For the driver to accommodate to the automated driving task, the first signs do not contain errors.

- $number\_of\_correct\_last\_signs = 2$
  It may be necessary to shift an error to another position in order to avoid too many consecutive errors. Therefore we keep a few correct signs at the end to allow for that.

- $start\_changing\_lanes\_distance = 60$
  The distance towards the road sign when signs become visible and the lane change starts.

- $signs\_minimum\_distance = 100$, $signs\_maximum\_distance = 140$
  The minimum and maximum distance between two consecutive road signs. The distance is varying randomly between these values.

---

[1] Controller Area Network
[2] http://www.vector.com/vi_canoe_de.html

- *constant_driving_time* = *true*
  For comparison reasons the total driving time for a run is kept constant. This requires a special algorithm for the placement of the road signs (cf. 4.1.2).

- *relation_change_or_straight* = 0.8
  With a probability of 80% a lane change occurs, with 20% the car drives straight.

- *relation_left_or_right* = 0.5
  Driving on the centre lane with a decided change of lanes, it is equally likely to change to the left or to the right.

The described configuration values were found after extensive iterative testing with different parameter sets involving a large number of different test drivers. Experimenting with showing only one road sign on a random side of the road – in order to avoid a predictable area on the screen to check for an emerging sign – resulted in strong confusion of the participants. Some participants implicitly assumed that the road side where the sign appeared indicated the direction the car had to change to without noticing the content of the sign. Therefore this idea was not pursued any further.

Metrics

The LCT's main measurement is the mean deviation between the positions of the model path trajectory and the actual driven course. This is not applicable for the ALCT as lane changes are performed automatically. Therefore we developed for ALCT a set of discrete objective measurements (cf. Fig. 4.2):

- **Mean response time**: Response time is the measured time span between the beginning of an incorrect lane change action (t_0, revealing the road sign) and the driver's reaction by reaching a steering wheel angle of 90 degrees (t_2). For each course the mean response time of all response times is calculated.

$$mean\_response\_time = \frac{1}{n}\sum_{i=1}^{n} rt_i$$

with n as the $(number\_of\_total\_errors - number\_of\_missed\_errors) > 0$ and rt as the response time for one error. Additionally, the mean response time for each error category can be calculated as a sub-measurement.

- **Number of missed errors**: If the driver shows no reaction in case of an error (t_2) until the next road sign is revealed ($t_4 = t_0$), the number of missed errors is incremented. Basically, an omission error occurs by not detecting an incorrect manoeuvre. After passing the road sign (t_3) a valid reaction is still possible.

4.1 System Design

- **Number of false interventions**: A false intervention means turning the steering wheel even if the lane change action is correctly executed and there is no need to intervene, which corresponds to a commission error. Also a reaction in the wrong direction, e.g. when a correction to the left is required and the driver steers to the right, increments the number of false interventions. In that case this does not count as a missed error and the response time will be measured. But because of the incorrect steering direction, a false intervention is also registered.

Furthermore, we calculate the time to the first gaze to the driving scene, when the road signs are revealed (t_1). We assume an additional time of 200 ms to be necessary in order to perceive the contents of the driving scene (first fixation, cf. 4.2.2).

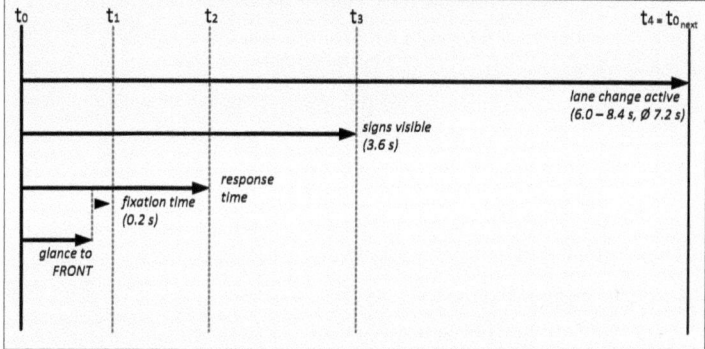

Figure 4.2: Temporal course of the ALCT. At t_0 the current road sign is revealed and is visible until t_3. In case of an error an intervention takes place at t_2, which can be as late as just before the t_0 of the next sign. t_1 indicates the first glance at the driving scene.

LO version

As described in 4.1.1, the more basic version only uses binary steering wheel input and does not allow the driver to influence the car's trajectory. Therefore all necessary information (position and contents of the signs, correct and incorrect lane changes) can be computed in advance. SPIDER requires predefining static content (signs) and allows to script dynamic behaviour (lane changes) which have to be stored in separate files. Road signs are defined in an XML dialect, lane changes have to be scripted in a proprietary signal-based scripting language. Of course, we cannot use always the same sequence of lane changes and road signs, so these files have to be generated prior to each run. We chose the platform-independent programming language Java[3] to build a tool for automatically creating files containing the road sign definitions and the lane change commands. The tool takes the set of parameters described above from a configuration file as input.

The following algorithm generates the necessary files in five steps:

Step 1: Input. The provided parameter set is parsed and all necessary variables are initialised.

Step 2: Error indices. We create a randomly distributed list of indices at which positions incorrect lane changes are supposed to occur. Several constraints apply for that list: there cannot be more than a certain number of errors in a row (*max_consecutive_errors*). It is not possible that two category 3 errors occur in a row, because error 3 requires the car to be on the centre lane and after the error occurred the car is on the left or the right lane. A number of signs at the beginning cannot be errors, in order to avoid accidentally missed errors at the very beginning of the run. If one constraint is violated, the list is shuffled again as long as all requirements are met.

Step 3: Car path. The path of the car on the track is generated. Following the previously generated list of errors, it is checked if for the current lane change an error is supposed to occur. If not, it is randomly decided whether the car goes straight or it changes the lane (*relation_change_or_straight*), as well as what is the corresponding road sign to place on the track. On the centre lane the chance is 50% (*relation_left_or_right*) for a change to the left or to the right. In case of an error, it is also decided which is the next lane to take depending on the predefined error category and what road sign to show with the same probabilities as previously mentioned (cf. Table 4.1).

Step 4: Road Sign Positioning. We determine the positions of the road signs on the track. The distance between road signs can vary between 100 m and 140 m, i.e. 120 m on average. In order to keep a constant driving time for each run, we always take a pair of signs, randomly choose a distance for one sign between the minimal and the maximal distance, and assign the difference to the average value to the other sign:

---

[3]http://java.sun.com

4.1 System Design

```
for i = number_of_signs
    if (i % 2)
        d[i] = random(sign_min_distance, sign_max_distance);
        d[i+1] = (sign_min_distance + sign_max_distance) - d[i];
    end if
end for
shuffle(d)
```

Thus, two signs are placed in an average distance of 120 m which in the end adds up to always the same total distance. Finally the list is shuffled. The position of the road signs determines the point on the track when the virtual vehicle begins a lane change ($start\_changing\_lanes\_distance = 60$).

Step 5: Output. Signs and lane changes are transformed into SPIDER-formatted code files.

HI version

Velocity and heading of the virtual vehicle are again controlled by an automated system. In contrast to the LO version, in the HI version the steering wheel is directly coupled with the driving environment and therefore able to influence the heading angle. The corresponding steering wheel angle is induced by an electric motor on the steering column which causes the steering wheel to turn itself according to the car's trajectory in the virtual scene. The automation always keeps the car in the middle of the current lane and performs lane changes automatically dependent on the road sign contents as described above. The current lane is determined by the centre point of the simulation car. The driver can at anytime take control over the car by steering in the desired direction.

In order to provide the described functionality, we had to use a different way of controlling the car on the track than we did in the LO version. The SPIDER framework offers an interface for a so-called **co-simulation** to be embedded into the driving dynamics program that allows modifying driving dynamics parameters of a simulated car during a running simulation. The co-simulation is implemented as Matlab/Simulink[4] model. Simulink is a graphical programming environment for modelling, analysing and simulating dynamic systems and is mainly used in control engineering. The Simulink model can be transformed into C-code using the toolbox Real-Time Workshop[5], compiled on the Linux operating system of the driving simulation and executed as a modular extension of the driving dynamics program in real-time.

---
[4]http://www.mathworks.com/products/simulink/
[5]http://www.mathworks.com/products/rtw/

4. Development of the Automated Lane Change Test

On the highest level the Simulink model contains only two functions, a **control function** and a function for **data exchange** with the driving dynamics program the model is communicating with. The data exchange function allows to pass a set of parameters from the mock-up car to the driving simulation, e.g. acceleration pedal state, steering wheel angle, controller operations, etc., but also receives various information from the simulation about the environment, lane data, other vehicles, etc. The control function contains the functionality to compute the car's driving behaviour from this information. Moreover, within this function the actuation of the steering wheel is controlled. The driver is always able to overrule the automated lateral guidance by turning the steering wheel with a momentum greater than 3.0 Nm for more than 0.2 s. When overruling, normally in case of an erroneous lane change, the applied torque is ramped down within 0.2 s to 0.0 Nm and the driver takes over steering manually for 2.0 seconds (3.0 seconds in case of error 3) before the momentum on the steering wheel is ramped up again within 1.5 s. When overruled, we use the same sound as in the LO version in order to convey appropriate feedback to the driver. We use a Kollmorgen Inland BL electric hollow shaft motor type RB01815-D00[6] (cf. Fig. 4.3, left), that is mounted on the steering column. This motor can apply a permanent torque of 6.0 Nm. It is connected via serial line to a Maccon SWM48-50-R-CT control unit, which can be controlled via CAN from the Simulink model running within the driving simulation environment (cf. Fig. 4.3, right). The described parameters of the model have been determined and adapted after an iterative test phase with several test subjects.

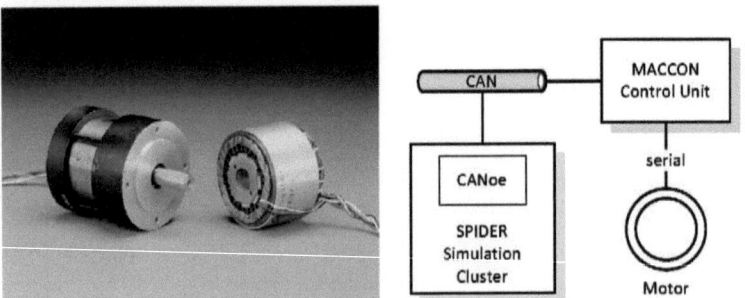

Figure 4.3: Left: Kollmorgen hollow shaft motor used to apply torque on the steering wheel. Right: Schematics of the signal chain to control the motor.

We used an existing model providing longitudinal and lateral control routines as provided by Waldmann et al. [170] and adapted it to the given driving scenario. Longitudinal

---
[6] http://www.kollmorgen.com/

4.1 System Design

control is mainly accomplished by accelerating the car at the beginning of the test run to 60 km/h and then keeping the speed constant. The foot pedals have been disabled so that the driver cannot influence the speed. For lateral control the most important information is to what lane the car is supposed to change. The trajectories for the lane change manoeuvres to the left and to the right are defined by a linearly increasing offset starting from the centre of the lane. This offset is smoothed using a PT1 low pass filter, which outputs a trajectory as shown in Fig. 4.4. Because of the driver's option

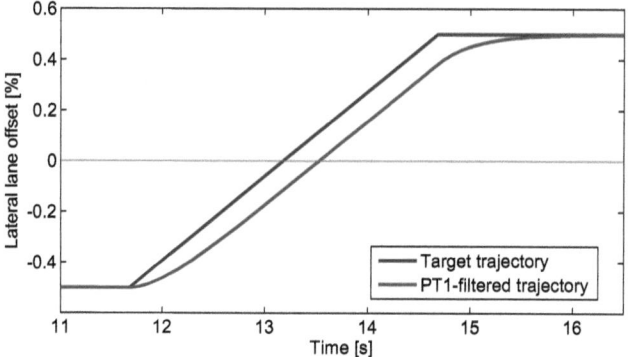

Figure 4.4: Lane change trajectories of the ALCT HI version. The PT1-filtered lane offset is used as input for lateral control.

to influence the car's trajectory and take over steering, the content of road signs cannot be entirely pre-computed, otherwise we cannot prevent changes across two lanes. We compute a preliminary sequence of correct changes and errors (using the algorithm in the LO version, step 2). At the time the signs are to be revealed (60 m before passing the sign), it is decided – based on the current lane the vehicle is in – what sign contents are to be shown in order to match the pre-computed change. If this is not possible, e.g. when the car is on the left lane and error 3 is supposed to occur which is only possible from the centre lane, the due change is delayed to the next possible position in the computed sequence array. When a target lane is determined, the lane change manoeuvre is initiated. We use the same seven lane change identifiers as described in the LO version.

We used the Simulink toolbox Stateflow[7] for the implementation of the road sign algorithm. Fig. 4.5 shows the central functions of the implementation, the complete Stateflow chart containing the road sign logic is shown in Figure A.2 in the appendix. However, the road sign positions can be entirely computed in advance; we used the same

---
[7] http://www.mathworks.com/products/stateflow/

74   4. Development of the Automated Lane Change Test

algorithm described in the LO version, step 4.

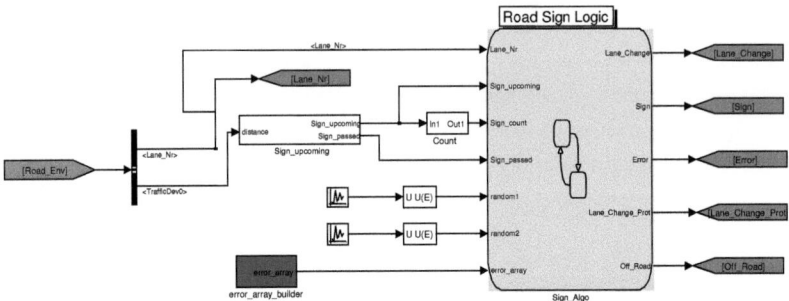

Figure 4.5: Simulink functions containing road sign computation algorithms.

4.1.3 Discussion of Differences between LCT and ALCT

Although the ALCT is systematically based on the LCT, there are some clear differences we would like to point out. Conceptually the most important difference is the way of interaction. The LCT is a permanent control and manoeuvre task (tracking/decision) whereas the ALCT requires automation supervision and only situational correction (detection/decision) as it would be the case with potential automated control systems.

Another obvious difference is the overall environment. The LCT is designed as a PC-based system; the ALCT is set in a more "realistic" environment with a car mock-up, a genuine steering wheel and large display of the driving scene presented on three plasma screens (cf. Fig. 4.6). This is done in order to create deeper involvement with the driving task and to potentially contribute to establishing more trust in the automation. This is also the cause for a longer run time with more signs (and lane changes respectively). With an error rate of 10% there is the need of a certain number of critical events in order to extract sufficient reaction data. The longer run time also required to reduce the average distance between the road signs.

We introduced the possibility of a straight driving manoeuvre. In the ALCT road signs do not always require a lane change as in the LCT, it is also likely that the driver is supposed to stay in the same lane. This makes the ALCT less predictable and requires exact comparison of signs and vehicle behaviour, since not changing at a road sign does not automatically imply an error. In the original design all upcoming road signs are always visible (although in the far distance and blank) and the content becomes visible

4.1 System Design

before passing. We decided to show only the next upcoming sign when reaching a certain distance and display the contents immediately to avoid drivers being able to expect and prepare for an error. This also contributes to less predictability. We increased the distance when the road signs are shown to 60 m in order to give the test subjects more time to perceive the content. Out of clarity reasons, we did not include the change across two lanes, as it is common in the LCT. An overview of all major differences is shown in Table 4.2.

	LCT	ALCT
Environment	PC	driving simulator
Type of interaction	manoeuvre and control	supervision and correction
Frequency of interaction	permanent	situational
Track length	3,000 m	11,000 m
Test duration	3 mins	11 mins
Total number of signs	18	90
Signs visible	always	60 m before passing
Sign contents visible	40 m before passing	60 m before passing
Sign distance	144 – 188 m	100 – 140 m
Possible manoeuvres	6	7
Change across 2 lanes	yes	no
Straight driving	no	yes
Measurements	mean lane deviation, standard lane deviation	mean response time, missed errors, false interventions

Table 4.2: Overview of the differences between the LCT and the ALCT implementation.

In summary, a direct comparison of the LCT and the ALCT, for example in a comparative user study, is not possible out of several reasons. The LCT measures the mean deviation of a manual tracking task, the ALCT measures the response time to a detected error. In theory, it would be possible to extract a response time in case of a lane change in the LCT, too, but since the ALCT requires the test subject to wait for the automated lane change in order to judge the correctness of the action, this comparison seems unfair. The internal model of the LCT assumes an optimal reaction time of 0.6 s (cf. 3.8), response times in the ALCT will show much longer response times (cf. 4.2.5, 4.3.4) because of the different character of necessary interaction and vehicle movement. The response time of the ALCT also includes that the test person does not see the upcoming road signs beforehand, which is also the reason for the introduction of the straight driving manoeuvre in the ALCT. Moreover, the overall length of the course and the number of necessary interventions differ widely between the two methods. The ALCT requires interaction to be seldom, only in case of a detected error, so an adaption to the shorter LCT is not reasonable. Vice versa, the measurement of the LCT is designed only for a three minutes drive.

4.2 User Study 1: LO version

This section describes the first user study that we did with the ALCT methodology. The primary goal was to prove effectiveness and feasibility of the method. This basically means it had to be shown that the chosen measurements are able to discriminate between different experimental conditions as well as objective and subjective results are consistent. Secondly we wanted to gain insight into the effects of secondary tasks on recognition of automation errors in a automated driving scenario. In this study we used the **LO version** implementation of the ALCT (cf. 4.1.2), i.e. with no feedback on the steering wheel and no possibility for the participants to influence the path of the virtual vehicle. Parts of this section have been published in [153, 154] and parts have also been described in a diploma thesis prepared by Marion Mangold under the supervision of the author [103].

4.2.1 Hypotheses

Based on the categorisation of secondary tasks and the implicit assumptions of overlapping resources in section 3.1.3, the following hypotheses were stated. Each hypothesis will be assessed using the metrics of mean response time, missed errors and false interventions.

1. H_1: Main effect: Simultaneously performing a secondary task results in a deterioration of the primary task performance as compared to only performing the primary task.

2. H_2: Interactive secondary tasks induce a worse primary task performance than passive tasks.

3. H_3: Visual secondary tasks induce a worse primary task performance than auditory tasks because of a stronger interference with the driving task.

4. H_4: Secondary tasks categorised as hard to interrupt induce a worse primary task performance than tasks categorised as easy to interrupt.

5. H_5: Secondary tasks with spatial information encoding induce a worse primary task performance than tasks with verbal information encoding.

4.2.2 Experimental Procedure

In the experiment we used the six tasks as described in section 3.1.4: Entering a destination into the navigation system (**navigation**), finding a target on an interactive map (**interactive map**), reading of short lines of text (**short text**), reading of long paragraphs of text (**long text**), having a conversation on the phone (**phone call**), listening to an audio book (**audio book**).

The study consisted of seven blocks, one for each secondary task and one with no secondary task to perform as a baseline. We applied a within-subject-design, so that each test person completed all seven blocks. The order of the blocks was counterbalanced across all subjects (cf. permutation table A.1). The overall study duration was about two hours.

At the beginning of the experiment, we made the test persons familiar with the driving simulator and the ALCT. We explained to them in detail how the ALCT works, what to do in case of an error and to react as fast as possible. Prior to each test run, the participants had a chance to practise every secondary task statically until the they felt securely familiar with it. During a run, the test subjects were constantly occupied with a task. That means, the task was continuously running (audio book) or after one completed subtask immediately the next subtask followed (navigation, interactive map, question in the phone call conversation). The reading tasks were self-paced, but instructed in a way that the test subjects were supposed to read as many pages as they could.

After each block the participants answered questions about their subjective workload estimation. For that we used again the **Driver Activity Load Index** (DALI, [128], [127]), as described in section 3.1.2. Since not all dimensions apply for all tasks (e.g. the phone call task has no visual dimension) we did not use the global demand score but focused on the general dimensions mental effort, stress and interference. We did not ascertain the DALI after the baseline run, because this was only a single task condition. Additionally we asked the test subjects to estimate their current level of tiredness from zero (wide awake) to 100 (extremely tired) in order to determine potential fatiguing effects imposed by the automation. Finally after all test runs the participants had to rank all secondary tasks according to their perceived imposed workload from place one (least) to six (most).

During all visual tasks we recorded the participants' gaze data in order to determine when the test subjects looked where. Gaze data analysis has been identified as a valuable means of attention assessment (e.g. [80]). We divided the field of sight into two areas of interest (AOIs): the central information display (CID) and the driving scene (FRONT, cf. Fig. 4.8, right). To be precise, for consistency reasons we created one more area (ELSE) to capture all gazes. For simplicity we assumed that a gaze on the driving scene (i.e. inside the AOI *FRONT*) is identical with the perception of a road sign, if visible, since there is no other stimulus in the driving scene (cf. Cohen1991). We also assumed a certain time span for the test subjects to actually see the content of the driving scene. This is defined by the term *fixation*. The duration of a fixation can be interpreted as a measurement of depth of perception. Perception can be described as the sum of the phases selection, organization, and interpretation [60]. Fixations can take between 100 and 2000 ms with a concentration between 200 and 600 ms [90, 183]. Image perception has a mean fixation time of 330 ms, visual search 275 ms and reading 225 ms [134]. Based on this, a fixation onto an AOI was defined as a gaze that stayed uninterruptedly inside an AOI for a minimum time of 200 ms.

4.2.3 Technical Realisation

We implemented the experimental setup in the driving simulation environment of BMW Research and Technology. Fig. 4.7 shows the overall hard- and software architecture. We used a mockup car equipped with fully functional foot pedals, steering wheel and steering column that were connected to the driving simulation control computer via CAN. The mockup also comprised a 10" display with a resolution of 1280 × 480 pixels mounted to the right of the driver where we showed the content of the visual secondary tasks (cf. Fig. 4.6). The interactive map task was implemented as a Adobe Flash[8] simulation running inside a C# wrapper process that enables the Flash movie to receive UDP[9] packets. For the navigation task we used a standard simulation of the BMW iDrive menu that can be operated via keyboard input. The short and long text reading tasks were realised as simple Microsoft PowerPoint slide sets which also can be operated via key strokes. The phone call task was realised by a two-way audio communication channel between the experiment control centre and the mockup room. The audio book was played as a simple audio stream via the same channel.

Since a standard keyboard is not suitable for a driving environment, we used a multifunctional controller (BMW iDrive controller) that can be pushed, rotated and

---

[8] http://www.adobe.com/flash/
[9] User Datagram Procotol

4.2 User Study 1: LO version

tilted as input device for the secondary tasks (cf. Fig. 3.4). The controller is able to communicate via a local CAN connection with a Windows PC that also runs the described secondary tasks. We created a program that acts a as proxy between the controller and the different secondary task programs. The proxy consists of several C++ modules encapsulated as DLL[10] files able to receive and transcode CAN messages from the iDrive controller into Windows key events and into UDP packets to be received by the secondary task applications. The proxy also had to contain a *bus simulation* module emulating communication with the control unit the controller is normally connected to in the car.

Figure 4.6: ALCT experimental setup. Test participant driving the ALCT LO version. He is operating the interactive map using the iDrive controller and wears a head-mounted eye-tracking system.

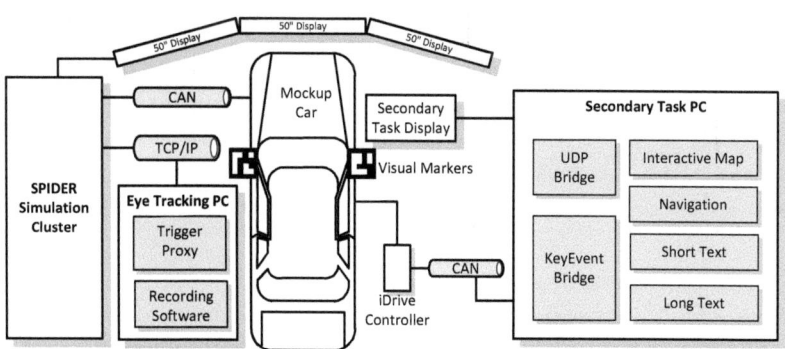

Figure 4.7: Schematics of hardware and software architecture in the driving simulation environment.

In front of the car mockup we had three 50" plasma screens aligned in an angle of 34°

---
[10]Dynamic Link Library

next to each other displaying the driving scene. Since the ALCT setting does not include other cars the front view is sufficient.

As mentioned above, we recorded gaze data. For that we used a Dikablis[11] head-mounted eye-tracking system (cf. Fig. 4.8, left). The head piece basically consists of two cameras and a communication unit. One camera is directed towards the user's eye, another camera captures the user's field of view. Using a calibration software running on a PC the head piece is connected to, it is possible to determine a single point where the user's gaze currently rests upon. With another software tool we can define certain areas of interest (AOIs) within the video feed captured by the field camera. These can be anchored in the real world by using visual markers containing a specific pattern (cf. Fig. 4.7 and 4.8, right). Postprocessing the video stream after recording detects the position of the visual markers in the video image. Knowing the position of the markers and their relative offset to the defined AOI enables us to automatically determine if, when and how long the user has looked into a certain AOI.

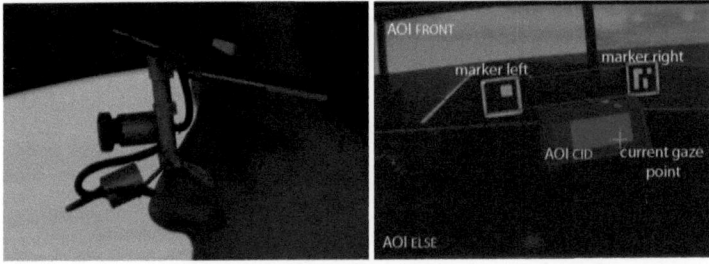

Figure 4.8: Left: Dikablis eye-tracking system. One camera tracks the user's eye, the field camera captures the environment. Properly calibrated we know what the user looks at. Right: Analysis view. The screen can be subdivided into areas of interest (AOIs). Visual markers anchor AOI positions on the screen for automated analysis. The cross-hair shows the test subject's current gaze point.

For an in-depth analysis of gaze data it is necessary to be able to assess certain conditions in more detail. For instance in order to analyse the gaze behaviour during an error condition, the data must be marked. To do so we used another proxy program running on the eye-tracking PC that receives trigger messages via a TCP/IP network connection and adds these messages to the protocol data. From the driving simulation we submitted messages containing information about when a road sign is visible, what the content of the sign is, when an error occurs and when the driver intervenes by turning the steering

---

[11]http://www.ergoneers.com/de/products/dlab-dikablis/overview.html

4.2 User Study 1: LO version 81

wheel. Thus the data recorded by the driving simulation and the eye-tracking software are synchronised.

The main challenge in the technical realisation was to establish stable communication between various heterogeneous hardware and software components. We also recorded audio and video from the experiment to be able to trace back and correct potential data inconsistencies.

4.2.4 Sample

We had 28 test persons (19 male, 9 female) participating in our study with an average age of 29.4 years ($SD = 6.03$, $min = 19$, $max = 47$). All 28 produced a fully valid data set and could be taken into analysis. 24 have been recruited from a BMW test subject database, 4 subjects were not BMW employees. All participants were in possession of a driving license for 1 to 21 years with an average of 10.75 years ($SD = 5.73$). Since we were using a head-mounted eye-tracking system, participants in need of spectacles were excluded from the study, as long as they were not able to wear contact lenses.

4.2.5 Results

The following section reports the results from the described study. First we present objectively measured results (response times, error data and gaze data, etc.), then subjective statements from the test subjects.

Gender and Age

In order to determine if the age or gender of the test subjects had an effect we performed preliminary tests. An ANOVA showed that there was no significant difference between male and female in the mean response times ($F[1,26] = 4.059; p = .054$). Male subjects show faster response times by tendency, but in all tasks there is only a significant difference in the navigation condition ($t[26] = -3.783; p = .001$) in favour of male test subjects. Also regarding missed errors and false interventions we did not find significant differences. So the gender does not generally have an influence on the measured values.

Also the age of the participants showed no significant correlation with the mean response time. Regarding missed errors and false interventions we found significant correlations in the long text and in the short text task, but since these were very rare events in the whole experiment, this result is probably not too meaningful. In summary it can be said that also the age had no influence on our measurements. Therefore we can perform the following tests without consideration of gender and age.

Reaction Data

As described in 4.1.2, the response time means the time span between the appearance of a road sign and the turning of the steering wheel by 90° in case of a recognised error. Since every test subject performed all conditions we ran a repeated measures analysis of variance (ANOVA). Sphericity was not met, so we used the Greenhouse-Geisser correction. This showed a significant main effect of performing secondary tasks on mean response time with $F[3.644, 98.389] = 9.545; p = .000$ (cf. Fig. 4.9). Driving without secondary tasks (baseline condition) showed the shortest mean response time ($M = 1.71$, $SD = .14$), finding locations on an *interactive map* resulted in the longest mean response time ($M = 2.06$, $SD = .34$) which means an increase by 20.5%. Performing a post-hoc pairwise comparison of all conditions using Bonferroni alpha correction we found all tasks except the *audio book* task differ significantly from the *baseline* regarding the mean response time. Furthermore the *audio book* condition shows significantly shorter mean response times compared to the *navigation* task ($p = .023$) and the *interactive map* ($p = .018$). Also, the *short text* task has significantly shorter mean response times than *navigation* ($p = .002$) and *interactive map* ($p = .010$). During the experiment a total

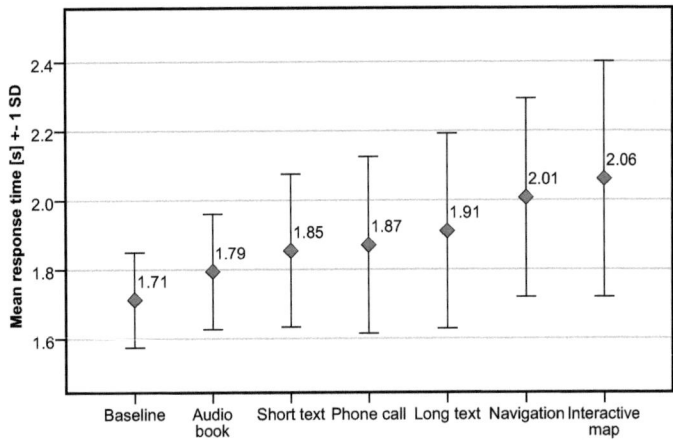

Figure 4.9: Mean response time and standard deviation for the baseline and all secondary tasks (sorted in ascending order).

number of 64 errors ($M = 2.29$ per person, $SD = 2.31$) were missed (i.e. not corrected by turning the steering wheel) with zero missed errors in the audio book condition up

4.2 User Study 1: LO version

to 26 errors in the interactive map (cf. Fig. 4.10). 26 of in total 252 (28 test subjects × nine errors per test run) occurred errors also means that more than 10% of all errors in the interactive map condition have not been corrected. As indicated by the standard deviation there are also enormous interindividual differences in the number of missed errors ranging from zero misses to ten missed errors by one test subject summed over all conditions. We found a significant main effect of secondary tasks on missed errors using cross tables and a chi-square test ($\chi^2[6] = 73.414; p = .000$).

We recorded a total number of 44 false interventions ($M = 1.57$ per person, $SD = 1.60$) in the experiment ranging from one in the baseline condition to 19 during the phone call condition (cf. Fig. 4.11). This resulted in a significant main effect of secondary tasks on false interventions ($\chi^2[6] = 38.413; p = .000$). Again we found differences between single test subjects, from zero to six incorrect interventions summed over all conditions.

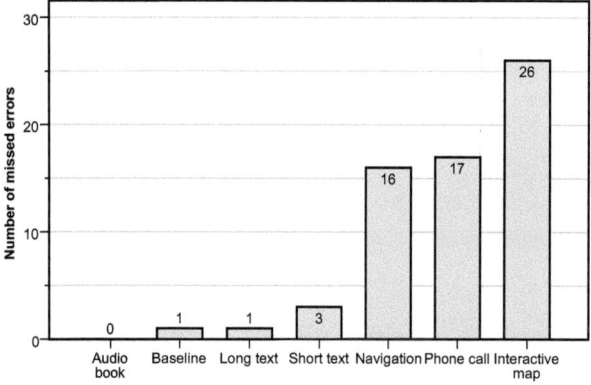

Figure 4.10: Number of missed errors in each condition summed over all test subjects (sorted in ascending order).

For a more detailed insight into what kind of secondary tasks influence the recognition performance on automation errors, we analysed the reaction data in terms of the categorisation in chapter 3. In each case we only considered one dimension independently from the others that also applied. Figure 4.12 shows all dimensions compared below.

Degree of Interaction A grouped comparison of **active** (*phone call, navigation, interactive map*) vs. **passive** (*audio book, short text, long text*) tasks using a repeated measures ANOVA revealed that the dimension degree of interaction (active vs. passive) has a significant effect on response times ($F[1.645, 44.417] = 26.220; p = .000$, Greenhouse-Geisser). A post-hoc Bonferroni analysis showed significantly longer mean response

4. Development of the Automated Lane Change Test

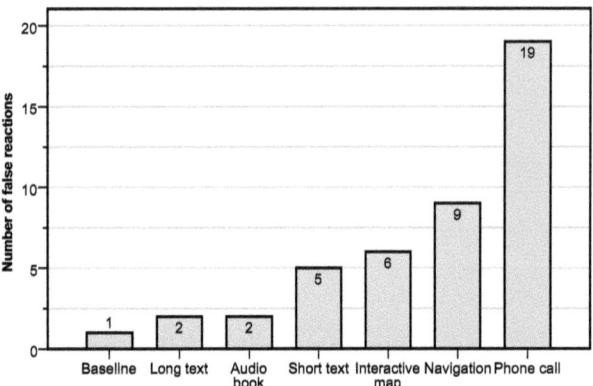

Figure 4.11: Number of false interventions in each condition summed over test subjects (sorted in ascending order).

times for active than for passive tasks ($p = .001$), as well as for the baseline condition ($p = .000$). Passive tasks also differ from the baseline condition ($p = .001$). There are clear differences regarding the number of missed errors. With only four errors missed in passive tasks, we recorded 59 misses in active tasks. This means a significant higher number of mean missed errors for active tasks ($Z = -4.072, p = .000$). Analogously we found significantly more false interventions in active (34) than in passive tasks (nine, $Z = -3.450, p = .001$).

Modality Analysing the modality of information transfer, **visual** (*short text, long text, navigation, interactive map*) vs. **auditory** (*audio book, phone call*), we found a significant main effect of the modality on mean response times ($F[2, 54] = 19.361; p = .000$). Visual tasks show significantly longer times than auditory tasks ($p = .013$) and than the baseline ($p = .000$). Auditory tasks also have significantly longer response times compared to the baseline ($p = .003$). Regarding missed errors there is no significant difference between visual and auditory tasks ($Z = -1.039, p = .299$). Regarding false interventions there is no significant difference between visual tasks and auditory tasks ($Z = -1.659, p = .097$).

Information Encoding Comparing five tasks with **verbal** information encoding (*audio book, phone call, short text, long text, navigation*) with the **spatial** task (*interactive map*) does not make much sense because of the one-side distribution of case numbers. Instead we compared two tasks that only differ in the dimension of information encoding, interactive map and navigation task. We could not find significant differences regarding mean response time ($t[27] = -.881; p = .386$), missed errors ($Z = -1.378, p = .168$) or

4.2 User Study 1: LO version

false interventions ($Z = -.540, p = .589$).

Interruptibility We also compared tasks that are easy to interrupt (*short text, navigation, interactive map*) and tasks that are hard to interrupt (*audio book, phone call, long text*). Contrary to our assumption in H_5 we found that performing easily interruptible secondary tasks led to significantly longer response times compared to tasks that were hard to interrupt ($t[27] = 2.581; p = .016$)). Comparing directly short text and long text conditions which only differ in the dimension of interruptibility, there is no significant difference regarding mean response times ($t[27] = 1.319; p = .198$). Analogously to the response times, there are significantly more errors missed in easily interruptible tasks ($Z = -2.482, p = .013$). Regarding false interventions, there are no differences between conditions ($Z = -.440, p = .660$).

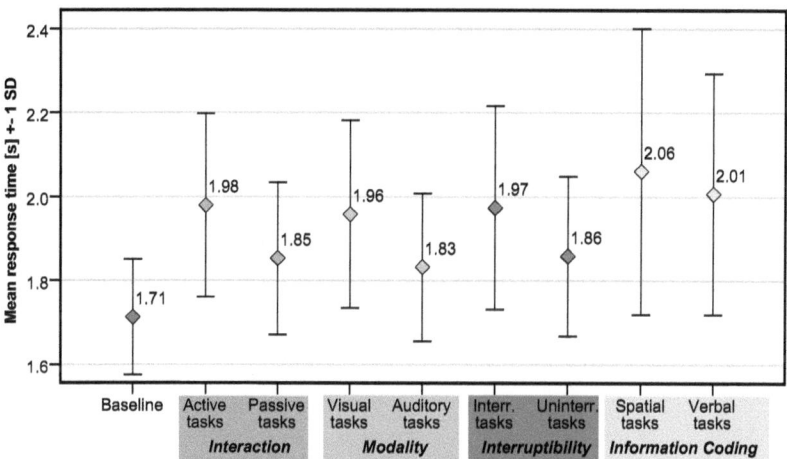

Figure 4.12: Mean response times in seconds and standard deviation of all conditions grouped by dimensions.

Error categories We also analysed the mean response time divided into the error categories (cf. 4.1.1, Fig. 4.13). Error category 2 (no change when required) showed the longest mean response time ($M = 2.09$, $SD = .26$), whereas error category 3 (change to the wrong lane) produced the shortest mean response time ($M = 1.93$, $SD = .20$). Times of error category 1 (change when not required) range in between ($M = 1.73$, $SD = .19$). A repeated measures ANOVA proves a significant main effect of the error category ($F[2, 54] = 41.263; p = .000$). We found significant differences between all error categories regarding the mean response time using a post-hoc pairwise comparison with a Bonferroni alpha adjustment. In category 1, 33 errors were missed in total ($M = 1.18$, $SD = .94$), in category 2 we found 23 misses ($M = .82$, $SD = 1.33$), and in the third category 8 misses ($M = .29$, $SD = .71$).

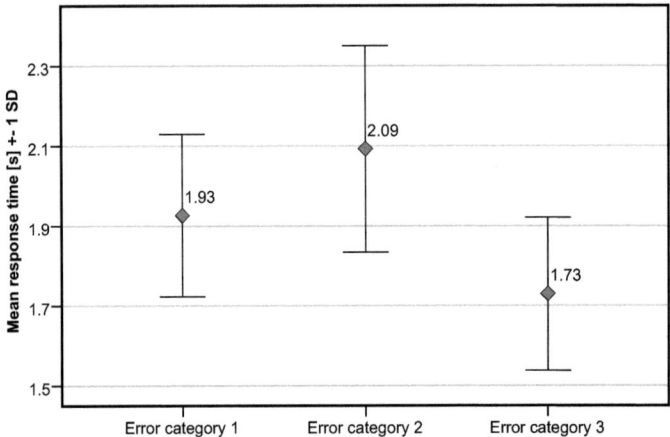

Figure 4.13: Mean response times in seconds and standard deviation of all conditions grouped to error categories.

Gaze Data

An analysis of gaze distribution regarding the **total gaze time** on the AOIs CID and FRONT showed an overall gaze ratio of approx. 3:1 in favour of the CID. The long text condition showed a distribution of 86% CID and 14% FRONT, whereas the map task showed 71% CID and 29% FRONT. Navigation and short text reveal an identical distribution of 73% CID and 27% FRONT (cf. Table 4.3). A repeated measures ANOVA showed a main effect of secondary tasks on total gaze time for both areas ($F_{FRONT}[3,81] = 44.210; p = .000$ and $F_{CID}[2.283, 61.650] = 53.455; p = .000$, Greenhouse-Geisser) with long text showing the shortest gaze times on FRONT and the longest gazes on the CID compared to all other tasks (each $p = .000$).

Mean gaze times on the CID ranged from $2.13s$ ($SD = .62$) in the interactive map condition to $4.24s$ ($SD = 1.31$) in the long text condition, on FRONT from $.90s$ ($SD = .35$) in the short text condition to $.71s$ ($SD = .19$) in the long text condition (cf. 4.14). This resulted in a main effect of secondary tasks on the mean gaze time on the CID ($F_{CID} = [1.754, 47.366] = 49.727; p = .000$, Greenhouse-Geisser). A post-hoc Bonferroni analysis showed that the long text has significantly longer total gaze times on

4.2 User Study 1: LO version

			Interactive map	Navigation	Short text	Long text
Total Gaze Time		CID	M=453.75 (SD=44.53)	M=467.42 (SD=42.73)	M=466.31 (SD=66.32)	M=553.38 (SD=36.79)
		FRONT	M=187.16 (SD=43.08)	M=175.55 (SD=42.55)	M=173.86 (SD=64.42)	M=91.52 (SD=45.42)
	% CID / % FRONT		71 / 29	73 / 27	73 / 27	86 / 14
Mean Gaze Time		CID	M=2.13 (SD=.62)	M=2.18 (SD=.58)	M=2.65 (SD=1.06)	M=4.24 (SD=.1.32)
		FRONT	M=0.83 (SD=.16)	M=0.78 (SD=.15)	M=.90 (SD=.35)	M=.71 (SD=.19)
Max. Gaze Time		CID	M=8.47 (SD=2.17)	M=8.07 (SD=2.85)	M=7.00 (SD=1.70)	M=8.38 (SD=1.88)
		FRONT	M= 4.71 (SD=2.11)	M=3.42 (SD=1.12)	M=3.82 (SD=1.68)	M=3.14 (SD=1.73)

Table 4.3: Total summed gaze times, mean gaze times and maximum gaze times (in seconds) on the AOIs CID and FRONT for all visual tasks.

the CID compared to all other tasks (each $p = .000$). The short text differs significantly from the long text ($p = .000$), the navigation condition ($p = .007$) and the interactive map ($p = .022$). Navigation and interactive map showed no difference. We also found general differences between the secondary tasks in the gaze times on the FRONT ($F_{FRONT}[1.989, 53.698] = 4.921; p = .011$, Greenhouse-Geisser). Here the short text showed significantly longer mean gaze times compared to the long text ($p = .007$).

Analysing the **maximum gaze times** on the CID, we found the shortest times in the short text condition ($M = 7.00$, $SD = 1.70$) and the longest in the interactive map ($M = 8.47$, $SD = 2.17$), whereas maximum gaze times on FRONT showed the shortest times in the long text condition ($M = 3.14$, $SD = 1.73$) and the longest in the interactive map ($M = 4.71$, $SD = 2.11$). A repeated measures ANVOA showed a significant influence of the task type on the maximum gaze times on CID ($F[3, 81] = 4.591; p = .005$) with a significant difference between the long text and the interactive map ($p = .004$). We also found a significant effect of the task type on the maximum gaze times on FRONT ($F[3, 81] = 5.591; p = .002$) with a significant difference between the short text and the interactive map ($p = .008$).

Test subjects are likely to miss an incorrect lane change when they do not attend to the driving scene as long as the road signs are visible. We rate a lane change (correct and incorrect) as overlooked, if we don't register a single fixation (gaze time > 200 ms) on FRONT during the time the road signs are visible (3.6 s). The overlooked lane changes ranged from six with zero incorrect changes in the short text condition up to 64

4. Development of the Automated Lane Change Test

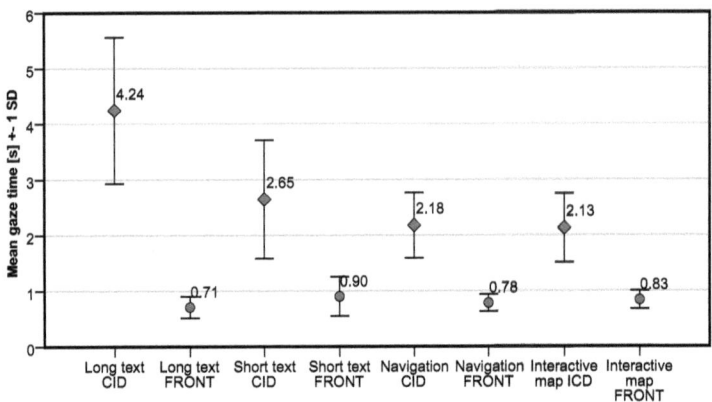

Figure 4.14: Mean gaze times and standard deviation (in seconds) of all visual tasks for AOIs CID and FRONT, sorted in descending order.

with eight incorrect changes in the interactive map, summed over all participants (cf. Table 4.4).

Lane changes overlooked	Interactive map	Navigation	Short text	Long text
correct	56	20	11	6
incorrect	8	2	0	0
Total	64	22	11	6

Table 4.4: Lane changes overlooked, summed over all test subjects.

Even more interesting is the number of missed errors if the test subjects actually had seen the road signs but yet not intervened in case of an incorrect lane change ("looked but not seen"). This number is basically the difference between the missed errors in that condition and the number of overlooked incorrect lane changes. Fig. 4.15 shows the comparison of total missed errors, overlooked errors and 'looked but not seen' errors.

In the map condition, participants missed 26 errors in total, which contained eight errors that had been overlooked by not watching the driving scene, whereas 18 errors were not corrected though participants had looked at the road signs at least once. The navigation condition showed 14 of 16 errors that were seen but not corrected compared to two errors overlooked, the short text showed three out of three and the long text one out of one seen, but not reacted to. A Friedman test showed a significant difference between

4.2 User Study 1: LO version

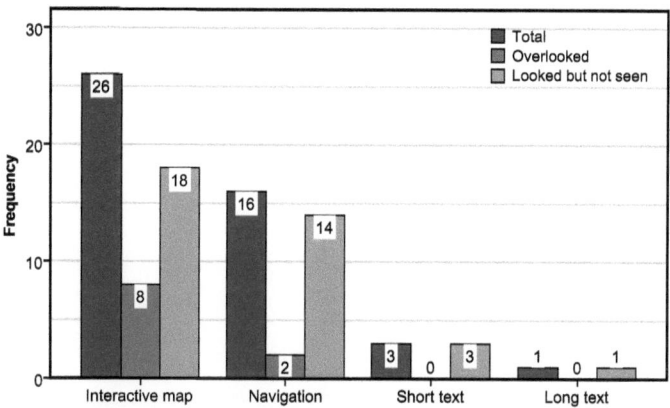

Figure 4.15: Gaze analysis of missed errors summed over all participants. All missed errors, overlooked errors and errors seen but not correct.

the conditions ($\chi^2[3] = 17.579; p = .001$). All pairwise tests showed a significant difference ($p < .05$) except interactive map and navigation, as well as short text and long text.

An analysis of the time to the first fixation on the driving scene when the road signs appeared (t_1, cf. Fig. 4.2) showed that the short text condition had the shortest ($M = .64$, $SD = .14$) and the interactive map the longest time ($M = .80$, $SD = .29$, cf. Fig. 4.16). We found a significant main effect using a repeated measures ANOVA ($F[3,81] = 5.627; p = .001$). This can be ascribed to the short text condition, which showed significantly shorter times compared to all other tasks (each $p < .014$). Beyond that there we no differences. We neither found differences when comparing correct versus the three types of incorrect lane changes ($F[2.244, 60.589] = 1.918; p = .13$, Greenhouse-Geisser).

Subjective Data

DALI The subjective rating using the DALI (cf. 4.2.2) on a 6-point scale (ranging from 0 = low and 5 = high) showed the least perceived workload in the audio book condition ($M = 1.71$, $SD = .56$) and highest workload in the interactive map ($M = 3.18$, $SD = .69$, cf. Fig. 4.17). As mentioned, the baseline drive comprised only a single task, so the DALI was not applicable. The different tasks showed a significant effect on the mean DALI score using a repeated measures ANOVA ($F[5,135] = 33.937; p = .000$). In a pairwise post-hoc Bonferroni analysis, the audiobook condition was rated significantly less demanding than all the other tasks (each $p < .05$). However, the navigation task and

4. Development of the Automated Lane Change Test

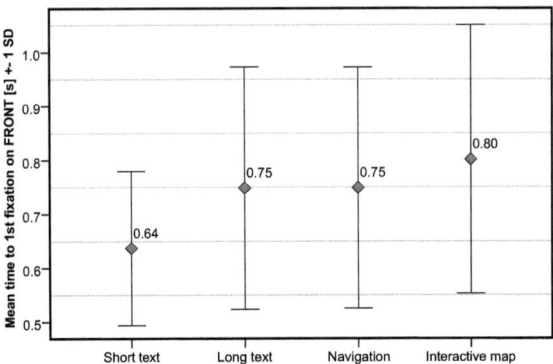

Figure 4.16: Time to first fixation on FRONT in seconds and standard deviation when road signs appear (all visual tasks, sorted in ascending order).

the interactive map – with no difference between each other – were rated significantly more demanding than all other tasks (each $p < .05$). The rating of the phone call task, the short text and long text condition did not differ significantly.

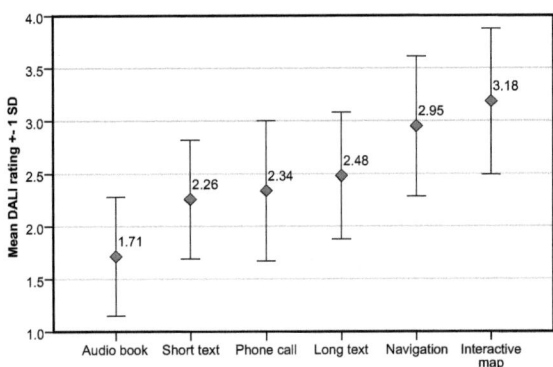

Figure 4.17: Mean DALI score and standard deviation, sorted in ascending order.

Fatigue We also assessed the participants' fatigue during the course of the experiment. After each run they were asked for their perceived level of tiredness on a scale from 0% (wide awake) to 100% (extremely tired). As described in 4.2.2, the order of tasks was counterbalanced across the test subjects, so that each task was performed equally distributed over the course of the study. The baseline condition turned out to be the most fatiguing task ($M = 41.57$, $SD = 23.33$), whereas the phone call task resulted in the lowest

4.2 User Study 1: LO version

perceived fatigue ($M = 28.86$, $SD = 18.70$, cf. Fig. 4.18, top). It appears that active tasks have a less fatiguing effect on the participants than passive tasks. However, these results must be treated with reservation, since these ratings are likely to be confounded with a fatiguing effect of the experiment duration. We analysed the tasks after their temporal course in the experiment. The fatigue ratings showed that the first performed task had the lowest mean level of tiredness ($M = 30.59$, $SD = 20.03$) and the last task the highest ($M = 41.04$, $SD = 20.59$). Fig. 4.18 bottom, shows the temporal progression of the perceived fatigue.

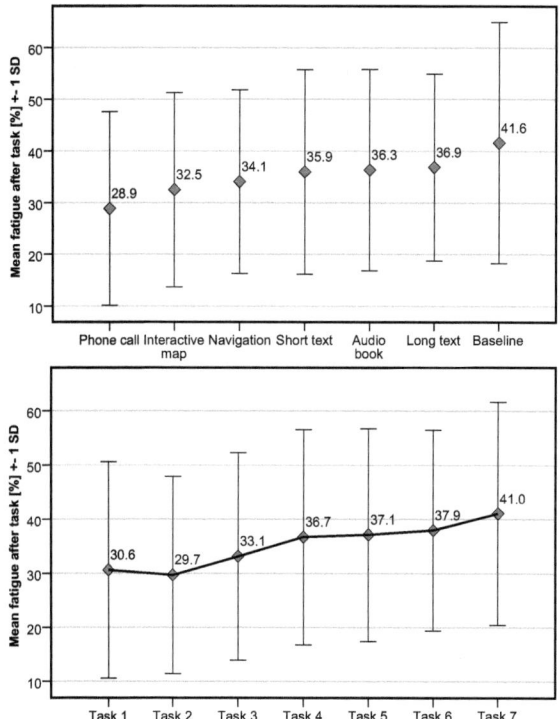

Figure 4.18: Top: Mean level of perceived fatigue and standard deviation, rated after corresponding task, sorted in ascending order. Bottom: Mean level of perceived fatigue and standard deviation, rated after corresponding task, temporal progression.

Task Ranking After finishing all test runs, the test subjects were asked to rank the experienced secondary tasks regarding the perceived difficulty and distraction from the primary task, from one (easiest, least distracting) to six (hardest, most distracting). We used a forced choice rating, so that each task had a place assigned. Fig. 4.19 shows the mean ranks. The audio book was rated as the least demanding ($M = 1.79$, $SD = 1.13$), the interactive map as the most demanding task ($M = 5.04$, $SD = 1.00$). The ascending order equals the order of the mean DALI scores. When applying the median instead of the mean function, the overall order stays the same, only long text and navigation swap places.

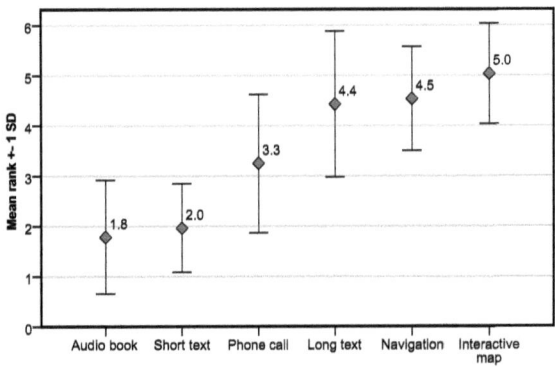

Figure 4.19: Mean assigned rank and standard deviation of all secondary tasks, sorted in ascending order from perceived easiest to hardest task.

Subjective Interruptibility Furthermore, the test participants judged the interruptibility of all secondary tasks on a 5-point Likert scale from one (hard to interrupt) to five (easy to interrupt). The long text task was rated with the lowest mean value ($M = 2.18$, $SD = 1.02$) and the short text as the highest ($M = 3.96$, $SD = .84$). Fig. 4.20 displays the obtained results. A repeated measures ANOVA showed an overall difference ($F[3.378, 91.204] = 0.042; p = .000$, Greenhouse-Geisser). The short text was rated significantly higher than all tasks previously categorised as hard to interrupt (each $p < .04$), whereas the long text was judged significantly lower than all tasks except the phone call (each $p < .03$). Between all other tasks were no significant differences. It became apparent that the test subjects in our study share principally, but not entirely, our categorisation into easy and hard to interrupt. The audio book task was rated as easier to interrupt than expected.

Further Results In the concluding questionnaire we asked the question how many errors the test subjects thought they had missed. The answers ranged from zero to eight with

4.2 User Study 1: LO version

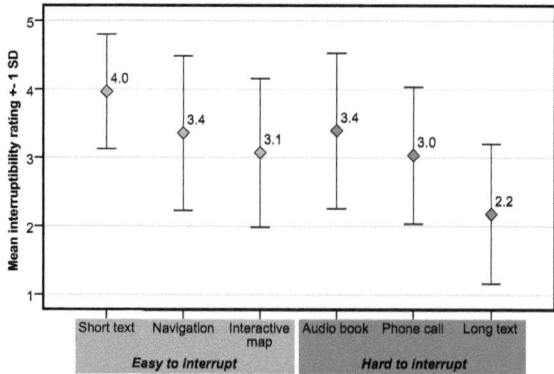

Figure 4.20: Mean rating of interruptibility and standard deviation. Sorted in descending order, grouped by categorisation into easy and bad interruptibility.

an average of 2.54 ($SD = 2.35$). We correlated their estimation with the actual number of missed errors and found no significant result ($Pearson - r = .299, p = .123$).

4.2.6 Discussion of Results

In this section the hypotheses stated in 4.2.1 will be discussed based on the previously presented results.

Main Effect We have seen very clear effects of performing secondary tasks simultaneously to the primary task of supervising automated vehicle guidance. The results in the baseline drive without an additional task show the fastest response times in case of an error, significantly different from all secondary tasks except the audio book task. This task has also subjectively been rated as the easiest task, so that we assume that this task can be performed effortlessly when supervising an automated driving task, and does not affect automation supervision and error recognition negatively. Expressed in a POC graph, the dual task of automated driving supervision and listening to an audio book would come close to the ideal point P in the upper right corner (cf. 2.1.2).

Also missed errors and false interventions appear in the baseline drive in very rare cases compared to the dual-task conditions. The single missed error was happening interestingly at a point of time when the test subject was yawning.

These results indicate that the measurements in the ALCT method are principally able to discriminate regarding different secondary tasks. Therefore, we regard H_1 as confirmed.

Degree of Interaction The newly introduced categorisation dimension proved to be helpful in explaining the obtained results. We found that tasks involving an active engagement with an operating element or an interaction with another person lead to a deterioration in the primary driving supervision task. We found significantly longer response times, more missed errors and more false interventions compared to tasks with passive, consuming characteristics. Consistently, active tasks have also been subjectively perceived as more demanding. We assume the reason for this lies in a deeper level of mental processing [157]. This is supported by the measured gaze activity. Active (visual) tasks imply frequent changes of AOIs, with mean gaze times of about 2s, which matches the upper recommended limit by the AAM for secondary tasks during manual driving [1]. Based on these results, H_2 can be confirmed.

Modality The dimension of modality categorising a secondary task has been adopted from Wickens [175]. Since the major amount of perceived information during driving is visual information [151, 162], the assumption that secondary tasks requiring visual attention result in a deterioration of the performance in the primary task is not far-fetched. We also assumed that tasks conveying information via the auditory channel result in a better performance than visual tasks. Indeed we found that visual tasks imply slower response times and induce more false interventions than auditory tasks. But we could not find a difference regarding missed errors. Even a direct comparison of the two tasks only differing in this dimension (audio book vs. long text) showed the same result. This is mainly due to the number of errors missed in the phone call task. So H_3 can be confirmed regarding response times and false interventions and must be rejected regarding missed errors.

Concerning auditory tasks, it is worth to have a look at the difference between listening and speaking. The phone call task always shows significantly worse results compared to the audio book task. This is a clear hint that the degree of interaction again plays an important role and has an confounding effect on the dimension of modality.

Interruptibility We assumed that tasks that can be easily interrupted and continued result in a better performance than tasks that are unwillingly interrupted because they cannot be continued as easily. The surprising result is that there is a significant difference in response times in favour of tasks that we categorised as hard to interrupt. There is no difference in missed errors and false interventions. So H_4 must be rejected. There are several potential explanations for our contradictory finding. The participants basically agree with our categorisation of secondary tasks, but their subjective ratings do not clearly separate tasks which are easy and hard to interrupt. Another likely reason might be the strong effects of the other dimensions confounding the measurements of interruptibility.

4.2 User Study 1: LO version   95

Moreover, it could be the case that during automated driving the interruptibility of a secondary task becomes less important, because of the different way of interacting with the vehicle.

Information Encoding Wickens considers the encoding of information as the main factor of interference of overlapping mental resources [172, 175]. Because of the spatial characteristic of the driving scene we hypothesised that a secondary task using spatial information encoding results in a worse performance in the primary task compared to tasks with verbal information encoding. This assumption could not be confirmed in the conducted study. To be fair, with the interactive map we only had one spatial task in the experiment, since there are not many common in-car tasks involving spatial information. Therefore we only compared the interactive map with the one corresponding task differing in the dimension of information encoding, the navigation task. These two tasks basically show very similar results regarding response times, gaze behaviour, and subjective rating, and slightly but not significantly different results in missed errors and false interventions. Since the interactive map also involved some verbal information (names of federal states and cities), it is possible that these two tasks were too similar to produce significantly different results. It is also likely that the other dimensions have strong confounding effects, so that potential differences did not become visible. Thus, we must reject hypothesis H_5.

General Discussion There are some interesting results that haven't been discussed so far. We find a remarkable match regarding objectively measured and subjectively rated data. Mean response times, the mean DALI score and the assigned rank show exactly the same order (cf. Fig. 4.9, 4.17, 4.19). Of course, there is not a significant difference between all items within these measurements, but nevertheless this is an indication that the chosen measurements are suitable.

Another interesting result is the coherence between missed errors and mean gaze duration in visual tasks. Surprisingly, the longer the mean gaze on the display, the lower the number of errors missed. The long text shows by far the highest mean gaze times on the CID ($> 4s$), the longest total gaze times on the CID, and was rated as task hardest to interrupt. However, we found medium response times and a single missed error in the whole study. We traced this finding back to the degree of dynamics in the display. The interactive map and navigation task involved constant changes in display contents, and also resulted in a high number of missed errors; the display contents within the long text task, however, remained unchanged for minutes at a time. This is tied to a different need for visual search on the display which is likely to lead to a different perception of the appearing road signs [13]. However, this does not necessarily mean that more errors were overseen by not watching the road during tasks with more visual search involved. The majority of the incorrect lane changes were perceived, but the participants often failed to react appropriately during the tasks they rated more mentally demanding. With resources of the working memory bound during a dual-task situation, people fail to connect visually perceived elements with knowledge structures in the long term memory. Superficial processing, in our case of the road signs and the vehicle's actual trajectory, results in an deficient model of the current situation and the appropriate action is not executed [6]. So the "lack of situation awareness may be directly responsible for much of the out-of-the-loop performance decrement" [51], p. 2.

At first appearance the obtained gaze data for the interactive map is contradictory. We found the shortest mean gaze times on the CID ($> 2s$), but the longest maximum gaze times on the CID ($> 8s$), the longest total gaze time on the FRONT and by far the most overlooked road signs. These results match the observation during the study, that this task, which was also subjectively rated as the most demanding one, was really stressful for the test participants. The nature of the task with permanent interaction, visual distraction and permanently changing display contents prevented the development of a suitable 'switching strategy' in order to share one's attention between the primary and the secondary task. Most of the time the test subjects frequently switched between FRONT and CID, but sometimes they seemed to 'forget' their primary task when they were searching for the next given target on the map. When they had found it, they tilted the controller in the direction of the target and then looked back to the driving scene. This is how very long single gaze times originated.

An analysis of the time to the first fixation on the FRONT after the road signs appeared proved the short text task to show significantly shorter times than the other visual tasks. We assume this is due to the AOI switching rhythm the average task duration induces. The fact that there were no differences between correct and incorrect lane changes is entirely plausible, since the test subjects could not know if it is a correct or incorrect lane change when they looked back to the FRONT.

The results obtained in the phone call condition were somewhat surprising, particularly regarding the missed errors and false interventions. This task showed the most false interventions and the second most missed errors, although there was no visual distraction and therefore no need to take the eyes off the driving scene. But, as previously mentioned, also the other tasks showed a number of missed incorrect lane changes when the eyes were actually on the road, and yet no intervention happened. This has been observed with all active tasks. Based on the results in our studies we recommend the degree of interaction and modality as the main criteria of secondary tasks in an examination in the context of automated driving.

Different levels of automation trust find expression in remarkable interindividual differences in our measurements, most visible in the number of missed errors. In terms of commission and omission we have seen that commission errors (error 1 and error 3, cf. Fig. 4.13) produce shorter response times than omission errors (error 2), since they involve active vehicle movement, which is apparently better perceivable. However, this does not lead to an increased number of errors in category 2 that are missed by the test subjects. It is possible that the found effects might mitigate with a longer period of practising.

The overall performance of the test subjects over time only shows a tendency of a fatiguing effect. We found the baseline drive as the most fatiguing condition, but the rate of nine errors in eleven minutes is probably still to high and the driving time per session too short, so that the test subjects are likely to range in the middle sector of the Yerkes-Dodson arousal-performance relationship in all conditions (cf. Fig. 2.10).

4.3 User Study 2: LO vs. HI version

This section describes a study where we contrasted the two implementation versions of the ALCT.

4.3.1 Experimental Goals and Hypotheses

After obtaining encouraging results in the first study, a second study was conducted primarily to prove the validity of the ALCT method and its metrics. Another important question involves the influence of direct haptic feedback from the steering wheel on error recognition. To enable better comparisons we adopted most of the first study's experimental procedure. We stated the following hypotheses for this study:

1. H_1: The HI version leads to shorter response times than the LO version, because the haptic feedback makes a lane change perceivable earlier and more clearly.

2. H_2: Response times in error category 2 will be the longest in both versions, because this kind of error does not involve haptic feedback.

3. H_3: Through the haptic feedback the HI version results in fewer missed errors than the LO version.

4.3.2 Experimental Procedure and Setup

Based on the results from the first study and the found differences regarding secondary tasks, we only chose three of the tasks for the subsequent examination: **interactive map**, **short texts** and **phone call**, since we have seen the most noticeable differences in the results. Those tasks were realised identically as in study 1 (cf. 4.2.3). There were two experimental blocks, one using the LO interaction version, the other using the HI version. In each block participants performed all three tasks. In the block using the HI version we added a baseline run without a secondary task, so that there were again seven test runs for each participant. We decided not to include a baseline run in the LO version, because of the results from the first study showing very clear differences between baseline and all dual-task conditions. Furthermore, we wanted to keep the study within a limit of two hours duration.

The order of the secondary tasks within each block was counterbalanced across participants (cf. Appendix Table A.2). Half of the participants started with the LO version, the other half with the HI version. We used same objective measurements as in study 1 (mean response time, missed errors, false interventions and gaze). As subjective measurement for task demand we used again the DALI questionnaire in all conditions involving a dual-task setup.

We also used an identical hardware setup with a mock-up car, plasma screens, central information display showing visual task contents, and the same centrally mounted input device (cf. 4.2.3). The only exception was the actuated steering wheel, realised as described in 4.1.2. Again, participants were required to wear a head-mounted eye-tracking system for gaze analysis.

4.3.3 Sample

In this experiment 29 test subjects (20 male, nine female) with an average age of 34.2 years ($SD = 8.53$, $min = 23$, $max = 53$) participated. All of them have been recruited from the BMW test subject pool. All participants were in possession of a driving license for three to 35 years with an average of 16.1 years ($SD = 8.79$). As in the previous study, we excluded participants in need of spectacles, due to the eye-tracking system.

4.3.4 Results

The following section reports the results from the study. We present objectively measured results (response times, error data and gaze data), then subjective statements from the test

4.3 User Study 2: LO vs. HI version

subjects.

Reaction Data

Mean Response Times We analysed the **mean response times** using a repeated measures ANOVA with the factors *version* (LO vs. HI), *task type* (short text, interactive map, phone call) and *error category* (1, 2, 3). We found a significant main effect of the version ($F[1,28] = 133.64, p < .001$), of the task type ($F[2,56] = 15.14, p < .001$) and the error category ($F[1.32, 36.88] = 38.42, p < .001$, Greenhouse-Geisser). Moreover, we found a significant interaction effect between version and error category ($F[2,56] = 3.8, p = .028$, cf. Appendix Fig. A.3). In total, the response times in the HI version are 0.62 s to 0.81 s shorter than in the LO version. In the LO version the short text showed the shortest ($M = 2.13, SD = .35$) and the interactive map the longest mean response time ($M = 2.31, SD = .45$), which proved to be a significant difference (post-hoc pairwise comparisons using the Bonferroni alpha correction, $p < .001$). In the HI version the shortest response times were found in the baseline drive ($M = 1.36, SD = .17$) and the longest in the interactive map ($M = 1.66, SD = 0.3$). We found significantly longer times for the short text task than for the phone call task ($p = .023$), which was not the case in the LO version. As in version LO, the interactive map produced significantly longer response times than the phone call task ($p < .001$). The baseline shows significantly shorter response times than the short text ($p < .001$) and the interactive map ($p < .001$), but there is no difference compared to the phone call task ($p = .81$).

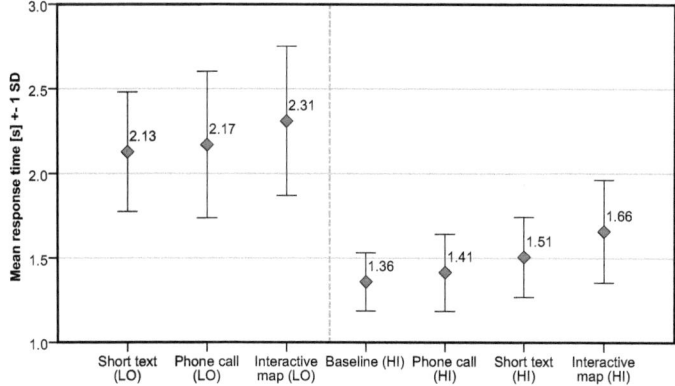

Figure 4.21: **Mean response time in seconds and standard deviation for version LO and HI. Grouped by version and sorted in ascending order.**

Table 4.5 shows the correlations of the mean response times within the secondary tasks.

In the corresponding ALCT version we found medium to high correlations in the mean response times. There were medium correlations between the same tasks in different versions.

	Phone call	Interactive map	Short text
Phone call	.54 (p=.002)	.6 (p=.001)	.61 (p<.001)
Interactive map	.68 (p<.001)	.53 (p=.003)	.78 (p=.001)
Short text	.73 (p<.001)	.79 (p<.001)	.41 (p=.027)

Table 4.5: Correlations of response times within the different secondary tasks (Pearson-r). The table shows correlations between tasks in the LO version (lower left), between tasks in the HI version (upper right) and pairwise compared between the versions (diagonally).

Error Categories When comparing response times regarding error categories, we found that in version LO, error 2 produced the longest response times ($M = 2.50$, $SD = .63$) and error 3 the shortest ($M = 1.95$, $SD = .28$). In version HI, also error 2 shows the longest response times ($M = 1.74$, $SD = .28$) and error category 3 the shortest ($M = 1.39$, $SD = .25$, cf. Fig. 4.22). For this analysis we excluded the response times from the version HI baseline, since there was no corresponding condition in version LO. We found significant differences in all pairwise compared error categories in both conditions (each with $p < .001$), except error 1 and error 2 in the LO version and error 1 and error 3 in the HI version. In reference to the interaction we found between error category and version, the difference between error 3 and other errors is more apparent in the LO version. In total there were 39 misses in error category 1, 40 missed in category 2 and four in category 3.

Missed Errors A total number of 55 errors were missed in the LO version, compared to 31 errors missed in the HI version (excluding the baseline). In both versions the task with the least missed errors was the short text (LO: ten, HI: seven, cf. Table 4.6). The phone call task induced the most errors in the LO version (24), whereas the interactive map showed the most missed errors in the HI version (13). There were no significant differences between tasks within the LO version (Friedman, $p = .096$), within the HI version (Friedman, $p = .185$), nor a main effect between both versions ($Z = -1.681, p = .093$).

4.3 User Study 2: LO vs. HI version

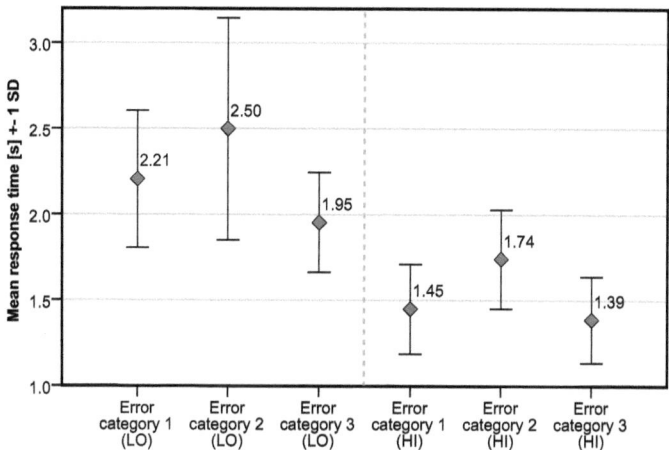

Figure 4.22: Mean response time in seconds and standard deviation for error categories in version LO and HI.

False Interventions In the HI version we registered a very high number of false interventions (190 in total, cf. Table 4.6) due to accidentally overruling the automation by holding the steering wheel too firmly. There were single test subjects overruling the automation more than 20 times, one even 33 times (cf. Fig. 4.23). Thus we decided not to analyse the data obtained in the HI version concerning false interventions. In the LO version we found only one false intervention in the short text task and eleven in the phone call condition.

Comparing Study 1 and Study 2 When comparing the measured values in the LO version of study 1, we can state the mean response times were 0.25 s to 0.30 s ($M = .29$) longer in the LO version of study 2 than in the LO version of study 1. In order to verify this, we used a multi-variate ANOVA with *study* as between-subject variable and *task type* as well as *error category* as within-subject factors. In particular, we were interested in potential interaction effects with the between-subject study. We found significant main effects of the factors task type ($F[1.69, 92.74] = 12.82, p < .001$, Greenhouse-Geisser) and error category ($F[1.53, 83.88] = 41.44, p < .001$, Greenhouse-Geisser), but no interaction effect of study (1 or 2) with the task type ($F[1.69, 92.74] = 0.28, p = .716$, Greenhouse-Geisser) or error category ($F[1.53, 83.88] = 1.47, p = .236$, Greenhouse-Geisser). As mentioned, there is a significant between-subject effect ($F[1, 55] = 12.26, p = .001$) showing that the participants in study 1 responded 0.29 s faster than the test subjects in study 2. We identified two main explanations for this finding. On the one hand we

4. Development of the Automated Lane Change Test

	Short text (LO)	Phone call (LO)	Interactive Map (LO)	Short text (HI)	Phone call (HI)	Interactive Map (HI)	Baseline (HI)
Missed error 1	4	13	6	4	5	5	2
Missed error 2	6	10	9	3	5	7	0
Missed error 3	0	1	1	0	1	1	0
Total missed	10	24	16	7	11	13	2
		50			31		
False interventions	1	11	7	24	74	34	58
		19				190	

Table 4.6: Number of missed errors and false interventions in each condition summed over all participants.

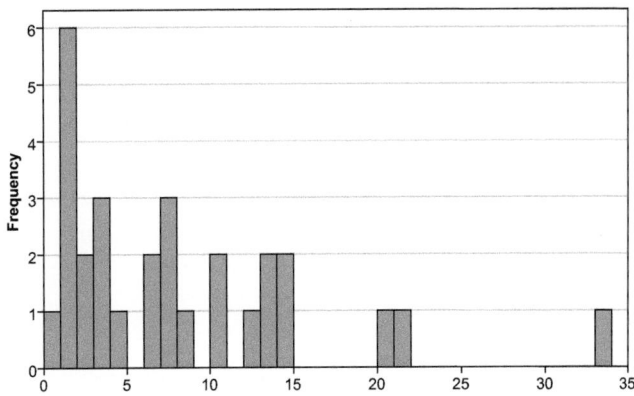

Figure 4.23: Histogram of false interventions. Number of times the automation was unnecessarily overruled by a given number of subjects. Only a single subject had no false interventions, another as much as 33.

found that three participants showed very long response times in almost all conditions (in single cases up to three times as long as compared to other participants). On the other hand, however, the participants in the second sample are roughly five years older on average compared to sample 1. Medium to high correlations of response times and age were found in most tasks (cf. Table 4.7). We also performed an analysis of covariance regarding the factor *age* and found that the adjusted difference averages 0.22 s. However, also with adjusted values, the between-subject factor is still significant

4.3 User Study 2: LO vs. HI version

$(F[1,54] = 6.91, p = .01)$.

	Short text (LO)	Phone call (LO)	Interactive map (LO)	Short text (HI)	Phone call (HI)	Interactive map (HI)
Correlation to age	.57 (p=.001)	.51 (p=.005)	.40 (p=.03)	.26 (p=.17)	.42 (p=.023)	.34 (p=.076)

Table 4.7: Correlations response times to age (Pearson-r).

In the LO version we found a higher number of total false interventions in the performed tasks in study 1, but with no significant difference to those in study 2, as shown by a Mann-Whitney-U test ($Z = -1.84, p = .066$). Comparisons of tasks in the LO version of study 1 and tasks of study 2 showed similar numbers of total missed errors (46 vs. 50). In study 1 the interactive map produced the most misses, whereas in study 2 the phone call task produced the most. A Mann-Whitney-U test did not show significant differences between the versions for the phone call task ($Z = -.653, p = .514$), the short text ($Z = -1.895, p = .058$) or the interactive map ($Z = -1.078, p = .281$).

Gaze Data

We recorded gaze data for both visual tasks: interactive map and short text. As in study 1, we assessed *total gaze times*, *mean gaze times*, and *overlooked lane changes*. Table 4.8 shows an overview. The **total gaze times** on the CID ranged from 397.19s ($SD = 73.59$) in the interactive map condition in the HI version up to 420.54s ($SD = 81.91$) in the short text condition in the LO version, whereas the short text in the LO version shows the shortest total gaze times on FRONT ($M = 199.65$, $SD = 75.41$) and the interactive map in the HI version shows the longest total gaze times ($M = 230.21$, $SD = 66.65$). For the CID, a repeated measures ANOVA with the factors *version* and *task type* showed a significant difference regarding the ALCT version ($F[1,25] = 5.17, p = .032$), but no effect of the task type ($F[1,25] = 0.59, p = .449$) and no interaction between version and task type ($F[1,25] = 0.23, p = .638$). Also, for the AOI FRONT, there is only a significant effect of the version ($F[1,25] = 6.79, p = .015$).

Mean gaze times on the CID ranged from 2.00 s ($SD = .71$) in the interactive map condition in the HI version to 2.51 s ($SD = .98$) in the short text condition in the LO version. Using a repeated measures ANOVA we found a significant main effect of the version on mean gaze duration ($F[1,25] = 12.09, p = .002$). Furthermore, both tasks showed significant shorter mean gaze times on the CID in the HI version than in the LO version (interactive map: $t[26] = 4.425, p = .000$, short text: $t[27] = 2.063, p = .049$). There are no differences regarding the AOI FRONT. We see an increased variance in

4. Development of the Automated Lane Change Test

			Interactive map (LO)	Short text (LO)	Interactive map (HI)	Short text (HI)
Total Gaze Time		CID	M=414.09 (SD=76.53)	M=420.54 (SD=81.91)	M=397.19 (SD=73.59)	M=407.07 (SD=82.04)
		FRONT	M=214.08 (SD=70.75)	M=199.65 (SD=75.41)	M=230.21 (SD=66.65)	M=217.42 (SD=79.82)
		%$_{CID}$ / %$_{FRONT}$	66 / 34	68 / 32	63 / 37	65 / 35
Mean Gaze Time		CID	M=2.24 (SD=.78)	M=2.51 (SD=.98)	M=2.00 (SD=.71)	M=2.26 (SD=1.03)
		FRONT	M=1.05 (SD=.34)	M=1.09 (SD=.36)	M=1.08 (SD=.36)	M=1.10 (SD=.42)
Max. Gaze Time		CID	M=8.54 (SD=2.80)	M=6.26 (SD=1.35)	M=7.13 (SD=1.59)	M=6.14 (SD=1.30)
		FRONT	M=5.53 (SD=2.58)	M=4.81 (SD=1.58)	M=6.91 (SD=2.94)	M=7.71 (SD=3.64)

Table 4.8: Total summed gaze times, mean gaze times and maximum gaze times on the AOIs CID and FRONT for all visual tasks in both versions, in seconds.

study 2 compared to study 1. The overall gaze times show a slight increase of times on FRONT and a decrease on the CID.

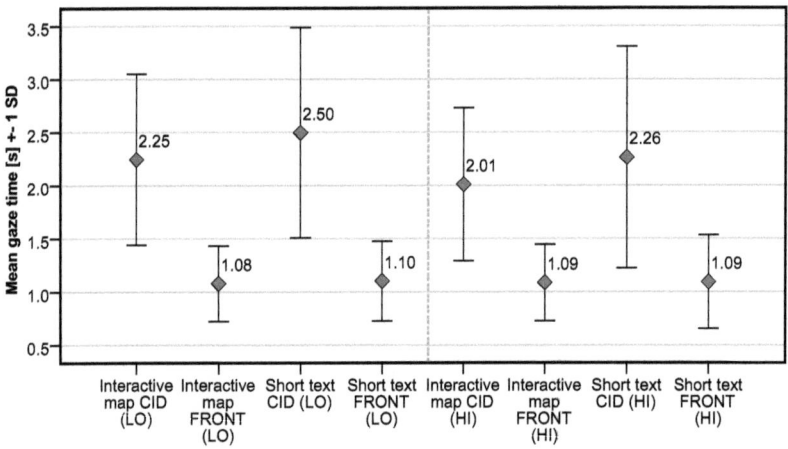

Figure 4.24: Mean gaze times on CID and FRONT in seconds with standard deviation.

Again, we analysed the lane changes that have been overlooked by not observing the driving scene. In the LO version we found 44 overlooked lane changes during the interactive map task with one error missed, compared to 33 missed lane changes (two

4.3 User Study 2: LO vs. HI version

errors) in the HI version (cf. Table 4.9). In the short text we counted 13 overlooked lane changes in the LO version and two in the HI version, each with one error overlooked. In both cases there were no significant differences. Compared to study 1, the number of overlooked lane changes in the interactive map task was lower (64 with eight errors in study 1), and almost equal in the short text task (eleven with zero errors in study 1).

Lane changes overlooked	Interactive map (LO)	Short text (LO)	Interactive map (HI)	Short text (HI)
Correct	43	12	31	1
Incorrect	1	1	2	1
Total	44	13	33	2

Table 4.9: Number of lane changes overlooked, summed over all test subjects.

Furthermore we ran an analysis of errors that have been missed although the test participants had looked at the road signs during a lane change (*looked but not seen*). Fig. 4.25 shows the comparison of total missed errors, overlooked errors and 'looked but not seen' errors. Of 16 missed errors in the interactive map condition in the LO version only one has been missed because of looking away from the driving scene, and 15 have actually been seen, but not reacted to. In the short text condition nine out of ten have been seen but not corrected. In the HI version we found similar but slightly lower numbers, with no significant difference. Finally the time leading up to the **first fixation** onto the road

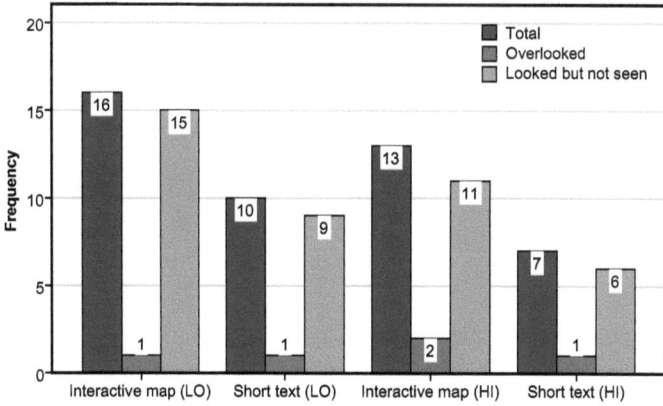

Figure 4.25: Gaze analysis of missed errors summed over all participants. All missed errors, overlooked errors and errors seen but not corrected, grouped by version.

when a road sign became visible was measured. The short text shows in both versions significantly shorter first fixation times than the interactive map ($t[28] = 5.325, p < .001$ and $t[26] = 5.357, p < .001$). These results are also consistent with study 1 as far as the LO version is concerned. Moreover, we found a significant main effect of the version on this measured time ($F[1, 13] = 73.23, p < .001$). A first fixation during a lane change occurred significantly sooner in the HI version than in the LO version for the short text condition ($t[28] = 7.922, p < .001$) and the interactive map ($t[26] = 4.176, p < .001$, cf. Fig. 4.26).

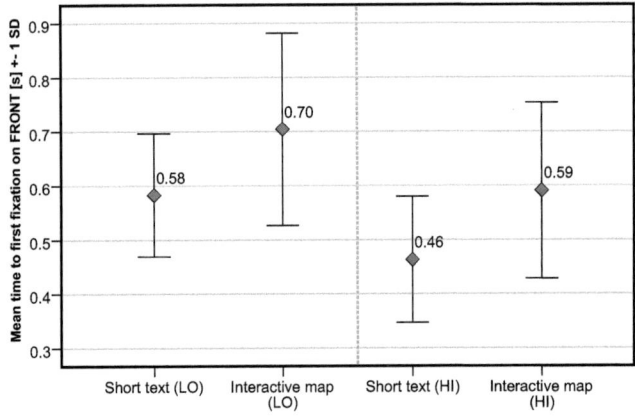

Figure 4.26: Time until the first fixation on AOI FRONT in seconds and standard deviation in the visual tasks, grouped by version.

Subjective Data

DALI As a subjective measurement we used again the DALI questionnaire. We did not compute the originally intended DALI score as the average of all seven assessed dimensions, but we only averaged the dimensions *mental effort, stress, temporal demand* and *interference*. We wanted to avoid a distortion in the calculated values due to the different nature of tasks. For instance, purely auditory tasks with no visual component are naturally rated low in the dimension of visual demand. So we excluded the modality and concentrated on the more general DALI dimensions.

On the computed alternative DALI score we applied a repeated measures ANOVA with the factors *task type* and *version*. There was no significant main effect of the ALCT version ($F[1, 28] = .68, p = .418$), but we found an effect of the task type ($F[2, 56] = 4.63, p = .014$). Also, there was a significant interaction effect which

4.3 User Study 2: LO vs. HI version

manifests itself as a bigger difference between the interactive map and the other tasks in the HI version. Post-hoc pairwise Bonferroni adjusted tests revealed that in the HI version the phone call task is rated significantly easier than the short text ($p = .016$) and the interactive map ($p < .001$), and the interactive map is significantly more demanding than the short text ($p = .001$) Fig. 4.27 shows the overall results. In comparison to study 1, the phone call is rated less demanding, with a significant difference to the short text, which was not the case in study 1.

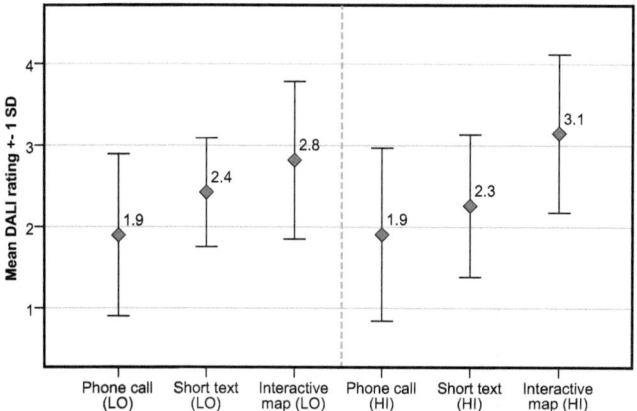

Figure 4.27: Mean DALI score and standard deviation, sorted in ascending order, grouped by version.

Task Ranking After the test runs the participants were asked to rank the experienced tasks regarding perceived difficulty from one (easiest) to three (hardest) task. The phone call task was ranked as the easiest task ($M = 1.25$, $SD = .59$) and the interactive map as the most difficult task ($M = 2.68$, $SD = .61$), cf. Table 4.10. A Friedman test showed significant differences ($\chi^2(2) = 28.79, p < .001$). Pairwise comparisons using a Wilcoxon test revealed significant differences between phone call and short text ($Z = -3.5, p < .001$), short text and interactive map ($Z = -2.8, p = .005$) as well as interactive map and phone call ($Z = -3.97, p < .001$). Compared to study 1, the phone call task was rated considerably better and swapped places with the short text. Furthermore, the test subjects had to estimate how many errors they believed to have missed without correcting during the experiment. The results ranged from zero to ten, with an average of 3.68 ($SD = 3.07$). On average, the test subjects estimated twice as much missed errors as they actually had ($M = 1.64$, $SD = 1.68$), but we found a significant correlation between the estimated number and the overall missed errors ($Pearson - r = .530, p = .020$).

Rank	Phone call	Short text	Interactive map
1	23	3	2
2	3	20	5
3	2	5	21
	M=1.25 (SD=.59)	M=2.07 (SD=.54)	M=2.68 (SD=.61)

Table 4.10: Ranking of tasks regarding the perceived difficulty.

Further Results Multivariate ANOVAs performed for mean response times, missed errors and false interventions showed no significant influence of **gender** in any of the seven task conditions.

In the concluding questionnaire the test participants had to answer the question with which ALCT version they thought they had missed more incorrect lane changes on a scale from -3 (more frequent in the LO version) to +3 (more frequent in the HI version). An average value of -0.75 ($SD = 1.46$) shows that the test participants believed they had missed more lane changes in the LO version. Statistically this value is significantly different from zero ($T = -2.73, p = .01$).

We also asked with which ALCT version they had recognised an incorrect lane change earlier on the same scale. The test subjects answered with an average value of 1.32 ($SD = 1.44$) that they had seen an incorrect lane change earlier in the HI version. A t-test showed that this value is significantly different from zero ($T = 4.85, p < .001$).

4.3.5 Discussion of Results

We found clear differences in **response times** comparing the two versions we implemented in this study. The HI version involving feedback from the steering wheel generated much shorter response times in comparison to the LO version without feedback. This is not a surprising result, as a lack of feedback and increased demands on vigilance can influence the drivers' reactions negatively [71]. Furthermore, the signal for a beginning lane change is in most cases more explicit. A movement in the steering wheel can be detected faster and with less cognitive demand than having to visually compare the road signs with the virtual vehicle's actual trajectory without haptic feedback. Therefore we can regard hypothesis H_1 as confirmed.

A number of test subjects showed in some cases clearly increased response times

4.3 User Study 2: LO vs. HI version

compared to the other participants. We decided not to exclude them from analysis, since not all measured values deviated strongly from other test subjects' response times. It seems they sometimes forgot to react as fast as possible.

The response times on an incorrect lane change are clearly dependent on the **error category**. We found the same differences in response times between the versions (up to 0.8 s) that we had measured individually also when grouping the times to the error categories. Error 2 shows consistently the longest times, since this error does not involve a movement of the steering wheel and can therefore be compared to all errors types in the LO version. So H_2 is confirmed. Nevertheless, even error 2 in the HI version induces significantly shorter response times compared to all error categories in the LO version. Through the haptic feedback there is obviously a stronger link between the driver and the driving respectively supervision task. The participants could not lean back to the same degree they did in the LO version. This is backed by the results of the analysis of the first fixation on the driving scene when a new lane change began. The participants used less time to redirect their attention toward the road, when driving with steering wheel feedback. Furthermore, also shorter mean gaze times on the central display and longer gaze times on the FRONT indicate that the test subjects remained more involved with the driving task in the HI version.

We did not see the expected differences between the ALCT versions regarding the missed errors. The total number of missed errors in the LO version were absolutely higher, but the differences were not significant. Consequently, H_3 must be rejected. We implicitly assumed that, analogously to the response times, the most missed errors would be in category 2. This also proved false, most errors have been missed in category 1. Moreover, most of these have not been overlooked by looking somewhere else, but missed with eyes on the virtual road. Revealingly, most errors in the HI version have been missed during the phone call task, where no visual distraction existed. These results again point clearly to the negative influence of cognitive workload on automation supervision. In category 3 almost no errors are missed. These seem to be recognizable very clearly despite cognitive workload.

We did not expect that the HI version would produce such a high number of false interventions (190 compared to 19 in the LO version, cf. Table 4.6). The participants had to manually force the steering wheel in the desired direction. We observed that in most cases the test subjects held the steering wheel too firmly when a lane change and a steering wheel turn was initiated. Increasing the momentum needed to overrule the automated steering would probably not have reduced the accidental interventions. We chose 3.0 Nm in the first place after an intensive testing phase experimenting with different momentums. We found that it is much easier to overrule the steering wheel by holding it tightly, rather than to apply a counterforce on the already turned steering wheel. Most of our test persons agreed that 3.0 Nm is already a strong resistance to work against. So we decided not to apply a higher momentum.

We found a good match between objectively measured results and the subjective estimations of the test persons. They mainly judged their own performance correctly when asked for subjective differences between the ALCT versions. But there is one point in that objective and subjective results do not match. The phone call task was rated as the easiest and least demanding task. However, in this task a remarkable number of missed errors happened. So the cognitive demand of this task has been underestimated. It is likely that having a conversation on the phone is assumed to be a well-known task that is also frequently performed in an automotive context. Also, the eyes are considered on the road, so the distraction is not perceived to the degree it actually subsists. Thus, no compensation effects occur that are common when the test persons are aware of being distracted [78]. Consequently, the subjects missed more errors without noticing afterwards.

In general, the results obtained for the LO version in study 2 had been established in study 1. Response times as well as missed errors seem very similar in both studies despite an increased variance due to the test sample and the test procedure. We also found very similar effects regarding the error categories. This supports the validity of the ALCT methodology and its metrics. A direct comparison of results can be done for some key measurements, but should not be overemphasised. This is mainly because of the different experimental procedure. In the second study the test subjects not only are confronted with two different versions of the ALCT, but they also perform every secondary task twice. It is likely that learning effects occur from the first to the second time the task is performed, and through the randomization the variance increases. This becomes visible in the gaze data, with clearly increased standard deviation mostly with gazes on the FRONT. Even if the secondary task types were not the focus of this study, we found results widely consistent with the first study, yet with minor differences in details.

4.4 Methodical Discussion

Driving with automated vehicle guidance systems requires supervision and selective intervention rather than permanent manual control and manoeuvring. In case of an automation error it is crucial to detect the error and react appropriately as quickly as possible. We tried to map these general concepts into a new methodology for laboratory assessment that is safe and easy to handle. Compared to the established LCT method, the ALCT incorporates event detection, supervision and choice reaction rather than control and reaction as in the LCT. During a drive with automated longitudinal and lateral control, the drivers' only task is to make sure the vehicle behaves as it is supposed to and doesn't leave its predefined path. This concept could be incorporated despite a virtual driving environment. Therefore the ALCT represents a more 'realistic' story than the LCT, especially the HI version, in a way that even when driving in an artificial environment, the driver's action would be very much the same as on the road, namely take over control and steer the vehicle in the correct direction.

The chosen setting and variables show plausible results with respect to the investigated subject, i.e. measuring the influence of secondary tasks on detecting and responding to automation errors. It is likely that different methods assessing driving performance (e.g. LCT, PDT, etc.) would have shown a similar tendency of overall workload imposed by most of the assessed secondary tasks. However, since they do not consider the context of automated driving and use different metrics, the results cannot be compared directly. The ALCT can provide detailed insight into how automation supervision and the comparison of normative and actual value are affected by tasks that are distracting in various aspects.

The ALCT covers commission errors (inappropriate action) and omission errors (no action when appropriate). This is mapped to erroneous lane changes. We deliberately only included lateral control errors not only for the purpose of simplicity. Automated longitudinal control systems have been in the market already for over a decade (cruise control, adaptive cruise control), and are widely accepted despite their imperfection. In theory it would also be possible to require longitudinal action in the ALCT, for example by introducing speed limits or brake signs. But the lack of kinaesthetic feedback in a static driving simulator when virtually braking can cause simulator sickness. Furthermore, changing speed is conceptually not trivial and would require profound changes in the overall methodology. If we introduced a brake sign, the automatically controlled vehicle would normally reduce its speed. This raised a number of questions: Down to what speed does the vehicle brake? Which deceleration is to be applied? Does the vehicle accelerate again and if, after what time? Does the participant have to use the gas pedal to speed up again? What if the brake sign is missed? Do we then also need an 'accelerate sign'? Can different types of signs interfere with each other? How can we avoid that? How many errors will occur in total and how do they distribute? Even if all those questions could be satisfyingly answered, changing the speed would disturb the continuity of the driving. Also the original LCT has no reason for altering the speed. Therefore we decided not to include longitudinal signals and action, respectively.

It could be argued that the driving scene is too simple and that the visual cue of showing road signs which can be anticipated to a certain degree, is too obvious, which is also true for the original LCT. The results of the experiments do not confirm this: although the driving scene is simple and despite the road signs are easy to spot when they appear, we found strong effects in response times and missed lane changes. So the depiction of the virtual driving scene itself does not seem to be adverse.

From a methodological point of view, both LO and HI version show plausible results and both can be used for examining the influence of arbitrary secondary tasks in an automated driving situation. For a more realistic, but technically more complex setup, we recommend the HI version with an actuated steering wheel. However, the HI version involves the danger of frequent false interventions if the participants override the automation accidentally. Since the results mainly differ in an absolute response time value, the LO version can also be used. Although we chose the setting in a driving simulator, the ALCT could also be implemented as a PC-based version. This would show if driving in large-screen simulation environment really creates a deeper feeling of immersion and higher trust in automation.

According to Bortz and Döring [15], a scientific measurement method must be *objective*, *valid*, and *reliable*. Objectivity means that the obtained results are not influenced by the experimenter and special circumstances during the experimental situation, analysis, or interpretation. The validity indicates that the method is suitable for measuring the desired criterion and actually is able to measure it. Finally, a method is reliable if it *reliably* measures the desired criterion and it is not subject to measurement errors to an unacceptable degree. The ALCT was designed so that the requirements are fulfilled in the best possible way. The virtual driving scene runs on a real-time simulation system with a jitter of less than 0.01 s. Measurements are triggered automatically when a certain condition is met unambiguously. So in the LO version the steering wheel angle and in the HI version the force applied to the steering wheel are measured by dedicated hardware and logged automatically. We unambiguously determined the points of time when the measurements are to be taken (cf. Fig. 4.2). Moreover, all data processing and analysis is done automatically, too. A crucial point is that the instruction is executed exactly identically with each test subject. If subjects do not entirely understand that their primary task is the supervision of the automation, this can distort the results, as we might have seen in the second study with some participants not intervening as fast as they possibly could. This is a common problem with most scientific measurement methods that assess human behaviour. It is also advisable that the participants do not know the total number of errors during one run. Clever participants might try to outwit the experimenter and dedicate to the secondary task more intensely only after the maximum number of errors is reached.

We tried to obtain results as objective, reliable and valid as possible. In the end, the ultimate validity of the ALCT cannot be proven unequivocally. Despite quite clear results in both studies, it is also not possible to make an absolute statement about the criticality of single tasks during automated driving, as there is no reference to compare to so far. In the studies, we focused on 'real-life' tasks that are likely to be performed during driving. We deliberately did not choose an artificial reference task (e.g. SURT, CTT, etc., cf. 2.1.3), since they do not really reflect a realistic in-car task. The CTT for instance would be categorised in our scheme as [visual, active, bad interruptibility, spatial], which means maximal overlap with the driving task and is therefore extremely distracting. We could not find a realistic, permissible in-car task comparable to that. The available reference tasks address very similar dimensions and do therefore not cover all dimensions that we wanted to assess. Nonetheless, for a complete judgement and reference of the results obtained in our studies, a real-life driving experiment with a real implementation of automated vehicle control would be necessary. We assume that the trust in automation and therefore involvement with secondary tasks will be lower in a real automated driving situation, since there is real danger tied to inattention in real traffic.

4.5 Summary

In this chapter we presented the Automated Lane Change methodology. We described the development, the technical features and requirements, the implementation, and explained why we designed it the way it was finally built. There are two versions regarding the interaction with the system. In the LO version turning the steering wheel does not effect the automatically controlled path of the virtual vehicle in the on-screen environment. The HI version offers feedback on the vehicles movement through the steering wheel and allows to take over manual control if the driver wishes to. Using this method, we conducted two comprehensive user studies assessing the effectiveness and feasibility of the methodology and to gain insights on how certain categories of secondary tasks influence the recognition of automation errors during an automated drive. The studies showed a clear effect of secondary tasks on automation error detection to a varying degree. Also haptic feedback as implemented in the HI version of the ALCT proved to be very helpful with keeping the driver aware of his primary task, the supervision of the automated vehicle guidance system.

Chapter 5

Magic Carpet – A Prospective Driving Path Display

This chapter describes the development and evaluation of a prospective driving path display – the **Magic Carpet** – as a means of supporting the recognition of errors occurring during automated driving. As mentioned earlier, we focus on lateral control errors. The driving path display specifically targets erroneous lane detection by the sensor system which results in a slow and continuous deviation from the centre of the lane. Opposed to the explicit incorrect lane change manoeuvres incorporated in the formal ALCT method, the driving path display aims at a more subtle – but also critical – type of automation error (cf. 3.3). The Magic Carpet makes the automated vehicle's future path visible to the driver and thus enables him or her to recognise a deviation from the course potentially earlier than without visual support. This concept has been implemented in a driving simulation environment.

In 5.1 we describe the basic principles, background information, the design process and how the driving path display is technically realised. Section 5.2 reports the procedure and results of a driving simulation user study we conducted with different versions of the driving path display.

5.1 Development of the Magic Carpet

5.1.1 Basic Principles and Related Work

The basic idea is to make the automated vehicle's near future path visible to the driver. This is similar to a so-called flight path vector (FPV) as used in aircraft head-up displays. As a minimal requirement, we assume a semi-automated system that is able to maintain the speed and keep the vehicle inside its definite lane. Extracted from sensor and camera data, an automated control system has an internal model of the road ahead (e.g. the next three seconds in the future) and computes a projected trajectory which the controller follows. We make this trajectory visible (cf. Fig. 5.1). Thus, in theory, the driver can recognise a deviation from the intended course potentially earlier than without support. The natural reaction – turning the steering wheel in the opposite direction – is located on Rasmussen's skill- or rule-based level (cf. Fig. 2.1). The concept of the prospective driving path display is based on **Augmented Reality** (AR) which means that virtual information is added to the real world. In our case, we add the projected future vehicle path virtually to the real road view. The path lies like a carpet on the road in front of the vehicle and moves itself with the car, which is why we call it the **Magic Carpet**. The concept has been filed for patent [152]. For simplicity, we will call the driving path display **carpet** from now on.

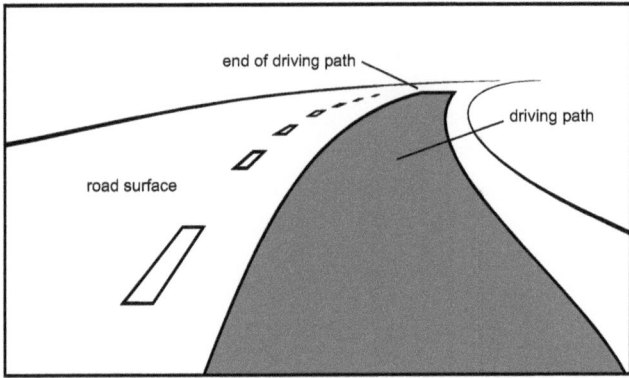

Figure 5.1: Sketch of a prospective driving path display. The internal representation of the vehicle's projected guidance trajectory is mapped onto the road in form of a virtual coloured area. The vehicle will take the projected path and in a few seconds reach the position where the end of the driving path currently is.

AR is a paradigm within the field of computer science and can be described as a computer-supported augmentation of real world elements with virtual elements. The term AR was coined in the early 1990's and was first classified by Milgram's *Virtuality Continuum*, with the real environment on the one end and the virtual environment on the other [109], cf. Fig. 5.2.

Although AR is not limited to a single sensory channel, most applications only

5.1 Development of the Magic Carpet

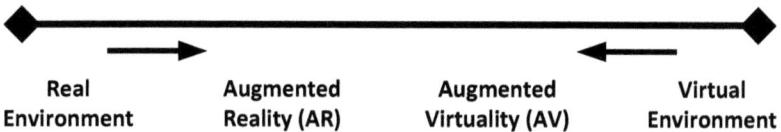

Figure 5.2: Milgram's Reality-Virtuality continuum (redrawn from [109]).

make use of visual content. AR does not replace, but rather enriches reality by adding information and creating a composite image of the real world and virtual objects. This can be achieved using different techniques. A common way of realising AR applications is the use of head-mounted displays (HMDs) showing a merged image of real and virtual content. The virtual elements are naturally only visible to the person wearing the HMD. Another approach is using a handheld display as a "magic lense". Virtual objects are overlaid onto a camera image and shown on the display. Today, mobile phones equipped with a camera are the standard platform for handheld AR applications, since they have become powerful enough to perform the necessary image processing routines. It is also possible to project virtual elements on two- or three-dimensional surfaces in the environment or to use 3D displays as an output medium for AR.

There are many examples of useful AR applications from various domains, but we want to focus on AR for automotive uses. For the use of AR inside a car, there is another technique available which can display images directly overlaid on reality through mirroring the virtual content in the windowpanes in a perspectively correct way (cf. Fig. 5.3). This technique is called **contact analogue** and is commonly realised by advanced head-up displays. Thus, the virtual image appears to be in fact merged with reality. A popular application using this technology is contact analogue navigation (e.g. [56, 92, 116, 180]) that does not only give navigational hints, but shows the driver which way must be taken on the road. A slightly different approach is the **virtual cable**[1], that appears as a red line high above the road to lead the driver the way.

Apart from navigation applications, there are several examples of automotive AR that support driving safety. As early as in the 1970's Bubb presented a contact analogue concept that displayed the safety margin in the form of a brake bar. The brake bar indicated the point on the road where the vehicle would come to a stop with full braking force applied [23]. This concept has been taken up by Tönnis et al. (cf. Fig.

---

[1]http://www.mvs.net/

5. Magic Carpet – A Prospective Driving Path Display

Figure 5.3: Augmented reality navigation. Left: Extra display (from [116]). Right: Contact analogue display (from [143]).

5.4, [160, 161]), also including the distance to other vehicles. Bergmeier explored the potential of contact analogue marking of pedestrians in the dark using a night-vision system [8]. As Fig. 5.3 and Fig. 5.4 show, such systems are mostly in a prototype stage,

Figure 5.4: Contact analogue brake bar indicating the stopping distance (from [161]).

not yet of high quality and not yet commercially available. Contact analogue displays are technically complex, require large installation space and suffer from some intrinsic problems. Inappropriate overlays are still an unsolved issue. When driving closely behind another vehicle, a virtual navigation path, for example, would be shown overlaid on the vehicle, not on the road. Moreover, not all desired content can be shown, due to limited display area (cf. [180]). Israel and Bubb show an overview of the potential and limitations of the contact analogue HUD in vehicles [83]. Stanton and Pinto present a study showing effects of risk homeostasis when using vision enhancement systems [155]. That means, drivers tend to compensate the gain of safety and comfort achieved through a supporting system by driving more risky.

5.1.2 Design Process and General System Description

We created several different versions of the carpet design. First, we tried to visualise the area on the road that will be occupied in the next seconds by the vehicle. This resulted in a simple polygon in the centre of the driving lane with the width of the vehicle ("carpet", cf. Fig. 5.1). Another design approach was the future trace of the wheels instead of a carpet ("wheel traces"), so that only the area of road contact is displayed. It follows the analogy of traces in snow, only projected to the future roadway (cf. Fig. 5.5, left). This concept resulted in negative feedback from our test drivers, because those traces looked like additional road markings, in some situations like those used as provisory lane markings in construction sites, so that the test drivers repeatedly got confused. We then tried to combine the carpet polygon with the wheel traces in order to avoid any ambiguity (cf. Fig. 5.5, right). The broad centre polygon had the width of the distance between the wheels and the slim lines left and right indicated the broadest lateral dimensions of the car, i.e. the border of the side mirrors. This depiction was judged as too overloaded, with no real extra value. Another version was the marking of the whole lane, from the right border of the road to the dashed line in the centre of the road with a width of 3.5 m. Also this depiction did not persuade our testers, because it had not a direct connection to the vehicle and its position, and was therefore judged as not useful enough. So in the end we decided to display the carpet only as a single polygon with the width of the vehicle in the centre of the lane, because this was understood intuitively by most of our test drivers.

Figure 5.5: Sketches of carpet alternatives. Left: Wheel traces. Right: Combination of wheel traces and carpet.

This concept of the carpet has been implemented in a driving simulation environment (5.1.3). As described above, there were several technologies available to realise the augmented image of the driving scene. One option was to use a HMD. For HMDs to work well they must provide minimal latency, otherwise there will always be a mismatch between the driving scene and the overlaid prospected driving path when the driver moves his or her head. Apart from that wearing an HMD for a longer period of time is not comfortable. A realisation using a real hardware contact analogue head-up display was not the adequate option for our goal to show and to evaluate the basic principle and the general effectiveness, since such displays are still expensive and complex to build. So, finally the carpet was realised as a video overlay in the driving simulation graphics as a simulated contact analogue head-up display. This gave us the freedom to display the carpet exactly as desired and to experiment with shape, colour and system behaviour, without having to take restrictions by optical hardware into account. Within the limits of this thesis, no more than a proof of concept can be provided.

The carpet display is designed to be visible when the vehicle drives with automated longitudinal and lateral control. The carpet is depicted as a coloured two-dimensional polygon with slight transparency, displayed on the road surface directly in front of the driver's vehicle. With activated automation the car is kept in the centre of its own lane, so that the carpet is also displayed in the centre of the lane. It has the width of the vehicle – in the driving simulation 1.79 m – and a variable length. The carpet length is determined by the time the vehicle's sensors are able to look ahead (e.g. three seconds), so that the length varies with the vehicle's speed. That means the vehicle will be at the position where the carpet ends within three seconds. This is true with straight driving as well as in curves. Fig. 5.6 shows a sample how the final carpet looks like in the driving simulation environment.

Figure 5.6: Front view showing the carpet display. It shows the vehicle's future path and position up to three seconds ahead.

5.1 Development of the Magic Carpet 121

Milgram defines a set of six classes describing different ways of realising Mixed Reality. In our case, the carpet is integrated with a rendered image of the driving simulation environment. This comes closest to Milgram's class 6: *"Completely graphic but partially immersive environments (e.g. large screen displays) in which real physical objects in the user's environment play a role in (or interfere with) the computer generated scene"* [109], p. 3. So in our case it helpful to speak of **Augmented Simulated Reality**.

5.1.3 Implementation

The carpet software is implemented as a Matlab/Simulink model that is executed in a driving simulation environment, similarly as described in 4.1.2. We used an existing model containing longitudinal and lateral control routines as implemented by Schaller et al. [142], adapted and extended by the desired functionality. We will not explain the details of the longitudinal and lateral controller, since those were not developed as part of this work and were only used as a means to provide the desired automation behaviour.

The SPIDER driving simulation (cf. Fig. 5.7) provides detailed data about the ego vehicle, road and lane positions, surrounding vehicles as well as arbitrary generic information which all serves as input for our computations in the Simulink model. From the mock-up car we get live input from the steering wheel (angle, angle speed and momentum), pedals and steering wheel buttons. All inputs are then processed and passed to SPIDER.

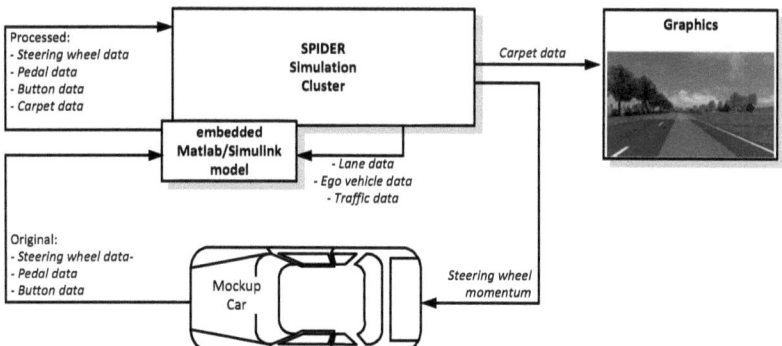

Figure 5.7: Realisation of the carpet in the driving simulation, overall hardware setup and information flow.

Carpet trajectory A trajectory is a functional graph describing an object's movement path. In order to determine the carpet's trajectory there are three parameters needed:

- Lateral offset y_0
- Heading angle θ
- Trajectory curvature κ

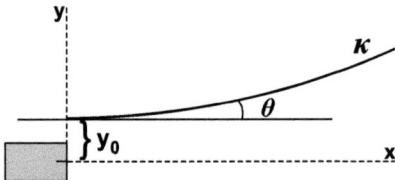

Figure 5.8: Vehicle trajectory determined by offset y_0, heading angle θ and curvature κ.

Fig. 5.8 shows a car's trajectory on the road described by those values. The lateral offset y_0 is the distance from the centre of the lane to the centre of the car related to the front tip. Heading angle θ means the rotation of the car with reference to the tangent of the trajectory with curvature κ. Those values are also needed as input for the lateral control of the virtual car. The trajectory can be calculated using a 2nd order Taylor polynomial:

$$y = y_0 + \theta x + \frac{1}{2}\kappa x^2$$

It is the task of the controller to keep y_0 as small as possible.

The carpet is displayed as a polygon based on an array of fixed points. The fixed points are placed in equal distance on the trajectory following the centre of the lane (cf. Fig. 5.9), with $y_0 = 0$, $\theta = 0$ and $\kappa_{carpet} = \kappa_{lane}$. The fixed points are then doubled and shifted $width/2$ to the left and to the right. The obtained points now enclose the carpet polygon and are filled with colour. We had to extend SPIDER by an extra interface for receiving and displaying the carpet polygon. Position and appearance can be determined by the following parameters:

- *number_of_points*: The number of points that span the carpet polygon.
- *width*: The lateral width of the carpet polygon in meters.

5.1 Development of the Magic Carpet

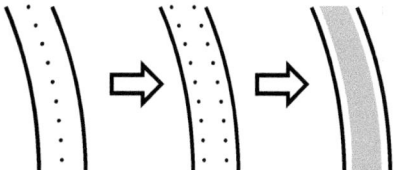

Figure 5.9: Principle how the carpet polygon is constructed.

- *redChannel*: Ratio of the colour red in the carpet colour [0..1].
- *greenChannel*: Ratio of the colour green in the carpet colour [0..1].
- *blueChannel*: Ratio of the colour blue in the carpet colour [0..1].
- *transparency*: The alpha channel of the carpet polygon [0..1].
- *zBuffering*: Display the carpet with or without depth information [0 | 1]. When displaying without depth information, the carpet will be painted over any object, with depth information, the carpet would potentially be occluded by other cars, as it would lay on the road and cars drive on it.
- *points*: For each point a pair of x- and y-coordinates. x indicates the distance from the centre tip of the car, y indicates the offset from the lane centre in meters (dx, dy).

All parameters except the points are predefined, but can be also changed at runtime. In every simulation cycle the Matlab/Simulink model computes the set of vertices of the carpet polygon and passes it via the newly introduced interface to the SPIDER simulation cluster. The carpet is then rendered integratedly with the virtual scene on the road. It is important to note that we do not use world coordinates, but coordinates relative to the virtual car's current lane. That makes it easier to induce incorrect lane keeping behaviour, as described in detail in 5.1.4. We have a set of global parameters we initialise the Simulink model with:

- *carpet_length*: The time it takes in seconds to reach the point on the road where the carpet currently ends with the centre tip of the virtual car ($default = 3$).
- *min_carpet_length*: Minimal length in meters of displayed carpet ($default = 20$).
- *max_carpet_length*: Maximum length in meters of displayed carpet ($default = 150$).
- *begin_carpet*: Starting point of the carpet in front of the virtual vehicle in meters ($default = 1$).

- *carpet_no_fixed_points*: Number of fixed points the carpet polygon consists of ($default = 10$).

- *error_polynomial_degree*: Polynomial degree of the error function: 1 (linear), 2 (squared) or 3 (cubic) ($default = 2$). The error function is described in section 5.1.4.

- *error_coefficient* Coefficient used in the error function ($default = 0.0000562$).

- *heading_limit* Maximum heading angle in radians. When reached, the gradient angle of the error function keeps this value ($default = 5° \cdot \frac{2\pi}{360}$).

5.1.4 Modelling of Automation Errors

The Magic Carpet mainly visualises lateral control errors caused by incorrect lane detection, i.e. lanes are detected, but not exactly where they actually are. This error is not unlikely to happen in a real vehicle that is not equipped with redundant high quality sensors. Through the filters and signal smoothing routines of the controller, the error is perceivable not as a sudden action, but as a slowly increasing deviation from the lane. Of course, in the driving simulation there is no incorrect lane detection, so that the automated control system would never deviate from the lane. We replicate this faulty control behaviour in a way that when we want a deviation to occur, the original lane data is manipulated by adding an increasing lateral offset. The controller then no longer keeps the centre of the lane, but takes the modified data as the correct lane centre and the vehicle drifts away to the left or to the right. In order to realise the modified lane data, we use different error functions inducing differently fast increasing deviations. The modified lane data is also visible in the carpet, also deviating from the actual lane (cf. Fig. 5.10).

Figure 5.10: Lane deviation resulting from manipulated lane information visible in the carpet.

5.1 Development of the Magic Carpet

Fig. 5.11 shows the top-level Simulink functions necessary for the computation of the carpet. The important functions are *error generation* and *vector generation*, which are explained in detail in the following section. The error generation function computes the data necessary for the incorrect lane keeping behaviour. It takes five arguments:

- x: A vector consisting of *number_of_points* points on the vehicle's trajectory that line out the carpet. Source: Self-generated.

- *lat_pos*: Lateral position within the current lane. Source: Driving simulation.

- *lane_width*: Width of the current lane. Important to determine the centre of the lane. Source: Driving simulation.

- *ego_vel*: Velocity of the ego vehicle. Important to determine the carpet length. Source: Driving simulation.

- *error*: Flag if an error is currently active. Source: Driving simulation.

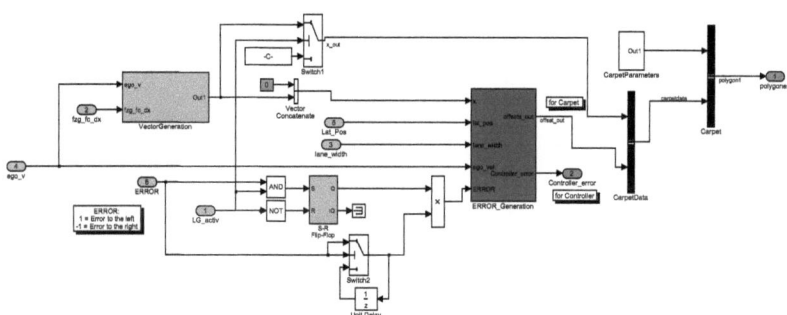

Figure 5.11: Simulink implementation of the generation of the data necessary to display the carpet polygon.

The error generation functions needs a vector of fixed points that describe the carpet polygon. Below an example is shown with the parameters of ten fixed points, a carpet length of ten meters (three seconds with ego velocity of 3.33 $\frac{m}{s}$) with a starting point of three meters in front of the vehicle.

1. Generate a vector with (*number_of_points* + 1) points dependent on vehicle speed and carpet length. Example output: $[3,4,5,6,7,8,9,10,11,12]$.

2. Add zero as first point for the controller. Example output: $[0,3,4,5,6,7,8,9,10,11,12]$.

The resulting vector now contains the x-values that are later passed to the driving simulation. The controller needs the first vector value to be zero, because this indicates the current x-position. Within the error generation function, this vector is further transformed:

1. Subtract the highest value from all values in the vector. Example output:
   $[-12,-9,-8,-7,-6,-5,-4,-3,-2,-1,0]$.

2. Add the driven distance. Example output for five meters:
   $[-7,-4,-3,-2,-1,0,1,2,3,4,5]$.

3. Set all negative values to zero. Example output: $[0,0,0,0,0,0,1,2,3,4,5]$.

This transformation is only executed when an error is active. If not, the output of this transformation always looks like $[0,0,0,0,0,0,0,0,0,0,0]$, since there is no offset added to any point. The resulting vector now serves as input for the actual error function. For a flexible deviation behaviour we implemented three different functions, making the error increase in a linear (coefficient a), squared (coefficient b, cf. Appendix Fig. A.4) and cubic (coefficient c) manner:

- Linear: $y = a \cdot x$

- Squared: $y = b \cdot x^2$

- Cubic: $y = c \cdot x^3$

Applying the error functions element-wise with coefficients $a = b = c = 0.001$, after five meters the y-vectors would look like this:

- Linear: [0, 0, 0, 0, 0, 0, 0.001, 0.002, 0.003, 0.004, 0.005]

- Squared: [0, 0, 0, 0, 0, 0, 0.001, 0.004, 0.009, 0.016, 0.025]

- Cubic: [0, 0, 0, 0, 0, 0, 0.001, 0.008, 0.027, 0.064, 0.125]

The output of the error generation is a vector with y-values containing the offsets from the centre of the lane for the next *number_of_points* points on the road. In the example, with the cubic error function after five meters the deviation is already 12.5 cm, whereas with the linear function only has produced a deviation of 0.5 cm. The controller needs this vector in a different format, therefore there are two output parameters in this function. The x and y vectors are then merged as *points*(dx, dy) together with the carpet parameters described in 5.1 and passed to the driving simulation in the given format.

5.1 Development of the Magic Carpet

Controller Input

Since the controller does not only use the lateral offset vector created by the error function, but also the heading angle and the curvature, we had to provide the controller also with these values. If the controller would only be provided with the lateral offset, it would try to compensate the resulting incorrect heading angle relative to the road, and as a consequence, the virtual vehicle would not drive exactly on the carpet. The heading angle is the tangent of the slope of a graph $f(x)$, and the slope θ is the first derivative of the graph: $\theta = tan(f')$. So:

- Linear: $f_1(x) = ax \Rightarrow \theta_1 = f_1'(x) = tan(x)$
- Squared: $f_2(x) = bx^2 \Rightarrow \theta_2 = f_2'(x) = tan(2bx)$
- Cubic: $f_3(x) = cx^3 \Rightarrow \theta_3 = f_3'(x) = tan(3cx^2)$

Heading Angle θ In order to avoid too strong increase of the lane deviation, which could possibly not be handled by the controller, we have to limit the also increasing heading angle in reference to the road. The point when a heading angle α is reached can be pre-calculated:

- Linear: n/a, since θ is constant.

- Squared:

$$tan(\alpha) = \frac{d\,offset}{dx} = 2bx \Rightarrow x_2 = \frac{tan(\alpha)}{2b}$$

  Example for $b = 0.001$, $\alpha = 5° \Rightarrow x_2 = 43.74$. In 43.74 meters the heading angle is reached.

- Cubic:

$$tan(\alpha) = \frac{d\,offset}{dx} = 3cx^2 \Rightarrow x_3 = \sqrt{\frac{tan(\alpha)}{3c}}$$

  Example for $c = 0.00001$, $\alpha = 5° \Rightarrow x_3 = 54$. In 54 meters the heading angle is reached.

As soon as the heading limit α is reached, the heading angle θ stays constant: $\theta_1 = \theta_2 = \theta_3 = tan(\alpha)$.

Curvature κ The curvature of a graph of a function f in the point $(x, f(x))$ is calculated by the formula:

$$\kappa = \frac{f''(x)}{(1 + f'(x)^2)^{\frac{3}{2}}}$$

So:

- Linear: $\kappa_1 = 0$
- Squared: $\kappa_2 = \frac{2b}{(1+(2bx)^2)^{\frac{3}{2}}}$
- Cubic: $\kappa_3 = \frac{6cx}{(1+(3cx^2)^2)^{\frac{3}{2}}}$

As soon as the heading limit α is reached, the curvature κ in all error functions $= 0$.

Calculation of Lane Deviation

The error function also allows to pre-calculate the lane deviation at a given point, i.e. how long it takes to reach a given offset, or, what offset s is reached after a given time t depending on the velocity v of the vehicle. For

$$v = \frac{s}{t} \Rightarrow t = \frac{s}{v}$$

- Linear:

$$offset_1 = ax \Rightarrow x = \frac{offset_1}{a} \Rightarrow t_1 = \frac{\frac{offset_1}{a}}{v}$$

Example: An offset of 1 meter with $a = 0.01$ and $v = 16.6 \frac{m}{s}$ (60 km/h) is reached after 6 seconds or 100 m.

- Squared:

$$offset_2 = bx^2 \Rightarrow x = \sqrt{\frac{offset_2}{b}} \Rightarrow t_2 = \frac{\sqrt{\frac{offset_2}{b}}}{v}$$

Example: An offset of 1 meter with $b = 0.0001$ and $v = 16.6 \frac{m}{s}$ (60 km/h) is reached after 6 seconds or 100 m.

- Cubic:

$$offset_3 = cx^3 \Rightarrow x = \sqrt[3]{\frac{offset_3}{c}} \Rightarrow t_3 = \frac{\sqrt[3]{\frac{offset_3}{c}}}{v}$$

Example: An offset of 1 meter with $c = 0.000001$ and $v = 16.6 \frac{m}{s}$ (60 km/h) is reached after 6 seconds or 100 m.

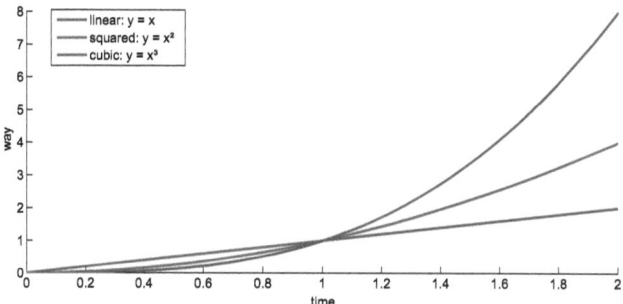

Figure 5.12: Exemplary plot of error functions with different polynomial degrees. In our case, the most adequate behaviour for the modelling of errors is reached by the squared function (red).

Eventually, we decided to use the **squared** error function with an error coefficient $b = 0.0000562$ in the user study described in the following section. This configuration produced subjectively the most realistic deviation behaviour. The linear error function did not allow for a smooth and unnoticeable beginning of an error and the cubic function resulted in a too strong increase in the deviation after almost no noticeable deviation in the beginning (cf. Fig. 5.12).

Using the formula above, one meter deviation is reached after eight seconds with $v = 16.6 \frac{m}{s}$ after 133.33 m. When run in real-time in the driving simulation it took approximately 6.7 seconds. This is due to the characteristics of the Simulink model when executed embeddedly and the clock of the driving simulation.

5.2 Evaluation of the Magic Carpet in a User Study

We evaluated the magic carpet in a comprehensive user study in order to get feedback on the idea of a prospective driving path display as a means to support the recognition of lateral automation errors by the driver. We wanted to show advantages and disadvantages of such a display, as well as obtain subjective opinions about this concept, to find out if this kind of support information bears potential. Moreover, we assessed different instantiations of such a display. We decided to implement two different versions of the carpet, i.e. we created two different ways of integrating the carpet information with the simulated reality. A contact analogue head-up display probably would be the best possible solution, since the carpet is shown directly overlaid over the real driving scene (cf. Fig. 5.13, left). As mentioned above, technologically this is today still very hard to realise and not available in the needed size. So we built an alternative version consisting of an extra display mounted in the centre console next to the CID (cf. Fig. 5.13, right). Shown on the display there is a live image of the driving scene, augmented with the carpet when the automation is turned on.

Figure 5.13: Different carpet versions. Left: Magic Carpet realised as contact analogue head-up display content merged with the driving scene. Right: Extra-display in the vehicle's centre console showing an augmented video of the driving scene with the driving path and no additional content on the front scene.

For the evaluation of effectiveness of the carpet display the ALCT was not the appropriate method, since they address different kinds of errors. In Rasmussen's 3-level model (cf. Fig. 2.1), a reaction to an ALCT errors happens on the knowledge-based level (comparison of road sign symbols with the actual driving path), a reaction to an error in the carpet setup happen on the skill- or rule-based level. Furthermore, ALCT and Magic Carpet serve a different purpose. The ALCT is a formal method to assess basic effects resulting from the situation of automated driving. The carpet display, however, is intended for use in a realistic setting. The concept of the carpet would not have worked when applied to the ALCT manoeuvres. Only when the road signs appear, the future course is decided, so the carpet could not have shown the future path beforehand. This is why we chose a different experimental setup and measurements, as described in the following sections. However, the results obtained in the ALCT studies influenced a number of decisions that concerned the evaluation design of the driving path display. Particularly, the use of haptic feedback on the steering wheel had been shown as effective, so that this was a basic requirement for the carpet experiment. Also the secondary tasks were chosen based on the results reported in section 4.2.5 and 4.3.4.

5.2.1 Hardware Setup and Human-Machine-Interface

The study took place in the driving simulation environment of BMW Research and Technology. The basic infrastructure has already been described in chapter 4. The main hardware was a mockup car, the front half of a reconstructed BMW sedan 5 series (cf. Fig. 5.14) with automatic transmission. The motor has been taken out and replaced by computers and interfaces connected to the SPIDER driving simulation. The interior, however, was completely identical with a genuine car. Only the originally analogue instrument cluster has been replaced by a digital display that showed the same instruments as an Adobe Flash[2] simulation. The mockup car was placed in front of a 220° curved canvas that showed the composite driving scene created by five projectors with a resolution of 1024×1920 pixels each (cf. Fig. 5.14).

The extra in-car screen that we integrated for the alternative version of the carpet was a 10.4" Nickl SunLight 10X automotive TFT display[3] with an XGA resolution of 1024×768 pixels. We created a very simple logic for enabling and disabling the

Figure 5.14: Driving simulator setup. Mockup car in front of a curved canvas displaying the driving scene.

automated driving function. There is an I/O-button on the left button panel of the steering wheel that toggles complete preset longitudinal as well as lateral automation with one button press, and switches it off again with another button press (cf. Fig. 5.15, left). When the automation is switched on, we replace the revolution counter on the right side of the digital instrument cluster by a large status information message as visual feedback.

---
[2] http://www.adobe.com/Flash
[3] http://www.nickl.de/Products/Displays/Sl10x/Sl10x_uk.htm

Moreover, the working automation becomes tangibly perceivable through a momentum applied to the steering wheel. A Kollmorgen Inland BL electric hollow shaft motor (Type RB01815-D00) is mounted on the steering column as already described in section 4.1.2 (cf. Fig. 4.3, left). Controlled by the Simulink model we can apply a permanent momentum of 3.0 Nm. In order to overrule the automation, this momentum has to be exceeded for at least 0.5 s, before the automation turns off. The time constraint has been introduced in order to avoid accidental overruling. When overruled, the momentum on the steering wheel is ramped down within 0.2 s, the automation is switched off and the rev counter reappears in the instrument cluster. The automation can also be switched off by pushing the brake pedal. The automation is then immediately disabled.

Figure 5.15: Left: Control buttons on the steering wheel, the I/O-key (bottom left) toggles longitudinal and lateral automation. Right: Digital instrument cluster, displaying current speed and status of the automated longitudinal and lateral control system.

5.2.2 Experimental Design and Procedure

Each test subject must complete one test run consisting of a track with a length of 32 km. The constant speed is 60 km/h, which results in a total test length of 32 minutes. The test subjects drive on a rural road with a lane width of 3.75 m and mainly easy curves with a radius from 150 to 700 m. They are always on the priority road with no need to stop at intersections. During the drive, the participants always drive with the automation switched on and at least one hand loosely on the steering wheel. There is no traffic on the road in the direction of the test vehicle, but frequent oncoming traffic in the left lane. We did not introduce a leading vehicle ahead of the ego vehicle in order to avoid potential negative effects of the carpet overlaying the vehicle ahead, even though it would have been reasonable to make the limited speed plausible despite a free road. With the automation turned on, the virtual vehicle is kept in the centre of the right lane and follows a pre-computed path. In case of an error this path deviates away from the lane centre to the

5.2 Evaluation of the Magic Carpet in a User Study 133

left, towards the left lane and continues to deviate with an increasing offset (as described in 5.1.4). This happens on seven locations on the track. In this case, the test subject must recognise this incorrect behaviour and overrule the steering wheel by turning it in the opposite direction. The test subject must then manually bring the vehicle back on the centre of the right lane and switch the automation on again. The errors have all been placed in curves with a radius of 300 m for comparability. However, the curves have been embedded in a changing surrounding environment so that it cannot be foreseen if the next curve will produce an automation error. We designed the error situations in a way that not overruling the steering wheel would result in a collision with the oncoming traffic. The oncoming vehicles have been programmed to control their speed so that they would hit the test vehicle when entering their lane. With that we prevent any ambiguity and avoid that the test subjects accept the deviation from their lane and react only when they would leave the road. We decided to place the error situations only in curves after having a test subject close his eyes before an error occurred on a straight section of the road. He could tell immediately when the error became perceivable by the slightest movements of the steering wheel. When placed in a curve, the steering wheel naturally turns and the error cannot be anticipated. Three errors occur in a right curve and four in a left curve. The first error occurring is treated separately as the *initial contact error*. The errors are located as follows:

1. Left curve: Initial contact error (after 5.48 minutes)

2. Left curve (after 7.50 minutes)

3. Left curve (after 13.50 minutes)

4. Right curve (after 16.01 minutes)

5. Left curve (after 23.23 minutes)

6. Right curve (after 24.55 minutes)

7. Right curve (after 31.01 minutes)

We applied a factorial **between-subject-design**, dividing our test sample into three groups according to the carpet version: Contact analogue head-up display (*HUD*, cf. Fig. 5.13, left), extra in-car display (*DISPLAY*, cf. Fig. 5.13, right) and a *Baseline* drive with no visual feedback at all.

Before the test drive there was a short demonstration drive during which we made the test subjects familiar with the driving simulator, the control, the overruling of the automated system, and if applicable, with the characteristics of the driving path display. They were instructed to keep the automation on all the time, but if they thought, something was going wrong, they were supposed to take over manual control. We told them their primary task was to make sure that the vehicle drives safely on the road. They were *not* shown and told how an automation error finds expression, in order to obtain genuine data on initial contact with an error.

Additionally there were two secondary tasks to accomplish that were selectively presented during the test drive: entering destinations into the navigation system using the iDrive controller (**navigation**) and answering questions in a phone conversation (**phone call**). These tasks were implemented identically as described in section 3.1.4. The tasks were chosen based on the results from the ALCT studies (cf. 4.2.5 and 4.3.4). We decided to include two active tasks, one visually and the other auditorily demanding that had also produced a significant effect in the ALCT setting. Each secondary task was performed once during an error in a left and in a right curve and randomly distributed over the locations with exception of the initial error location, which always occurred without a secondary task. In order to prevent predictability, each task had to be performed two more times placed on predefined locations on the road without an error occurring. Appendix Table A.3 shows the permutation table for all tasks in 12 different variants. Below follows an overview of the relevant factors in this study:

- **Carpet version** with the levels:

    – Contact analogue head-up display (HUD)

    – Extra in-car display in the centre console (Display)

    – No visual support (Baseline)

- **Type of curve** with the levels:

    – Left curve

    – Right curve

- **Type of secondary task** with the levels:

    – Phone call

    – Navigation

    – No task

5.2.3 Metrics

The main measurement in the study is the **lane deviation** in case of an error. The lane deviation is defined as the lateral offset to the centre of the right lane at the time when the automation is overruled in case of an error. Since the driver must apply a counterforce on the steering for 0.5 s in order to overrule the automation, we take the lane offset 0.5 s earlier than the automation is switched off. Thus, the actual maximum offset might be a little higher, but the vehicle is already turning to the right even if the automation is still active. We decided to take the measured offset when the test subjects decided to overrule the system. This measurement can also be dichotomised, i.e. divided into a *timely* and a *late* reaction, depending on a certain threshold determining if the reaction was soon enough, for instance before exceeding the left lane boundaries. Tightly coupled with the lane deviation is the **response time**, i.e. the time between the beginning of the deviation and overruling the automation. This time depends on the characteristics of the error addition. The faster the error offset grows, the shorter the time the test subjects have to respond. In other words, a long response time does not necessarily mean that the situation is highly critical, if the error offset increases very slowly. So the more meaningful measurement in this study is the lane deviation.

As in the studies described in chapter 4, we are using a Dikablis head-mounted eye-tracking system in order to obtain the gaze behaviour from the participants. We defined the AOIs FRONT (driving scene), CID (central information display in the dash board, IC (instrument cluster) and DISPLAY (the extra in-car driving display in the DISPLAY condition), cf. Fig. 5.16. Regarding the gaze data we measure the **total gaze time**, **mean gaze time** and the **gaze rate**.

5.2.4 Pre-study

During the implementation and testing of the driving path display we noticed that the lane deviation and response times varied depending on the direction of the curve. In order to determine potential differences between left and right curves (cf. Fig. 5.17), we decided to run a short, informal pre-study. We had seven test persons with an average age of 29.71 years ($SD = 6.21$, $min = 25$, $max = 42$) drive the implemented track and assessed the lane deviation during occurring errors in two left and two right curves. As described in 5.2.2, the test subjects were only told to drive with the automated guiding system and keep the car safely on the track. The participants had no secondary tasks to accomplish during the test run.

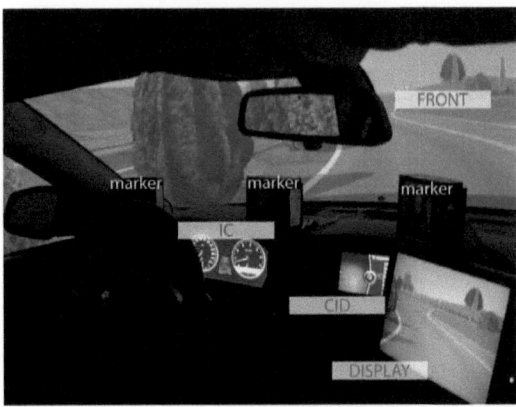

Figure 5.16: Mockup interior with the AOIs FRONT, IC, CID, and DISPLAY, and three visual markers on the dash board for automatic gaze detection.

Figure 5.17: Carpet deviating from the centre of the lane in a left curve (left) and in a right curve (right).

Results Despite the small sample size a one-way ANOVA showed clear evidence that the reaction times are longer in left curves than in right curves ($F[1,27] = 5.163, p = .032$), cf. Fig. 5.18. There was no significant difference between the first and the second left curve ($t[6] = -.134, p = .898$) and neither between the right curves ($t[6] = 2.110, p = .079$). This had the consequence that we had to distinguish between left and right curves and had to take this into account as a separate factor in our main study. A discussion of this result is presented together with the discussion of the results of the main study in section 5.2.8.

5.2 Evaluation of the Magic Carpet in a User Study

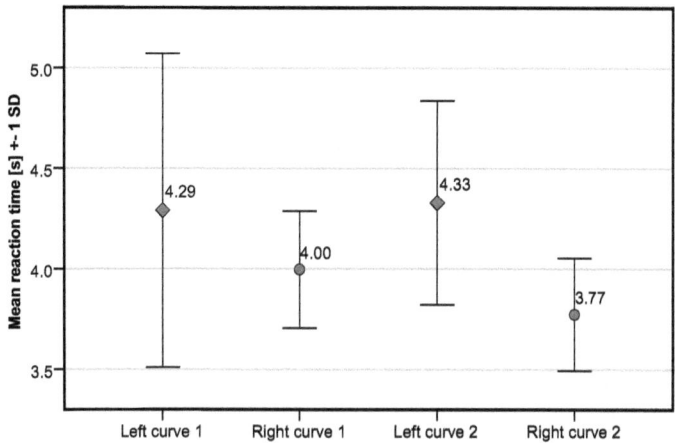

Figure 5.18: Pre-study: Mean reaction time in seconds and standard deviation in left and right curves.

5.2.5 Hypotheses

Before the study, we stated a number of hypotheses expressing the anticipated results:

1. H_1: In the HUD condition we will see the least lane deviation and the shortest response times of all conditions. In the Baseline without visual support we will see the highest lane deviation and the longest response times of all conditions. The DISPLAY condition will lie in between regarding lane deviation and response times.

2. H_2: We will see less lane deviation and shorter response times in right curves than in left curves, regardless of carpet version and secondary task type.

3. H_3: When secondary tasks are to perform, we will see higher lane deviation and longer response times, regardless of carpet version and type of curve.

4. H_4: In the DISPLAY condition, a visual task close to the carpet display will result in less lane deviation than without visual support.

5.2.6 Sample

In total 71 valid test subjects (60 male, 11 female) participated in our study with an average age of 31.94 years ($SD = 9.38$, $min = 22$, $max = 60$). Two participants had to be excluded beforehand from analysis, since they could not finish the experiment due to simulator sickness. All participants were in possession of a driving license for 4 to 42 years with an average of 14.20 years ($SD = 9.45$). As in the studies described in chapter 4, participants in need of spectacles were excluded from the study, as long as they were not able to wear contact lenses, because we used a head-mounted eye-tracking system again. The participants were randomly separated into three groups, 24 driving the experiment with the driving path shown in the contact analogue head-up display, 24 with in-car display and 23 without any visual support.

5.2.7 Results

The following section reports the results from the conducted study.

Reaction data

As previously mentioned, we had six error situations and a separate initial error situation. When reporting average values over all situations, we always exclude the initial error and mention this situation separately. The lane border is exceeded with a lane deviation greater than .98 m. The following charts show this border by depicting a red horizontal line at this value.

Response time and lane deviation are closely related. In order to validate our measured data we correlated those values in all conditions. The overall correlation shows consistently a very high value ($Pearson - r = .992, p = .000$). Table 5.1 shows the correlations in each error situation.

r	Initial error	Error 1	Error 2	Error 3	Error 4	Error 5	Error 6
HUD	.998	.984	.984	.990	.992	.997	.975
DISPLAY	.992	.970	.985	.992	.990	.979	.975
Baseline	.998	.996	.998	.994	.996	.984	.987

Table 5.1: Correlations between lane deviation and response time, Pearson-r.

Main Effects In order to determine the effect of the predefined factors *carpet version*, *type of curve* and *type of secondary task*, we ran a mixed model $3 \times 2 \times 3$ ANOVA on the mean lane deviation. The between-subject factor was the carpet version. Carpet version showed a significant main effect ($F[2,68] = 23.414, p = .000$, *partial* $\eta^2 = .408$). We also found a main effect of secondary task ($F[1.604, 109.099] = 11.680, p = .000$, *partial* $\eta^2 = .147$) and of curve ($F[1,68] = 50.270, p = .000$, *partial* $\eta^2 = .425$).

5.2 Evaluation of the Magic Carpet in a User Study

Carpet Version We analysed the overall mean lane deviation in all three conditions varying the carpet version. We found a mean lane deviation of 0.55 m ($SD = .21$) in the HUD condition, 0.90 m ($SD = .33$) in the DISPLAY condition and 0.99 m ($SD = .13$) in the Baseline condition (cf. Fig. 5.19). The HUD condition induces significantly less deviation than the DISPLAY ($p = .000$) and the Baseline condition ($p = .000$). There is no difference between the DISPLAY and the Baseline condition ($p = .532$) regarding the overall mean lane deviation in case of an error.

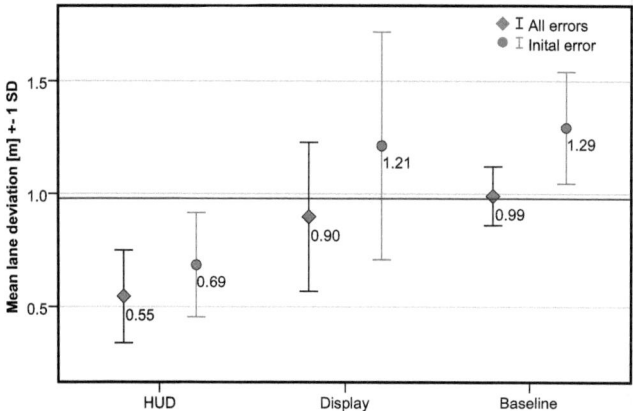

Figure 5.19: **Mean lane deviation and standard deviation of all errors (excluding the initial error) and the initial error (in meters), grouped by carpet version. The red horizontal line indicates the lane border.**

Initial Contact Error Only considering the initial error in each group, we found analogously to the overall lane deviation the least deviation in the HUD condition ($M = .69, SD = .23$), then the DISPLAY condition ($M = 1.21, SD = .50$) and the highest deviation in the baseline ($M = 1.29, SD = .25$). An ANOVA shows a significant effect of the carpet version ($F[2,68] = 20.942$), with a significant difference between HUD and DISPLAY ($p = .000$) as well as HUD and Baseline ($p = .000$), but no difference between DISPLAY and Baseline ($p = 1.000$). The initial error shows in all three conditions a significantly higher deviation compared to the average of all other situations (cf. Fig. 5.20, HUD: $t[23] = 3.375, p = .003$, DISPLAY: $t[23] = 3.820, p = .001$, Baseline: $t[22] = 7.432, p = .000$). Furthermore, we found a high correlation between the overall deviation and the initial error deviation ($Pearson - r = .750, p = .000$). This means, subjects showing a late reaction resulting in a high lane deviation in the initial error situation also show a high deviation in the other error situations.

5. Magic Carpet – A Prospective Driving Path Display

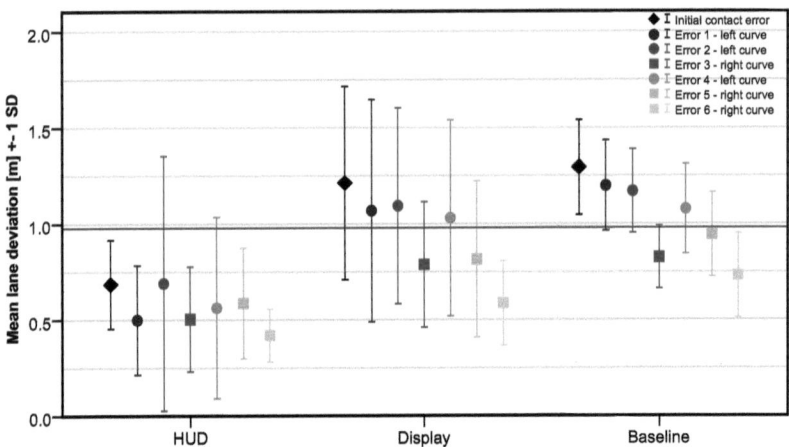

Figure 5.20: Mean lane deviation and standard deviation in error situations grouped by carpet version. The initial error results in the highest, errors in right curves in the least lane deviation. The red horizontal line indicates the lane border.

Curves As the pre-study showed, the type of curve has a measurable effect on the lane deviation. In left curves the test subjects had a mean lane deviation of 0.93 m ($SD = .42$) and in right curves 0.69 m ($SD = .24$), which results in a significant difference using Bonferroni alpha correction ($p = .000$). Expressed as response times, the left curve shows an average of 5.81 s ($SD = .89$) and the right curve 4.85 s ($SD = .64$). In the HUD condition the difference between left and right curve is not significant ($t[23] = 1.257, p = .222$), in the DISPLAY condition there is significantly less deviation in right curves ($t[23] = 4.436, p = .000$), as well as in the Baseline condition ($t[22] = 12.029, p = .000$). In right curves the test subjects mostly reacted fast enough to stay inside their own lane (cf. Fig. 5.21).

Secondary Tasks Also secondary tasks show a significant effect ($F[1.739, 118.283] = 11.485, p < .001$, partial $\eta^2 = .144$) on the lane deviation (cf. Fig. 5.22). Driving with no task resulted in a mean lane deviation of 0.76 m ($SD = .33$), during a phone call 0.76 m ($SD = .36$) and when entering a navigation destination 0.91 m ($SD = .36$). Phoning and performing no task did not differ from each other ($p = 1.00$), but implicate significantly less lane deviation than the navigation task (each $p < .002$).

Regarding H_4, we tested if the navigation task showed a difference between the

5.2 Evaluation of the Magic Carpet in a User Study 141

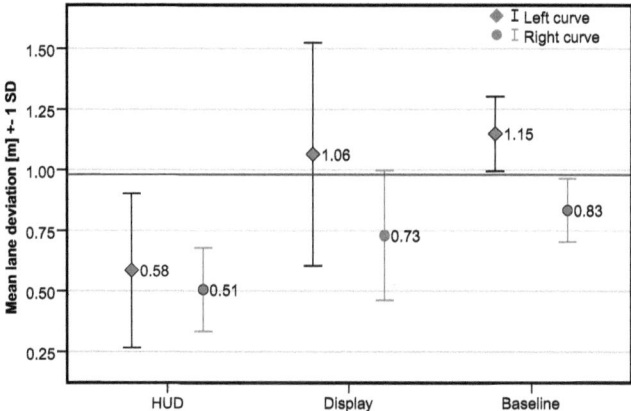

Figure 5.21: Mean lane deviation and standard deviation in meters grouped by carpet version and curve. The red horizontal line indicates the lane border.

DISPLAY condition and the Baseline using a one-way ANOVA with Bonferroni post-hoc test. Even if there is a significant effect of the carpet version on lane deviation during performing the navigation task ($F[2,70] = 7.063, p = .002$), there is no difference between DISPLAY and Baseline condition ($p = .471$).

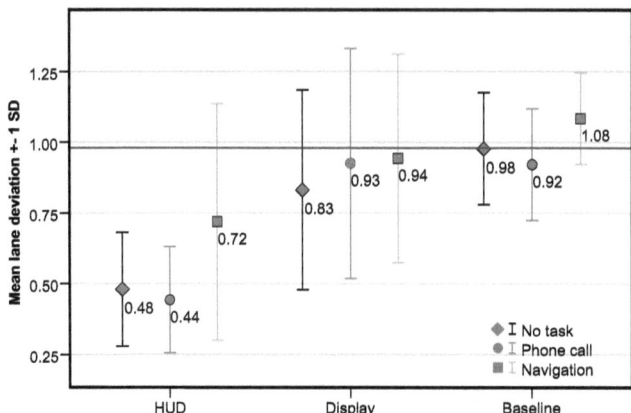

Figure 5.22: Mean lane deviation and standard deviation in meters grouped by carpet version and secondary tasks. The red horizontal line indicates the lane border.

Interactions The mixed-model ANOVA revealed a number of interactions between the different factors. We found a three-way interaction between all three factors $(F[3.003, 102.087] = 4.435, p = .002$, partial $\eta^2 = .115)$. During the study, participants in the HUD condition deviated significantly less than those in the Baseline condition, regardless of curve and secondary task.

- There was a two-way interaction between *carpet version* and *type of curve* $(F[2, 68] = 5.731, p = .005$, partial $\eta^2 = .144$, cf. Appendix Fig. A.5). We ran unpaired t-tests to investigate the differences between the different carpet versions. In both left and right curves participants driving in the HUD condition deviated less than those in the DISPLAY condition $(t[46] = -4.195, p = .000$ and $t[46] = -3.448, p = .000)$. In the HUD condition the test subjects also deviated significantly less than in the Baseline condition, regardless of curve with $t[45] = -7.683, p = .000$ in the left curve and $t[45] = -7.335 p = .000$ in the right curve. There were no differences between DISPLAY and Baseline regarding the type of curve (left: $t[45] = -.841, p = .405$, right: $t[45] = -1.686, p = .099)$.

- There was no interaction between *carpet version* and *secondary task* $(F[3.209, 109.099] = 2.462, p = .062$, partial $\eta^2 = .068$, cf. Appendix Fig. A.6).

- We found another interaction between *secondary task* and *type of curve* $(F[1.501, 102.087] = 5.233, p = .013$, partial $\eta^2 = .071$, cf. Appendix Fig. A.7). To further investigate this, we conducted paired sample t-tests. In all three secondary tasks, participants deviated further in the left curve than in the right curve (Phone call: $t[70] = 6.148, p = .000$; Navigation: $t[70] = 5.199, p = .000$; No task: $t[70] = 3.369, p = .001$). The participants reacted quicker during the phone call task than during the navigation task, regardless of type of curve with $t[70] = -2.828, p = .006$ in the left curve and $t[70] = -2.726, p = .008$ in the right curve. There was no difference regarding lane deviation between the phone call and no task, regardless of the type of curve with $t[70] = 1.672, p = .099$ in the left curve and $t[70] = -1.587, p = .117$ in the right curve. Only in the left curve, participants deviated less when performing no task than during the navigation task $(t[70] = 4.070, p = .000)$. There was no difference between no task and navigation in the right curve $(t[70] = 1.552, p = .125)$.

Situations Passed/Failed In order to understand the lane deviation and reaction in a temporal course, we created a graphical plot of each condition and situation from the beginning of the error until ten seconds after. For the initial error situation, Fig. 5.23 shows the deviation progression in the Baseline condition, Fig. 5.24 of

5.2 Evaluation of the Magic Carpet in a User Study

the DISPLAY condition, and Fig. 5.25 of the HUD condition. It becomes clear that the DISPLAY condition shows the highest variance, which we also found in the measured data. In the Baseline condition without visual support for recognising an error situation, the lane deviation shows a very homogeneous course, since most subjects seem to react at a similar point of time when the error becomes clearly perceivable by the deviation of the virtual car in the driving scene. Compared to the other conditions, this is very late, mostly between 1.0 and 2.0 m deviating from the center of the own lane.

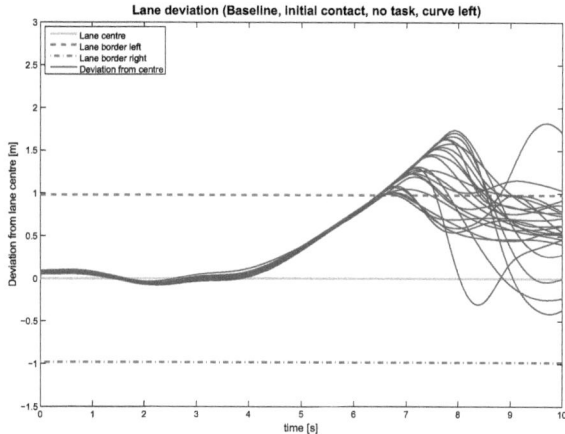

Figure 5.23: Plot of lane deviation during the initial contact error in the Baseline condition. The upper dashed line indicates the lane border of the right lane.

If staying inside the own lane (deviation $\leq$ 0.98 m) is the strict pass/fail criterion for each error situation, we can determine the percentage of situations that have been resolved successfully. Table 5.2 and Fig. 5.26 show an overview. During the HUD condition the majority of situations is successfully mastered ($M = 89.3\%, SD = 12.92$), from 63% in a left curve navigation task to 100% in a right curve during a phone call. In the DISPLAY condition only 53% ($SD = 26.31$) of all situations can be resolved timely from 17% to 79%. The Baseline shows even lower values with 36.6% ($SD = 28.3$) from 13% to 78%.

Gaze Data

Of all 71 test subjects the data of 61 participants was usable for analysis. The datasets included 20 participants driving in the HUD, 22 driving in the DISPLAY and 19 driving in the Baseline condition. We had to exclude the rest of the datasets due to incomplete

144　　　　　　　　　　5. Magic Carpet – A Prospective Driving Path Display

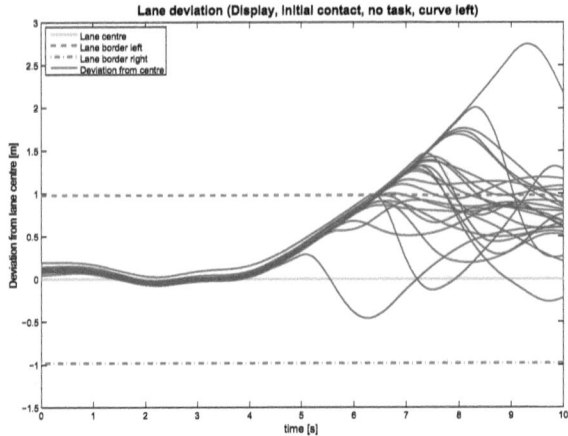

Figure 5.24: Plot of lane deviation during the initial contact error in the DISPLAY condition. The upper dashed line indicates the lane border of the right lane.

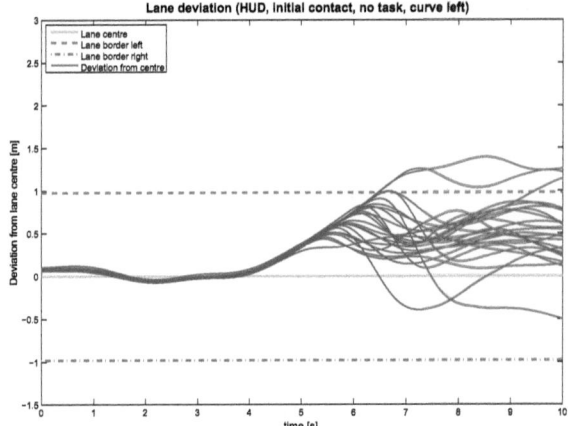

Figure 5.25: Plot of lane deviation during the initial contact error in the HUD condition. The upper dashed line indicates the lane border of the right lane.

recordings. All datasets pooled together revealed that participants looked to the FRONT for an average of 74.88% ($SD = 14.13$) of the entire experiment time, with a mean number of 420.8 ($SD = 168.22$) fixations that had a mean gaze time of 4.0 s ($SD = 1.7$). The CID showed a mean 11.71% ($SD = 2.51$) with a mean number of 168.23 ($SD = 43.03$) fixations that had a mean duration of 1.44 s ($SD = .45$). The IC showed an average of

5.2 Evaluation of the Magic Carpet in a User Study

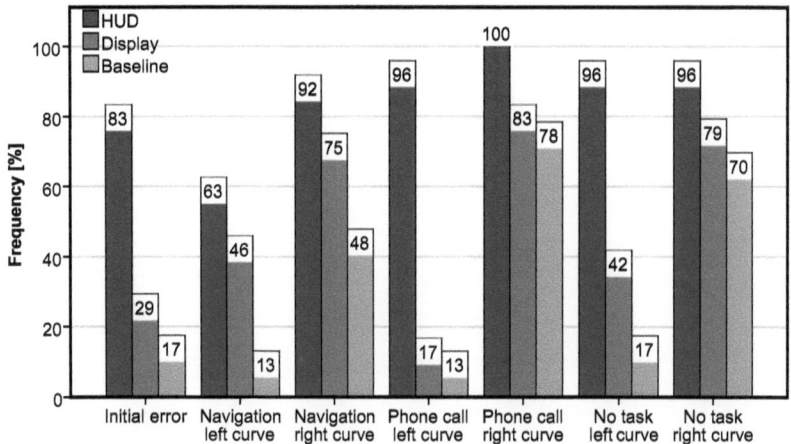

Figure 5.26: Percentage of situations successfully resolved before leaving the own lane, grouped by version.

	n = 24		n = 24		n = 23	
	HUD	HUD [%]	Display	Display [%]	Baseline	Baseline [%]
Initial error	20	83.3	7	29.2	4	17.4
Navigation left curve	15	62.5	11	45.8	3	13
Navigation right curve	22	91.7	18	75	11	47.8
Phone call left curve	23	95.8	4	16.7	3	13
Phone call right curve	24	100	20	83.3	18	78.3
No task left curve	23	95.8	10	41.7	4	17.4
No task right curve	23	95.8	19	79.2	16	69.6

Table 5.2: Situations successfully resolved (and percentage) before leaving the own lane, grouped by version.

2.56% ($SD = 1.58$) time, with a mean number of 73.2 ($SD = 38.67$) fixations with a mean duration of 0.68 s ($SD = 0.16$). Table 5.3 shows a detailed overview of the mean gaze time and the mean gaze distribution in all conditions. An ANOVA was run in order to investigate differences between the different carpet versions in number, duration and percentage of fixations on the CID and FRONT during different times of the experiment. The percentage of the entire experiment in which the participants looked at the CID differed significantly across carpet versions ($F[2,58] = 5.991, p = .003$). Post-hoc pairwise comparisons revealed that participants driving in the DISPLAY condition spent

5. Magic Carpet – A Prospective Driving Path Display

			HUD	Display	Baseline
Mean gaze time [s]	All	FRONT	4.81 (SD=1.70)	3.17 (SD=1.37)	4.13 (SD=1.69)
		CID	1.41 (SD=.57)	1.55 (SD=.46)	1.33 (SD=.24)
		Display	—	1.28 (SD=.89)	—
	during phone call task	FRONT	5.64 (SD=4.05)	4.60 (SD=4.25)	4.99 (SD=4.93)
		CID	.59 (SD=.29)	.59 (SD=.30)	.53 (SD=.14)
		Display	—	1.19 (SD=.81)	—
	during navigation task	FRONT	1.16 (SD=.68)	.94 (SD=.72)	.95 (SD=.40)
		CID	1.21 (SD=.66)	1.93 (SD=1.08)	1.59 (SD=.60)
		Display	—	.59 (SD=.70)	—
Mean gaze distribution [%]	All	FRONT	81.75 (SD=5.54)	62.97 (SD=17.22)	81.44 (SD=3.95)
		CID	11.24 (SD=2.73)	13.05 (SD=2.34)	10.65 (SD=1.78)
		Display	—	13.15 (SD=15.87)	—
	during phone call task	FRONT	88.28 (SD=11.21)	75.46 (SD=23.01)	85.60 (SD=11.04)
		CID	3.51 (SD=5.76)	3.15 (SD=3.36)	3.22 (SD=5.10)
		Display	—	7.12 (SD=15.79)	—
	during navigation task	FRONT	45.33 (SD=17.71)	29.10 (SD=18.47)	35.86 (SD=11.14)
		CID	44.96 (SD=16.21)	57.15 (SD=17.05)	53.89 (SD=10.10)
		Display	—	3.99 (SD=5.36)	—

Table 5.3: Mean gaze time in seconds and mean gaze distribution in % (with standard deviation) during phone call and navigation task grouped by carpet version.

a significantly higher percentage of the entire experiment looking at the CID than those driving in the HUD ($p = .044$) and the Baseline condition ($p = .005$). There was no difference in percentage between the Baseline and the HUD condition ($p = 1.000$). In addition there was a significant difference in mean length of fixation to front between the three carpet version conditions ($F[2,58] = 5.64, p = .006$). Post-hoc pairwise comparisons using the Bonferroni alpha correction showed that participants driving in the HUD condition had a longer mean gaze time to the FRONT than those driving in the DISPLAY condition ($p = .004$). There was no difference in mean gaze time to FRONT between subjects driving in the HUD condition and the Baseline condition ($p = .565$), nor between DISPLAY and Baseline condition ($p = .177$).

A further effect of the carpet version was found when comparing the percentage of the entire experiment in which participants looked at the FRONT ($F[2,58] = 19.979, p < .001$). A post-hoc pairwise comparison showed that the test subjects driving in the DISPLAY condition spent significantly less time in the experiment looking at the FRONT than in the HUD condition and the Baseline condition (each $p < .001$). There was no difference between the Baseline and the HUD condition ($p = 1.000$). There were also no significant differences between the carpet versions in the number of fixations onto the CID ($F[2,58] = .634, p = .534$), the mean gaze time onto the CID ($F[2,58] = 1.273, p = .288$),

5.2 Evaluation of the Magic Carpet in a User Study

and the mean number of fixations onto the FRONT ($F[2,58] = 1.297, p = .281$).

DISPLAY Gaze Data We decided to analyse the obtained gaze data in the DISPLAY condition in more detail. Table 5.4 shows an overview of the most important measured variables over the whole experiment. It is common for all measurements that we see remarkable individual differences, manifesting in the range of minimum and maximum values and the standard deviation from the average. Some test participants did not use the display at all, others used it heavily and sometimes even as their primary display for the driving scene. Since the participants were not specifically instructed to make heavy use of the in-car display, these are all valid results. The total gaze time over the whole experiment ranges from 6.8 seconds to almost 22 minutes with a mean value of 4.3 minutes, which means a gaze rate of .35% to 67% of the experiment time. Also the single fixations show a wide spectrum of values. The maximum gaze times range from 1.16 seconds to more than one minute without interruption. When computing a correlation between the gaze rate on the display and their deviation from the lane, it shows that the longer the test subjects watched the carpet in the display, the less they deviated from the lane before overruling the automation ($Pearson - r = .653, p = .001$).

	N	Minimum	Maximum	Mean	SD
Total gaze time [s]	22	6.80	1312.08	258.30	310.75
Number of fixations	22	14	421	170.36	113.11
Mean gaze time [s]	22	.45	3.25	1.28	.89
Gaze rate [%]	22	.35	67.00	13.15	15.87
Minimum gaze time [s]	22	1.16	66.88	11.60	16.41
Maximum gaze time [s]	22	.16	.20	.17	.01

Table 5.4: Descriptives of gaze data in the DISPLAY condition over the whole experiment. The values show enormous individual differences.

In most cases we have not seen a significant difference between the DISPLAY condition and the Baseline. Due to the observation that some participants used the display heavily and others almost not at all, we ran a separate analysis only regarding error situations where we registered at least a single gaze onto the display. This was defined as a fixation of at least 200 ms during the eight seconds an error event was active. The lane deviation in these situations was then compared to the mean lane deviation of the participants driving in the HUD and Baseline conditions. An ANOVA showed indeed a significant difference in the factor carpet version ($F[2,64] = 27.067, p < .001$). Post-hoc pairwise comparisons conducted using the Bonferroni alpha correction revealed that, when participants driving in the DISPLAY condition had looked at the display at the time of an error, they showed significantly less lane deviation than participants driving in the Baseline condition ($p = .003$). However, consistently with our previous results, in the HUD condition the test subjects had significantly less lane deviation than participants in the DISPLAY condition even when recognizing the error on the display ($p = .003$).

Subjective Results

After the test run we asked the participants in a concluding questionnaire a number of questions addressing subjective opinions on the experienced situations.

- The first question was about the general trust in automated systems on a 5-point-Likert scale from 1 (*very weak*) to 5 (*very strong*). Participants driving in the HUD condition showed the highest mean value ($M = 3.25, SD = .61$) compared to the DISPLAY condition ($M = 2.88, SD = 1.15$) and the Baseline ($M = 2.96, SD = .88$), but a one-way ANOVA showed no significant differences between the conditions ($F[2,70] = 1.129, p = .329$).

- To the question, whether the test subjects would use such an automated system as experienced in the daily traffic (yes/no/don't know), the answers were again very equally distributed between the groups. The majority said they would use such a system in daily traffic (11 to 13), four in each group would not use it and six to nine were undecided. Consequently, a one-way ANOVA did not show a significant effect of the carpet version ($F[2,70] = .183, p = .833$).

- We asked three more questions only to the participants driving the HUD or DISPLAY condition. On the question how helpful the carpet display was during the drive, on a 7-point-Likert scale from -3 (*very obstructive*) to +3 (*very helpful*), the HUD condition showed an average of 2.75 ($SD = .44$) and the DISPLAY condition 1.58 ($SD = 1.61$). An ANOVA revealed that participants driving in the HUD condition rated the carpet as significantly more helpful than those driving in the DISPLAY condition ($F[1,46] = 11.679, p < .001$).

- We also asked the participants in the concluding questionnaire *when* they decided to intervene and overrule the automation on a scale from 1 ('*As soon as a lane deviation was noticeable in the carpet*') to 7 ('*As soon as the car crossed the centre line*'). In the HUD condition the average intervention point was at a mean 2.25 ($SD = 1.15$), whereas in the DISPLAY condition the average was at 3.54 ($SD = 1.47$). An ANOVA showed that participants driving in the HUD condition

5.2 Evaluation of the Magic Carpet in a User Study

indicated that they reacted significantly sooner to the system failure than those driving in the DISPLAY condition ($F[1,46] = 11.446, p < .001$). Interestingly, in the DISPLAY condition we found a high correlation between the time of intervention and the gaze rate on the display ($Pearson - r = -.611, p = .003$). That means, the longer the participants watched the in-car display, the earlier they indicated to have reacted. This matches the results from above, confirming that longer display attention implicates less lane deviation.

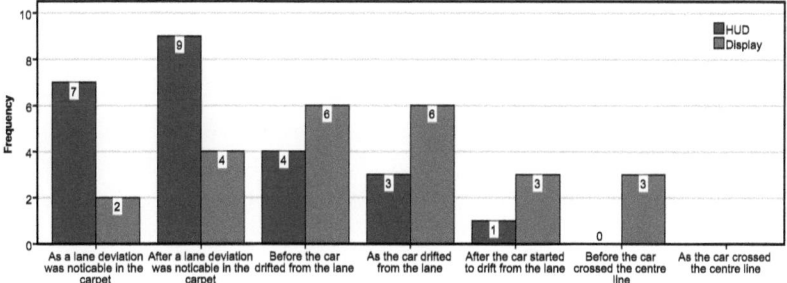

Figure 5.27: Answers to the question, at what point of time did the test subjects overrule the automation in case of an error.

- The last question concerned the participants' willingness to drive with a carpet in daily traffic (yes/no/don't know). In both conditions the answers were almost equally high. With *yes* answered in the HUD condition 62.5%, in the DISPLAY 58.3%, with *no* 20% in the HUD condition and 16% in the DISPLAY condition. A χ^2 test showed no significant difference ($\chi^2[2] = .236, p = .889$).

Further Results

- An analysis of covariance revealed no significant effect of gender on the mean lane deviation ($F[1,67] = 1.591, p = .211$). However, another analysis of covariance showed a signficant effect of the age on the lane deviation ($F[1,67] = 17.779, p = .000$). This means, the mean deviation increases with increasing age of the participants, which was also shown with a medium Pearson correlation ($r = .275, p = .020$).

- A repeated measures ANOVA was run in order to examine if there was an effect of progression, i.e. whether the lane deviation changed with number of errors already experienced. In fact, we found a significant main effect ($F[2.951, 212.465] =$

$15.643, p < .001$, *partial* $\eta^2 = .178$). That means in detail, the lane deviation decreases with the number of times an error has been experienced.

- Due to the found effect of progression we investigated whether there was a correlation between time lapse before an error and the corresponding lane deviation. We imagined that a longer time lapse between two errors would lead to a greater lane deviation. We found that in the Baseline condition there is a high correlation in each single error situation ranging from .693 to .841. However, in the HUD and the DISPLAY there is almost no correlation at all.

- We also recorded the number of times the test subjects overruled the automation even if there was no need to, comparable to the 'false interventions' metric in the ALCT (cf. 4.1.2). The mean values ranged from 3.21 ($SD = 2.19$) in the HUD condition, 2.79 ($SD = 1.82$) in the DISPLAY condition and 3.43 ($SD = 1.73$) in the Baseline condition. A one-way ANOVA did not show a significant effect of the carpet version ($F[2,70] = .679, p = .511$). So the carpet version does not influence the number of false interventions.

- Since it was possible to overrule the automation by using the brake pedal, we analysed the number of times the participants braked in case of an error. This has been done beforehand, because overruling the steering wheel requires to apply a force for a certain time before the overruling is registered. Braking by contrast is registered immediately. It turned out that not a single test subject had braked during a single error situation. So in all situations the steering wheel served as means to overrule the automation.

5.2.8 Discussion of Results

Hypotheses

In H_1 we stated in the HUD condition we would see the fastest response / the least deviation from the lane in case of a system error then in the DISPLAY condition, and the highest deviation in the Baseline condition. It is true that showing a prospective driving path as a contact analogue head-up display clearly proved to be a very good means for our test participants for recognising an automation error. On almost every factor level (curve and secondary task) we found significantly faster responses / less deviation from the lane than showing the carpet on an extra display or driving without any additional information. However, on most factor levels we could not find a significant difference between DISPLAY and Baseline. Only when separating out single situations where the test subjects have actually looked onto the display during an error, we found the DISPLAY condition

5.2 Evaluation of the Magic Carpet in a User Study

to be superior to the Baseline. Consistent to this finding, we found a negative correlation between gaze times on the in-car display and lane deviation. This means that the more the participants were involved with the display, the faster they responded to an error. So for the HUD condition H_1 can be confirmed, for the DISPLAY condition H_1 is rejected.

As anticipated in the pre-study, also in the main study we found clear differences in error situations between left and right curves. On average, the test subjects reacted almost one second faster in right curves than in left curves. So in general H_2 can be confirmed. The reason for this result is not quite obvious, since the deviation behaviour of the carpet is exactly the same in both cases. We ascribe this to the fact how the error originates. The steering wheel angle in a left curve error is greater than the trajectory requires in order to follow the lane in the centre, i.e. the steering wheel is turned too far. In a right curve error, however, the steering angle is smaller than the trajectory requires, i.e. the steering wheel is not turned far enough. As a consequence, a left curve error is mainly perceivable in the carpet as a too strong curvature, whereas in the right curve error the whole carpet seems to shift towards the left lane (cf. Fig. 5.17). We suppose that the difference in this visual characteristic is better visible in the right curve error. Aside from that, from a daily driving experience, in a curve one is usually being carried out of the curve by not turning the steering wheel far enough (right curve), rather than being drawn into the curve by turning the steering wheel too far (left curve). So this effect can probably be explained by very basic control mechanisms naturally occurring during driving, but since the differences between left and right curve are so prominent, it cannot be left aside.

With respect to secondary tasks we found that there is an effect of secondary tasks on the recognition of lane deviation, but it is not quite as strong as expected. The navigation task induced the highest lane deviation in all conditions. Phoning and no task at all performed similarly, both better than the navigation task in most cases. So H_3 proved only to be valid for the visual and active navigation task, and must be rejected for the phone call task. It is interesting that phoning sometimes even produced better results than having no secondary task. In the ALCT studies, the phone call task got mediocre results, in the carpet study it didn't seem to have a negative effect. We attribute this mainly to the mentally more challenging detection and decision task that was implemented in the ALCT (knowledge-based behaviour). The deviation from the lane in the carpet study is a more regulatory task without the need to compare explicit instructions (road signs) with the car's automatically taken path (skill- or rule-based behaviour). This seems to invoke the natural reaction of compensating the lane drift with a correcting steering action without being too much negatively influenced by a mentally distracting secondary task. From that point of view, this result is consistent with the theory of the driving task (cf. 2.1.1, Fig. 2.1). Another reason might be an expectancy effect. Some participants commented that they have been waiting for an error to happen when a secondary task was to perform and so they were extra alert. One test subject who paid extra attention, noticed an error in the last navigation task very late because he was watching the CID for a few seconds, and almost shouted: "Now you got me! And I've been waiting for this to happen the whole drive." Despite the number of distractors, some participants tried to apply a compensation strategy. They knew that they were being distracted and tried hard to focus on both, task and automation supervision. This was not possible in our ALCT studies, since the test subjects were occupied with a secondary task all the time and they were not able to sustain that shared attention during the whole drive to the same extent.

We assumed that when we show the carpet on a display close to the content of a visual task in the centre console, a deviation in the carpet is earlier visible and will lead to faster reactions than without visual support. This assumption was disproved in our study, the variance in the DISPLAY condition was simply too large, as already mentioned above in the discussion of H_1. So H_4 must also be rejected.

Gaze data

Particularly in the DISPLAY condition we found a huge range of usage time in the gaze data. Some participants used the display extensively, others almost not at all. We did not force the test subjects to use it, but we suggested to use it as a better means of discovering potential problematic situations. Nevertheless, some drove effectively without visual support, even though they had the in-car display available. As we observed this, some participants seemed overcharged with the whole experiment, since they often came the first time in touch with a driving simulator and simultaneously with a fully automated vehicle guiding system. Probably a number of participants was overcharged with using the in-car display as an auxiliary means to supervise the automation. However, it is yet an important finding that even if the potential benefit of such a display is obvious, some drivers might not want to change their behaviour, because they feel safer with their eyes on the road. This is why we analysed the reaction data in the respect of existence of fixations onto the display in case of errors. This shows that for those who want to use such a display, it actually has an advantage over no visual support. Another reason for this might be that the position of the carpet screen was not optimal. As described, we initially also tried to position the carpet display directly below the CID. This was perceived as too close to the driver, because of the mounting frame in front of the centre

5.2 Evaluation of the Magic Carpet in a User Study

stack. The position on the right hand side of the CID (cf. Fig. 5.16) obviously was not perfect either, as the test subjects had to turn their head quite far to the right to be able to see the screen. We could observe this in the recorded eye tracking videos. An integration of the carpet display within the CID could have produced better results in favour of the DISPLAY condition, but due to the small screen size (10") the image of the carpet next to the navigation content, a deviation in the carpet would have been hardly recognizable (cf. Fig. 3.9). So perhaps a larger display offering more space for the task content and a carpet display positioned in the centre console, or the carpet display shown instead of the instrument cluster in order to avoid too far head turning, could have performed better, since the time needed to look back to the driving scene after recognizing an error, adapt to the scene on the front and intervene adequately would be shorter.

Driving in the DISPLAY condition also had the effect of significant longer overall gaze time on the CID than in the HUD or Baseline condition, in particular during the navigation task. We judge this as a symptom of a difficult mental attention shift process. The primary task is to make sure that the vehicle stays safely on the road. Simultaneously there is at least one other task with visual feedback on different positions in the vehicle to accomplish. Dedicating to up to three tasks demanding visual attention results in a massive resource conflict in the sense of Wickens' MRT, which leads to increased mental workload that manifests itself in longer gaze times on the CID. We judge this as a hint that our categorisation established in 3.1 is valid in terms of modality. This is backed by equally long gaze times on the CID in the (auditory) phone call task over all conditions. Even if there is no need to watch the CID, 3% of all gazes are on the CID in all conditions (cf. Table 5.3).

General Discussion

It is interesting that even though the objective results are quite distinct over the conditions, in particular in the HUD condition compared to the others, the trust in the automation does not differ significantly, regardless of the experienced support. Even the willingness to use such as system in daily traffic despite of the occurred errors is equally high in all conditions. There appears to be a principal receptiveness for automated vehicle guidance systems throughout our test sample. However, in the HUD condition the carpet proved to be subjectively more helpful than in the DISPLAY condition and the participants indicated that they also reacted earlier when driving with the carpet in the HUD.

By our deliberate decision to locate errors only in curves, haptic feedback from the steering wheel did not show as effective as it did in our ALCT study (cf. 4.3), since the turning of the steering wheel was naturally induced by the curvature of the road and could not be used as a hint to a potential erroneous situation. Even if we required our participants to keep their hands on the steering wheel and therefore cannot make an empirically proven statement, we assume that the lane deviation would have been larger in all conditions when the test subjects would not have had their hands on the steering wheel during the automated drive. Unfortunately, we did not ascertain the acceptance of this requirement. However, we did not receive complaints, either.

Throughout the study it became clear that when driving without any visual support, the lane drift error was recognizable later than under all other conditions. This can not only be derived from the average deviation value but also from the small variance this condition induced compared to the other conditions and is directly visible in the deviation plots (cf. Fig. 5.23). The majority of test subjects reacted within a time frame of less than 0.5 seconds in this conditions in all errors. Until they showed a reaction, most of them had deviated already 0.8 to 1.1 meters from the centre of the lane to the left. This is a clear evidence that some form of support is necessary. As already mentioned, haptic feedback from the steering wheel is probably not sufficient in this scenario against this kind of automation error.

We introduced seven lane drift errors during a drive of 32 minutes, which is probably far from acceptable for an automated vehicle guidance system that is actually deployed on the road. However, for an empirical study we needed a critical mass of measuring points. The degression over time in response times to errors and lane deviation respectively as more errors have been experienced, showed that our test drivers were able to improve their error recognition performance. However, it is advisable to regard the worst case which is when an error is experienced for the first time.

We have seen the driving path display having a positive effect, particularly in the form of a contact analogue, augmented image of – in our case simulated – reality. Results in the HUD condition showed earlier recognition of errors, thus less deviation until an intervention, even in dual-task situations and with the initial contact error. We also found less gaze times away from the driving scene, so the carpet overlay on the road surface also acts as a visual anchor that keeps the driver's eyes on the road. This is not the case with an in-car screen showing a video image of the driving scene augmented with the driving path, due to the reasons described above. We have not seen convincing results in our study in favour of this version. So we strongly advocate the contact analogue form of a driving path display.

Of course, such a display can only be effective when it is actually watched and when the driver is mentally in 'driving mode', so that the driver can actually detect a potential lane drift and react appropriately. Therefore, a carpet display cannot be the sole solution to the problem of imperfect and failing automation, but it can contribute to an awareness of the overall driving situation and a better understanding of automated vehicle guidance systems and its limits.

5.3 Summary

In this chapter we described the development of a prospective driving path display as a means of support to recognise automation errors. In particular we target incorrect lane detection that results in a slow drift out of the lane which is one of the most critical errors possible. The driving path display visualises the future path of the automatically controlled vehicle. Thus the driver is able to detect a deviation from the course earlier than without visual support. We implemented the driving path display ("Magic Carpet") as a contact analogue head-up display – virtually in a driving simulation environment – and as an augmented video image on a separate screen mounted in the centre console of the vehicle mockup. A comparative study showed a clear positive effect of the carpet display in the contact analogue form. The in-car display could not contribute significantly to better error detection, it rather induced a remarkably large variance in the reaction data. However, the more the test subjects used the in-car display, the better were the reaction results.

Chapter 6

Contributions and Conclusion

This chapter summarises the contents of this thesis and explicitly discusses the innovative contributions made. Also, we conclude with a final discussion and point towards future developments in the field of automated driving research.

6.1 Discussion of Contributions

Picking up the research questions stated in 1.2, the contributions made in this work are concisely summarised and discussed in the following. Each question has been thoroughly addressed in the work presented in chapters 3, 4 and 5 against the background of chapter 2.

Assessment Methodology

By which methodology can human recognition of automation errors in an automated driving situation be suitably assessed?

One of our goals was to find a feasible, safe and cost-effective way of assessing the capability of humans to detect erroneous behaviour of vehicles under automated driving conditions. It is important that the intended methodology adequately models the key mechanisms of driving with a semi-automated control system in a real car as closely as possible. In the design of the **Automated Lane Change Test, (ALCT)**, we transferred these concepts to the best possible extent into the laboratory in the form of a driving-simulator-based methodology (cf. chapter 4). The ALCT is intended to be used as a basic evaluation tool for the assessment of effects induced by a highly automated driving situation, in particular in different dual-task conditions involving a secondary task.

During an ALCT drive, a virtual vehicle performs automated lane changes on a three-lane road in a simulated driving environment. The test subjects' task is to recognise incorrect automated driving – with the focus on incorrect lateral control – and to intervene manually when required. This corresponds to a signal detection task including choice-reaction. Incorrect driving has been incorporated in the form of different categories comprising commission and omission errors (cf. 2.3) by changing to the wrong lane or staying on the same lane when a change was due. Based on an approved standardised test setting, we built the ALCT as a flexible, configurable tool for easy and quick testing of different parameter sets, regarding speed, error rate, sign visibility times, etc. We also implemented different feedback modalities: visual feedback through the display of the driving scene (LO version), haptic feedback through the steering wheel (HI version) and acoustical feedback as affirmation of a successful intervention (LO and HI version). We carefully defined unambiguous objective metrics in order to measure error detection performance. These are: the time until an error is recognised as such and the proper reaction is carried out (response time), the number of situations in a given time where there was no response to an error (missed errors), and the number of responses that were not correct (false interventions).

In two studies using the ALCT we assessed the effectiveness of the method itself and the discriminatory power of the defined measurements regarding different conditions. In the studies, different conditions were established using various secondary tasks to accomplish simultaneously to the tasks to supervise the automated lane changes. The studies showed that the ALCT method discriminates between different conditions using the named metrics in both implemented versions. As the most useful metric, we identified the measurement of the average time of responding to occurring errors. We consistently found that in both versions – with or without haptic feedback – the longest response times occurred in situations when the supposed action was not carried out, so that no obvious change was perceivable (error category 2, cf. 4.1.1). Correspondingly, the shortest response times were measured when an unambiguous incorrect action was taken (error category 3). Conforming to our expectations, almost all dual-task conditions resulted in significantly increased response times and could be clearly separated from the single-task baseline condition.

The measurement of missed errors correlates quite well with the mean response times and the perceived mental workload. This is supported by the number of missed errors during the phone call conditions. However, we have seen remarkable differences between the single test subjects. Since missing an error in an ALCT session is a rare event, probably the sum of all missed errors in a certain condition over the whole

6.1 Discussion of Contributions

experiment is a better comparison criterion. This has to be taken into account when interpreting missed error results.

The results of measuring the false interventions were not entirely convincing, especially in HI version this metric could not be used due to too many accidental occurrences. Furthermore, in reality it is the driver's liberty to overrule an automated system at any time, may it be out of automation distrust or another reason. We therefore recommend not to focus on the metric of false interventions in the ALCT.

As for the length of the ALCT test runs, we suppose the testing of seven different tasks resulting in a total experimental time of about two hours to be the upper limit that should be assessed for each test subject. We detected slight fatigue effects that might influence the test subjects' performance and motivation.

The LO and the HI version implementation of the ALCT produce widely consistent results. The HI version, however, showed the metrics ranging on a clearly lower level, particularly regarding response times. This is backed by our findings in the gaze data. With haptic feedback there was more attention to the driving scene than without. This can be judged as a hint towards improved situation awareness when haptic feedback is available (cf. 2.3). Thus, as many researchers have stated in the past, haptic feedback turns out to be extremely helpful as an information channel and keeps drivers mentally more in their driving task, also (or perhaps specifically) in the context of automated driving.

Error Recognition Support

By which means can human recognition of automation errors in an automated driving situation be supported?

It is not sufficient to determine human capabilities of recognizing automation errors. The next logical step is to improve this performance by all means available. In section 3.3.2 we presented different approaches and discussed the basic idea, potential and drawbacks. In the end, we chose two measures that are considered to be most effective. First, we required the driver to **permanently keep at least one hand on the steering wheel** in all our studies. This contributes on one side to a reduction of response times, because in case of a necessary steering action the driver does not need time to reach for the steering wheel in the first place. On the other side, as mentioned above, haptic feedback from the actuated steering wheel is valuable information about driving dynamics. Thus, vehicle movement – even if only virtually – is directly perceptible and also contributes to shorter response times, as we could show in ALCT study 2 when comparing the LO and the HI version of the ALCT (cf. 4.3.4).

As a second measure we implemented a **prospective driving path display (Magic Carpet)** showing the path of the automatically controlled vehicle in the near future based on the information available to the longitudinal and lateral controllers. Deployed in a driving simulation environment, we assessed the potential of the driving path display in the form of a large-scale merged video projection recreating a contact analogue head-up display and on an in-car mounted screen.

The basic results obtained in the ALCT studies influenced several decisions regarding the evaluation of the driving path display. In particular the found effectiveness of haptic feedback on the steering wheel and therefore the design of the overall experimental procedure, as well as the selection of secondary tasks have been essentially motivated by the results reported in section 4.2.5 and 4.3.4.

Independent from the type of support, without knowing the exact characteristics of a potential error beforehand, the test participants showed the greatest deviation from the lane at the very first occurring error. The more errors had been experienced, the smaller the deviation until a reaction. Interestingly, we also found that the direction of road curves has an effect on the point in time when an error becomes recognizable as such, independently from the level of support. Although the vehicle always deviated from its lane towards the oncoming lane, in right curves this has been noticed significantly earlier.

We could show that the driving path display has a positive effect on the recognition of slow, automation induced lane departure. Especially when the driving path display is shown directly overlaid with the driving scene, a significantly improved response behaviour in all conditions is measureable. The in-car display was also found to be effective, but not to the same extent as the overlay and not for all test participants. We observed that the in-car display showing the driving path polarised our test subjects: some used it heavily, some rejected it almost utterly. This resulted in a wide variance. In the end, we could only find the in-car screen helpful for those test subjects who really made use of it. We suppose that the declining attitude is due to the whole situation of an unfamiliar way of driving and the unusual position and content of the in-car screen. Despite the quite different results for the two versions, in the subjective feedback participants expressed an equal desire for a driving path display showing the future path of the vehicle.

6.1 Discussion of Contributions

Implicitly, all 'support measures' point towards the imperfection and error-proneness of automated control systems. With perfect automation, no support would be necessary.

Categorisation and Role of Secondary Tasks

To what extent do secondary activities influence humans in the recognition of automation errors in an automated driving situation?

Since there is a huge variety of potential secondary activities to be performed during driving, it is crucial to specify the question: what kinds of tasks influence the recognition of automation errors to which extent?

The most important step towards an answer is to find a way to reduce the magnitude of tasks to a manageable set. We achieved this on the one hand by focussing on a reasonable subset of relevant tasks. In section 3.1, we described the the selection of in-car tasks other authors made for judging their influence on driving performance. They also chose tasks that are likely to occur sometimes during a drive (unfold tissue, unwrap sweets, etc.), but are little more than single, punctual events and, moreover, cannot be legally regulated, nor influenced by the car manufacturer in any way. Therefore, we confined our set of tasks to activities that are enabled by driver information systems. There are legal regulations and design recommendations for such systems (cf. 2.1.3) and they are under control by the car manufacturer. On the other hand, in the process of grouping similar tasks, we created a formal categorisation of tasks based on established concepts, mainly inspired by Wickens' model of multiple resources (cf. 2.1.2) which was originally not intended for the description of tasks in our sense. We adapted and extended this model and eventually put up a scheme categorising in-car tasks in four dichotomous dimensions: **modality, degree of interaction, interruptibility** and **information encoding**.

In the next step, the found categorisation was applied in a number of experimental studies using the ALCT methodology and the Magic Carpet setting. The ALCT studies showed that not all of our introduced dimensions proved useful. While the distinctions within interruptibility and information encoding did not show measurable effects, the modality and the degree of interaction of a task could be clearly be identified as decisive factors. So we recommend to focus on the degree of interaction and modality when selecting tasks for evaluation in an in-car dual task scenario.

In all our studies, we particularly addressed the role of secondary tasks on the performance of automation error recognition. From the literature it is known that secondary activities can have a distracting influence on manual driving. We could find clear evidence that also the capability of automation supervision is impaired by common in-car side tasks. In all studies, the undistracted baseline drive consistently induced the best reaction performances in terms of response times and less missed errors in case of automation failure. The sharing of mental resources with a side task resulted in almost every condition in a deterioration in performance. More precisely, tasks involving active engagement and visual attention away from the driving scene show the highest negative influence. However, also verbal and mentally demanding tasks, such as conversing on the phone, should not be underestimated. Interestingly, the influence of the same tasks varies in different conditions. It appears that the higher the degree of realism of the driving task is, the lower is the influence of secondary tasks. We witnessed the highest increase in response times in the first ALCT study without haptic feedback through the steering wheel. Including this feedback, the response times compared to the baseline without a secondary task showed a significantly smaller increase. In the Magic Carpet study we saw only a slight increase in response time even when driving without the display of the driving path. We suppose that the effect of secondary tasks in a real driving environment with a real car will be even lower, if – and this is an important requirement – the automated guidance system has a similar reliability as our tested systems.

Nevertheless, haptic feedback through the steering wheel can contribute to mitigate those negative effects and help to prioritise the primary task, be it manual driving or automation supervision. Also other means, such as a driving path display, can help to keep the secondary task secondary and involve drivers more in their primary task for safe driving. With the ideas, concepts, experiments, and discussions presented in this work, we could contribute to a certain extent to these topics.

6.2 Conclusion and Future Work

It is important to understand that driving with highly automated vehicle guidance systems that execute longitudinal and lateral control is fundamentally different from manual driving from the driver's point of view. The permanent manual task to control the speed and the position within the lane is influenced or even completely replaced by a technical system. It is well acknowledged that machines are able to outperform human operators in reaction time and accuracy in clearly defined situations. Since the major part of road accidents is caused by human failure, it seems reasonable to reduce human control in

6.2 Conclusion and Future Work

cars when possible. Vollrath and Flemisch state that hypothetically the best measure to increase traffic safety would be to discharge the driver completely from control and replace him by automated vehicles [168]. The same point is made by the 2004 movie *I, Robot*. In the world of 2035, vehicles driving autonomously are the standard way of transportation. Driving manually is considered to be unsafe and dangerous to other road users. Of course, this assumes perfect automation.

Yet, the future of automated or autonomous driving is still up in the air. Looking back to the development of the automobile in the last 125 years since the invention of the **Patent-Motorwagen** by Carl Benz in 1886, the overall architecture and way of interaction has proven remarkably stable. So it might be doubted that the whole traffic system will profoundly change in the next years. Today, for car manufacturers it is probably not a medium-term goal to offer fully autonomous driving, but specific support in distinct situations in which drivers want to be highly assisted. In the end, the decision of driving automatically or manually is made individually and cannot not be forced. Certainly not every driver wants to be a passenger on the driver's seat, but to enjoy the power and dynamics of his vehicle and the manual control over it. It is not a small number of car manufacturers, whose unique selling point is the feeling of manual driving itself. So the chance for a completely automated traffic system is probably very low. The question is also whether the driver can ever be completely replaced. Machines are usually good for routine tasks under defined conditions; humans are unmatched in resolving non-trivial situations unconventionally or even irrationally. People are able to communicate with other drivers in a way machines will hardly ever be.

If highly automated vehicle control systems should become broadly available in the future, this cannot be reached in a revolutionary, but in a careful, stepwise approach. Highly automated control systems are likely to be introduced in expensive top-of-the-range vehicles first. When they have proven their effectiveness and usefulness, lower vehicle classes will also be equipped, as the deployment process of new technology in the automotive industry usually approaches. So a radical change is not to be expected, especially regarding the transportation domain, where everybody in the world is part of. It is possible that at first the driver is able to activate the automatic control only on roads with very distinct properties (e.g. only on highways, dedicated lanes providing special infrastructure, etc.) or for a very limited amount of time, as Parasuraman et al. suggest [123]. It would be also imaginable that in a transition period motor traffic could be separated into automated and non-automated vehicles, for instance on structurally separate lanes which can only be accessed by vehicles meeting a certain automation standard.

For such a scenario to become more realistic and for the advantages we described in section 2.2.3 to become effective, there are a number of challenges to overcome. There is the need for redundant and heterogeneous automotive sensor systems that are able to perceive the environment and the position of the vehicle in this environment with very high reliability. Currently available systems are susceptible to incorrect lane information – especially under adverse environmental conditions (night, rain, snow, fog, etc.) – that can result in erroneous lane guidance. This is difficult to control by the driver, as we could prove in this work (cf. 5.2). Furthermore, vehicle-local information is probably not sufficient, because the sensory horizon of these system is limited. We need sophisticated and reliable communication systems that interchange up-to-date information in real-time about the situational traffic conditions, surrounding cars, potential road hazards, etc. with infrastructure or other vehicles. For this, we also need standards, regulations and protocols that enable this communication in an unambiguous and robust way. This information must be carefully assessed and checked for plausibility, in order to achieve the best possible decision basis for automated vehicle control. At best, for safe and efficient driving for all road users, all motorised traffic participants should be equipped with the named systems. Of course, all the legal questions of responsibility, as mentioned in 2.2.4, have to be solved first. It is possible that in the future driving with highly automated control systems requires the proof of certain skills or knowledge of how to handle such systems, and maybe a special training or driver's license.

It is necessary to thoroughly research the field of automated driving and to discuss positive and negative ramifications. It would be interesting to know if the overall traffic safety increases with the introduction of highly automated control systems, even if they are still prone to errors. Unfortunately, there are no reliable figures on that question available.

Outlook

On the basis of considerations above, we proceeded on a number of assumptions in this work:

- On the one hand, situationally relieving the driver from unpleasant driving conditions by automation under certain circumstances does not seem unrealistic.

- It is obvious that automated vehicle control systems will not be perfect for the time being.

6.2 Conclusion and Future Work

– A potential shift of attention towards secondary activities in the car has to be considered, since today's cars offer a large variety of tasks.

From that point of view, all addressed topics offer a number of possible future developments and research directions.

ALCT We have mainly dealt with the problem of imperfect automation resulting in errors and the human capabilities to recognise these. For that, we have proposed a first methodology for laboratory assessment. The studies we presented in chapter 4 have produced plausible results with respect to our established secondary task categorisation. However, the results do not allow for an absolute judgement of the criticality of these tasks in an automated driving situation. Eventually, the obtained results should be verified in a real automated driving scenario as a reference, which was not feasible during this work. A really interesting, but probably very costly, project could be the replication of the ALCT as a real-life test method. Against this reference, a further assessment of the ALCT method could be done and an absolute statement about the validity could be given. Further future work also implies the replication of the ALCT as a PC version, similar to the LCT setting. If we find similar results in a lower fidelity setup, the method would be easier to use for other researchers, since a driving simulation environment would not be necessary. It would also be interesting to see an alternative methodological approach towards the assessment of human capabilities of automation error recognition. This method should be compared to the proposed ALCT. The flexible, and configurable design of the ALCT and the simple driving scene allow for many more options for a modification of the test itself. It could be extended to more complex situations, including other vehicles, etc., potentially incorporating different kinds of errors. Of course, care has to be taken that the fundamental character of test is not impaired by such modifications.

Magic Carpet The development of the Magic Carpet in the driving simulation environment has revealed interesting insights how visual feedback on automated control systems can keep drivers attached to the driving task. But simulations can only provide a proof of concept and give hints about the potential effectiveness. Also in this case a real implementation of a contact analogue head-up display showing the vehicle's driving path should be tested under real driving conditions. This is not an easy thing to do, though, since the technology needed for this is still not broadly available. Furthermore, it must be determined what the ideal projection distance of the virtual image is, how the correct position of the virtual image can be found in order to match the driver's perspective, how drivers cope with the obstruction of objects by the virtual image, etc. There are already works that deal with these questions (cf. [8, 83, 143]). Apart from the technical issues that have to be solved, such a display can form an extra value to an automated driving function, since it visualises the presence and activity of otherwise invisible underlying mechanisms. Probably feedback on future actions is even vital to the acceptance of the automated control systems, even when we have reached a very high degree of reliability and the displayed content is not there for error recognition. Of course, the carpet display itself must be further evaluated. It would be interesting to know, how drivers react to errors in the depiction of the carpet, i.e. in situations where the car drives correctly, but the carpet shows another way. Also, if a contact analogue HUD is available the carpet is likely to be not the only content to be shown. It must be integrated with other kinds of contact analogue content, for instance navigational guiding hints. In the future, it would be even imaginable that a driving path display is realised not as a virtual image mirrored into the windscreen, but projected directly onto the road using extra (maybe coloured) headlights or lasers. This would solve a lot of technical issues regarding the contact analogue displays, but naturally it would also create new research questions.

Beyond this Work Beyond the topics addressed above, many general research questions arise in the near future regarding automated driving. We only want to name a few. Generally, more complex situations than the above described should be examined: automated driving in heavy traffic, in traffic congestions, in cities with mixed traffic where also vulnerable road users and traffic regulation systems are involved, etc. will be a considerable challenge. Not only in an technical aspect, also the acceptance of automated vehicle control systems in situations where errors are more likely, is interesting.

Another issue that should be investigated in the context of automated driving is the role of the driver's age. We have seen a significant increasing effect of age on response time in our ALCT study with the largest age span (cf. 4.3) and other studies have found similar effects (cf. [38]). With the current trend of aging societies, such questions gain in importance.

The automated systems that we have assumed as state-of-the-art in this work are able to keep the lane, the speed and a certain distance to other vehicle on the stabilisation level. The ALCT introduced automatically performed manoeuvres. There are already approaches for automated systems on the manoeuvring level (cf. [178]), e.g. an emergency stop system that safely brings a vehicle to a standstill in case of an emergency [170]. In the future, it would be imaginable the driver only has to push a button and the vehicle perform an automated overtaking manoeuvre, merges automatically into running traffic from the acceleration lane, etc.

6.2 Conclusion and Future Work

Automated driving is by far not only a technological issue. The functional interplay of sensors, cameras, control routines, and actuation is undoubtedly highly complex. But the even more interesting questions arise in the interaction between man and machine. Automation should never be an end in itself, but serve humans in the best possible way.

Appendix A

Appendix

Delphi Study

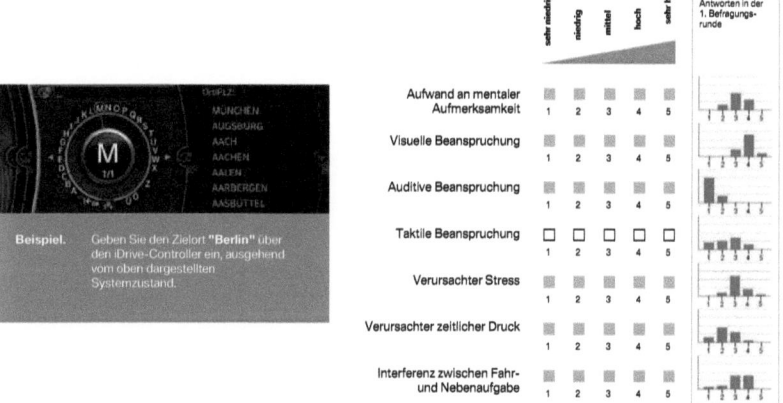

Figure A.1: Sample of 21 questions in the Delphi study. On the right, the second Delphi round is shown with the results from the first round.

ALCT

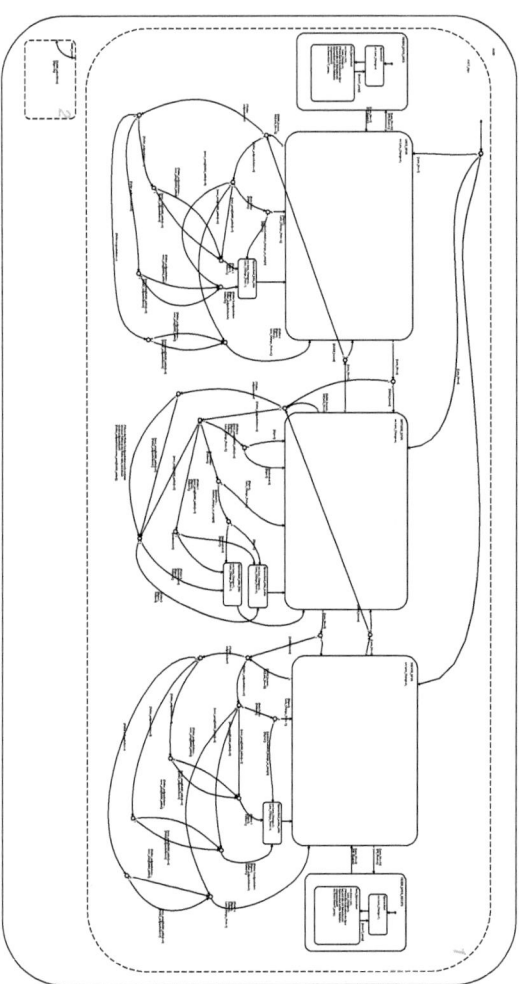

Figure A.2: Computation of road sign contents implemented as Stateflow chart.

Variant	1	2	3	4	5	6	7
Task 1	Baseline	Short text	Interactive Map	Audio book	Long text	Phone call	Navigation
Task 2	Short text	Baseline	Long text	Interactive Map	Phone call	Navigation	Phone call
Task 3	Navigation	Long text	Baseline	Phone call	Audio book	Short text	Interactive Map
Task 4	Interactive Map	Audio book	Phone call	Baseline	Navigation	Long text	Short text
Task 5	Audio book	Phone call	Short text	Navigation	Baseline	Interactive Map	Long text
Task 6	Long text	Navigation	Audio book	Short text	Interactive Map	Baseline	Audio book
Task 7	Phone call	Interactive Map	Navigation	Long text	Short text	Audio book	Baseline

Table A.1: **Permutation of secondary tasks during the test runs in seven variants in the first ALCT experiment.**

Variant	Task 1	Task 2	Task 3	Task 4	Task 5	Task 6	Task 7
1	Phone	Map	Short text	Baseline	Phone	Map	Short text
2	Baseline	Phone	Map	Short text	Phone	Map	Short text
3	Map	Short text	Phone	Map	Baseline	Short text	Phone
4	Map	Phone	Baseline	Short text	Map	Phone	Short text
5	Short text	Phone	Map	Short text	Phone	Baseline	Map
6	Short text	Phone	Baseline	Map	Short text	Phone	Map
7	Short text	Map	Phone	Short text	Map	Phone	Baseline
8	Short text	Map	Phone	Baseline	Short text	Map	Phone
9	Phone	Short text	Map	Baseline	Phone	Short text	Map
10	Baseline	Phone	Short text	Map	Phone	Short text	Map
11	Map	Phone	Short text	Map	Phone	Baseline	Short text
12	Map	Baseline	Short text	Phone	Map	Short text	Phone
13	Phone	Map	Short text	Phone	Baseline	Map	Short text
14	Phone	Baseline	Map	Short text	Phone	Map	Short text
15	Map	Short text	Phone	Map	Short text	Baseline	Phone
16	Map	Short text	Baseline	Phone	Map	Short text	Phone
17	Short text	Phone	Map	Short text	Phone	Map	Baseline
18	Short text	Phone	Map	Baseline	Short text	Phone	Map
19	Short text	Map	Phone	Baseline	Short text	Map	Phone
20	Baseline	Short text	Map	Phone	Short text	Map	Phone
21	Phone	Short text	Map	Phone	Short text	Baseline	Map
22	Phone	Short text	Baseline	Map	Phone	Short text	Map
23	Map	Phone	Short text	Map	Baseline	Phone	Short text
24	Map	Baseline	Phone	Short text	Map	Phone	Short text
25	Phone	Map	Short text	Phone	Map	Short text	Baseline
26	Phone	Map	Short text	Baseline	Phone	Map	Short text
27	Map	Short text	Phone	Baseline	Map	Short text	Phone
28	Baseline	Map	Short text	Phone	Map	Short text	Phone
29	Short text	Phone	Map	Short text	Baseline	Phone	Map
30	Short text	Baseline	Phone	Map	Short text	Phone	Map
31	Phone	Map	Short text	Baseline	Phone	Map	Short text
32	Phone	Baseline	Map	Short text	Phone	Map	Short text

Table A.2: Permutation of secondary tasks during the test runs in the second ALCT experiment. Light cells indicate the LO version, dark cells indicate the HI version.

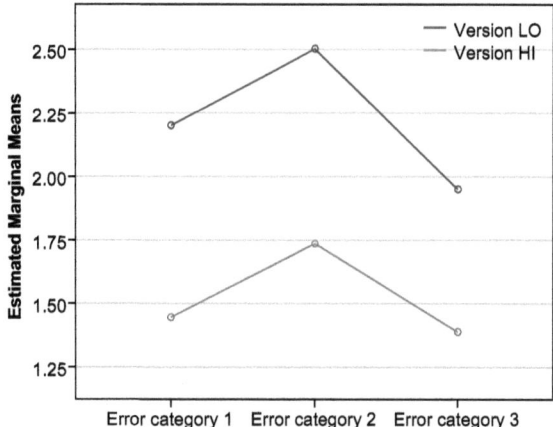

Figure A.3: Second ALCT experiment: Interaction Version × error category.

Magic Carpet

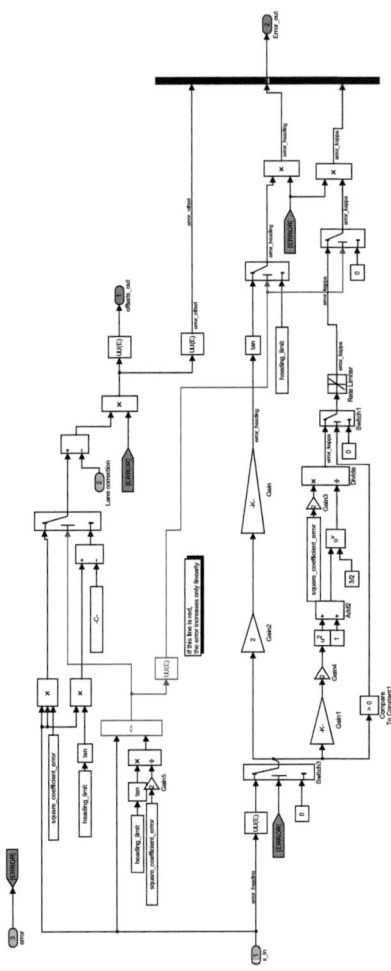

Figure A.4: Carpet error computation as implemented in Simulink, depicted for the squared error function $y = b \cdot x^2$.

Variant	1	2	3	4	5	6	7	8	9	10	11	12
Distractor 1	N	T	N	T	N	T	T	N	T	N	T	N
Distractor 2	T	N	T	N	T	N	N	T	N	T	N	T
Initial Error	-	-	-	-	-	-	-	-	-	-	-	-
Error 1 (left)	N	N	T	T	-	-	N	N	T	T	-	-
Distractor 3	N	T	N	T	N	T	T	N	T	N	T	N
Error 2 (left)	T	-	N	-	N	T	T	-	N	-	N	T
Distractor 4	T	N	T	N	T	N	N	T	N	T	N	T
Error 3 (right)	N	N	T	T	-	-	N	N	T	T	-	-
Distractor 5	N	T	N	T	N	T	T	N	T	N	T	N
Distractor 6	T	N	T	N	T	N	N	T	N	T	N	T
Error 4 (left)	-	T	-	N	T	N	-	T	-	N	T	N
Error 5 (right)	T	-	N	-	N	T	T	-	N	-	N	T
Distractor 7	N	T	N	T	N	T	T	N	T	N	T	N
Distractor 8	T	N	T	N	T	N	N	T	N	T	N	T
Error 6 (right)	-	T	-	N	T	N	-	T	-	N	T	N

Table A.3: Permutation of secondary tasks during the test run in 12 variants in the carpet experiment (N = navigation, T= phone call).

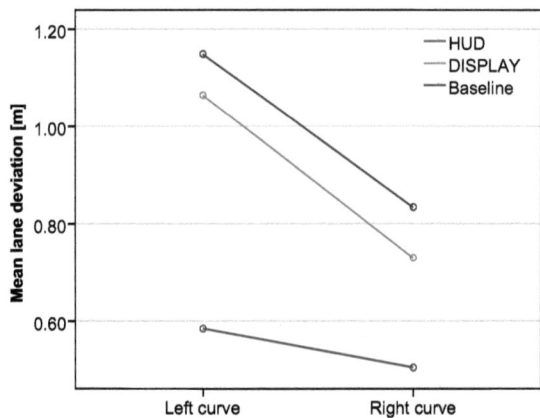

Figure A.5: Carpet experiment: Interaction Carpet version × Type of curve.

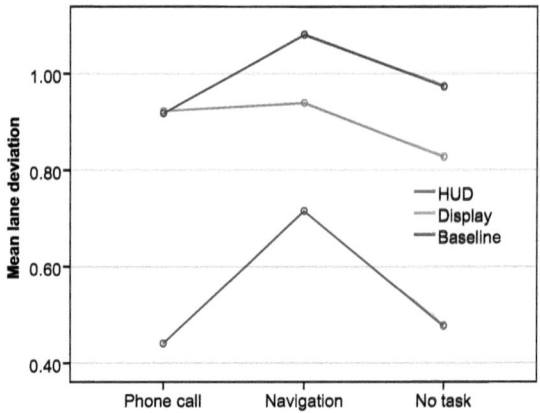

Figure A.6: Carpet experiment: Interaction Carpet version × Type of secondary task.

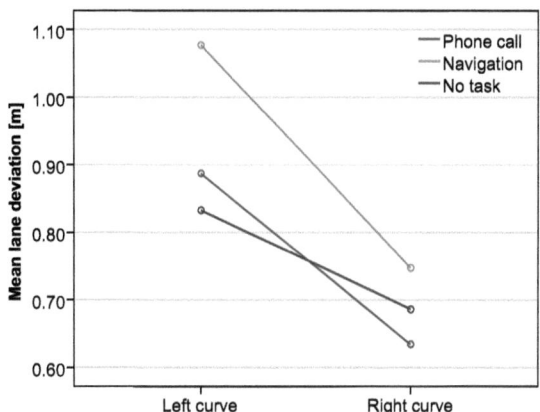

Figure A.7: Carpet experiment: Interaction Type of secondary task × Type of curve.

Bibliography

[1] AAM Driver Focus-Telematics Working Group. Statement of Principles, Criteria and Verification Procedures on Driver Interactions with Advanced In-Vehicle Informationand Communication Systems, 2006.

[2] D. A. Allport, B. Antonis, and P. Reynolds. On the division of attention: A disproof of the single-channel hypothesis. *Quarterly Journal of Experimental Psychology*, 24(2):225–235, 1972.

[3] S. Ashley. Smart Cars and Automated Highways. *Mechanical Engineering Magazine*, May 1998.

[4] N. Bagheri and G. A. Jamieson. The impact of context-related reliability on automation failure detection and scanning behaviour. In *IEEE International Conference on Systems, Man and Cybernetics*, pages 212–217, 2004.

[5] L. Bainbridge. Ironies of Automation. *Automatica*, 19(6):775–779, 1983.

[6] M. Baumann, T. Petzold, and J. Krems. Situation Awareness beim Autofahren als Verstehensprozess. *MMI-Interaktiv*, 11:43–57, 2006.

[7] K. Bengler, A. Huesmann, and M. Praxenthaler. Investigation of Visual Demand in a Static Driving Simulator within the ADAM Project. In H. Strasser and Heiner Bubb, editors, *Quality of Work and Products in Enterprises of the Future*, pages 49–52. Ergonomia Verlag, 2003.

[8] U. Bergmeier. *Kontaktanalog markierendes Nachtsichtsystem - Entwicklung und experimentelle Absicherung*. PhD thesis, Technische Universität München, 2009.

[9] R. Bernotat. Anthropotechnik in der Fahrzeugführung. *Ergonomics*, 13(3):353–377, 1970.

[10] M. Bertozzi, A. Broggi, G. Conte, and A. Fascioli. Obstacle and Lane Detection on ARGO. In *IEEE Conference on Intelligent Transportation System (ITSC '97)*, pages 1010–1015, 1997.

[11] C. E. Billings. Human-centered aircraft automation: A concept and guidelines. Technical report, NASA Ames Research Center, Moffet Field, CA, 1991. NASA Tech. Memorandum 103885.

[12] R. Bishop. *Intelligent Vehicle Technology and Trends.* Artech House, 2005.

[13] W. R. Boot, A. F. Kramer, E. Becic, D. A. Wiegmann, and T. Kubose. Detecting Transient Changes in Dynamic Displays: The More You Look, the Less You See. *Human Factors: The Journal of the Human Factors and Ergonomics Society*, 48(4):759–773, 2006.

[14] J. Bortz. *Statistik für Human- und Sozialwissenschaftler.* Springer Medizin Verlag, Heidelberg, 6th edition, 2005.

[15] J. Bortz and N. Döring. *Forschungsmethoden und Evaluation: für Human- und Sozialwissenschaftler.* Springer, Berlin, 4th edition, October 2006.

[16] H. H. Braess and G. Reichart. PROMETHEUS: Vision des "intelligenten Automobils auf der intelligenten Straße" - Versuch einer kritischen Würdigung. *ATZ*, 97(4):200–205, 1995.

[17] J. Breuer, K. Bengler, C. Heinrich, and W. Reichelt. Development of advanced driver attention metrics (ADAM). In H. Strasser, editor, *Proceedings of the Annual Spring Conference of the GfA on the Occasion of the 50th Anniversary of the Foundation of the Gesellschaft für Arbeitswissenschaft e.V. (GfA) and the XVII Annual Conference of the International Society for Occupational Ergonomics & Safety (ISOES)*, Munich, Germany, 2003.

[18] Broadbent. *Perception and Communications.* Permagon Press, New York, 1958.

[19] A. Broggi, M. Bertozzi, and A. Fascioli. ARGO and the MilleMiglia in Automatico Tour. *IEEE Intelligent Systems and their Applications*, 14(1):55–64, 1999.

[20] A. Broggi, M. Bertozzi, A. Fascioli, C. G. Lo Bianco, and A. Piazzi. Visual Perception of Obstacles and Vehicles for Platooning. *IEEE Transactions on Intelligent Transportation Systems*, 1(3):164–176, 2000.

[21] Lesley Brown, editor. *The New Shorter Oxford English Dictionary.* Clarendon Press, 1993.

[22] M.-P. Bruyas, C. Brusque, A. Auriault, H. Tattegrain, I. Aillerie, and M. Duraz. Impairment of lane change performance due to distraction: Effect of experimental contexts. In *Proceedings of Proceedings of the First European Conference on Human Centred Design for Intelligent Transport Systems*, pages 89–100, 2008.

BIBLIOGRAPHY 181

[23] H. Bubb. *Untersuchung über die Anzeige des Bremsweges im Kraftfahrzeug.* PhD thesis, Technische Universität München, 1975.

[24] H. Bubb. Systemergonomische Gestaltung. In H. Schmidtke, editor, *Ergonomie*. Hanser Verlag, München, 3rd edition, 1993.

[25] H. Bubb. Fahrerassistenz - primär ein Beitrag zu Komfort oder für die Sicherheit? In *Der Fahrer im 21. Jahrhundert. VDI Berichte*, number 1768. VDI Verlag, Düsseldorf, 2003.

[26] S. Buld, H.-P. Krüger, S. Hoffmann, A. Kaussner, H. Tietze, and I. Totzke. Wirkungen von Assistenz und Automation auf Fahrerzustand und Fahrsicherheit, Veröffentlichter Abschlussbericht Projekt EMPHASIS: Effort-Management und Performance-Handling in sicherheitsrelevanten Situationen. Technical report, IZVW Würzburg, 2002.

[27] S. Buld, H. Tietze, and H.-P. Krüger. Auswirkungen von Teilautomation auf das Fahren. In M. Maurer and C. Stiller, editors, *Fahrerassistenzsysteme mit maschineller Wahrnehmung*, pages 161–188. Springer, 2005.

[28] P. C. Burns, P. L. Trbovich, T. McCurdie, and J. L. Harbluk. Measuring distraction: Task duration and the lane-change test (LCT). In *Proceedings of the Human Factors and Ergonomics Society 49th Annual Meeting*, Orlando, Florida, USA, 2005. Human Factors Society.

[29] M. Campbell, M. Egerstedt, J. P. How, and R. M. Murray. Autonomous driving in urban environments: approaches, lessons and challenges. *Philosophical Transactions of the Royal Society A: Mathematical, Physical and Engineering Sciences*, 368(1928):4649–4672, 2010.

[30] E. C. Cherry. Some experiments on the recognition of speech, with one and with two ears. *Journal of the Acoustical Society of America*, 25:975–979, 1953.

[31] Commission of the European Communities. Commission recommendation on safe and efficient in-vehicle information and communication systems: Update of the european statement of principles on human machine interface, 2007. Brussels, Belgium: European Union.

[32] J. M. Cooper, I. Vladisavljevic, D. L. Strayer, and P. T. Martin. Drivers' Lane Changing Behavior While Conversing On a Cell Phone in a Variable Density Simulated Highway Environment. Technical report, University of Utah Traffic Lab, 2008.

[33] S. Cotter, J. Hopkin, A. Stevens, A. Burrows, M. Flament, and P. Kompfner. The institutional context for advanced driver assistance systems: A code of practice for development. In *13th World Congress & Exhibition on Intelligent Transport Systems and Services*, London, UK, October 2006.

[34] J. Coughlin, B. Reimer, and B. Mehler. Driver Wellness, Safety & the Development of an AwareCar. AgeLab White Paper, Dec. 2009.

[35] D. Damböck, M. Kienle, and K. Bengler. Die Zügel fest in der Hand halten - Automationsgradumschaltung durch Griffkraftmessung. In *Proceedings of USEWARE - Nutzergerechte Gestaltung technischer Systeme (USEWARE-2010)*, Baden-Baden, Germany, October 2010.

[36] D. R. Davies and R. Parasuraman. *The psychology of vigilance*. Academic Press, London, 1982.

[37] D. de Waard, M. van der Hulst, M. Hoedemaeker, and K. A. Brookhuis. Driver Behavior in an Emergency Situation in the Automated Highway System. *Transportation Human Factors*, 1(1):67–82, January 1999.

[38] G. Der and I. J. Deary. Age and Sex Differences in Reaction Time in Adulthood: Results From the United Kingdom Health and Lifestyle Survey. *Psychology and Aging*, 21(1):62–73, 2006.

[39] P. A. Desmond, P. A. Hancock, and J. L. Monette. Fatigue and automation-induced impairments in simulated driving performance. *Transportation Research Record*, 1628:8–14, 1998.

[40] J. A. Deutsch and D. Deutsch. Attention: Some theoretical considerations. *Psychological Review*, 70:80–90, 1963.

[41] S. Deutschle. Wer fährt? - Der Fahrer oder das System. *Straßenverkehrsrecht, Zeitschrift für die Praxis der Verkehrsjuristen*, 6:201–206, 2005.

[42] E. D. Dickmanns, R. Behringer, D. Dickmanns, T. Hildebrandt, M. Maurer, F. Thomanek, and J. Schiehlen. The seeing passenger car 'VaMoRs-P'. In *Proceedings of the Intelligent Vehicles '94 Symposium*, 1994.

[43] E. Donges. Aspekte der Aktiven Sicherheit bei der Führung von Personenkraftwagen. *Automobil-Industrie*, 27:183–190, 1982.

[44] E. Donges. Fahrerverhaltensmodelle. In H. Winner, S. Hakuli, and G. Wolf, editors, *Handbuch Fahrerassistenzsysteme*, pages 15–23. Vieweg+Teubner, 2009.

[45] L. Eckstein. *Entwicklung und Überprüfung eines Bedienkonzepts und von Algorithmen zum Fahren eines Kraftfahrzeugs mit aktiven Sidesticks*. PhD thesis, Universität Stuttgart, 2001.

[46] L. Eckstein, M. Heß, M. Rakic, and U. Petersen. Driver Distraction: Influence of secondary task performance on Real-World Driving. In H. Strasser and Heiner Bubb, editors, *Quality of Work and Products in Enterprises of the Future*, pages 45–48. Ergonomia Verlag, 2003.

[47] R. Elvik and T. Vaa. *The Handbook of Road Safety Measures*. Elsevier, 2004.

[48] M. R. Endsley. The application of human factors to the development of expert systems for advanced cockpits. In *Proceedings of the Human Factors Society 31st Annual Meeting*, pages 1388–1392, Santa Monica, CA, USA, 1987. Human Factors Society.

[49] M. R. Endsley. Design and evaluation for situation awareness enhancement. In *Proceedings of the Human Factors Society 32nd Annual Meeting*, pages 97–101, Santa Monica, CA, USA, 1988. Human Factors Society.

[50] M. R. Endsley and D. B. Kaber. Level of automation effects on performance, situation awareness and workload in a dynamic control task. *Ergonomics*, 42(3):462–492, 1999.

[51] M. R. Endsley and E. O. Kiris. The Out-of-the-Loop Performance Problem and Level of Control in Automation. *Human Factors*, 37(2):381–394, 1995.

[52] J. Engström and G. Markkula. Effects of visual and cognitive distraction on lane change test performance. In *Proceedings of the Fourth International Driving Symposium on Human Factors in Driver Assessment, Training and Vehicle Design*, pages 199–205, Stevenson, Washington, 2007.

[53] P. M. Fitts. Human engineering for an effective air navigation and traffic control system. Washington, DC: National Research Council, 1951.

[54] F. Flemisch, J. Kelsch, C. Löper, A. Schieben, J. Schindler, and M. Heesen. Cooperative Control and Active Interfaces for Vehicle Assistance and Automation. In *Proceedings of FISITA Automotive World Congress 2008*, Munich, 2008. VDI-FVT. F2008-02-045.

[55] F. O. Flemisch, C. A. Adams, S. R. Conway, K. H. Goodrich, M. T. Palmer, and P. C. Schutte. The H-Metaphor as a Guideline for Vehicle Automation and Interaction. Technical report, NASA, Langley Research Center, 2003.

[56] C. Ga and K. Yu. Design of real-view navigation system with virtual path-mapping technique. In *ASPRS/MAPPS 2009 Fall Conference*, San Antonio, Texas, USA, 2009.

[57] N. Galley. An enquiry into the relationship between activation and performance using saccadic eye movement parameters. *Ergonomics*, 41(5):698–720, 1988.

[58] G. Geiser. Mensch-Maschine-Kommunikation im Kraftfahrzeug. *Automobiltechnische Zeitschrift ATZ*, 87:74–77, 1985. GWV Fachverlage GmbH.

[59] D. N. Godbole and J. Lygeros. Safety & Throughput Analysis of Automated Highway Systems. Technical report, California PATH, University of California, Berkeley, 2000.

[60] E. B. Goldstein. *Sensation & Perception*. Thomson Higher Education, Belmont, CA, 2002.

[61] M. Gopal. *Control systems: principles and design*. Tata McGraw-Hill, 2nd edition, 2002.

[62] S. Graf, W. Spießl, A. Schmidt, A. Winter, and G. Rigoll. In-car interaction using search-based user interfaces. In *CHI '08: Proceedings of the twenty-sixth annual SIGCHI conference on Human factors in computing systems*, pages 1685–1688, New York, NY, USA, 2008. ACM.

[63] Etienne Grandjean. *Fitting the Man to the Task*. Taylor & Francis, London, 4th edition, 1988.

[64] J. Greenberg, L. Tijerina, R. Curry, B. Artz, L. Cathey, D. Kochhar, K. Kozak, and M. Blommer. Evaluation of driver distraction using an event detection paradigm. *Journal of the Transportation Research Board*, 1843:1–9, 2003.

[65] J. Grudin. Partitioning Digital Worlds: Focal and Peripheral Awareness in Multiple Monitor Use. In *Proceedings of the SIGCHI conference on Human factors in computing systems*, pages 458–465, Seattle, Washington, USA, March 2001.

[66] L. Gugerty and M. Falzetta. Using an event-detection measure to assess drivers' attention and situation awareness. In *Proceedings of the 49th Annual Meeting of the Human Factors and Ergonomics Society*, Orlando, Florida, USA, 2005. Human Factors Society.

[67] S. Hakuli, R. Bruder, F. O. Flemisch, C. Löper, H. Rausch, M. Schreiber, and H. Winner. Kooperative Automation. In H. Winner, S. Hakuli, and G. Wolf, editors, *Fahrerassistenzsysteme*, pages 632–656. Vieweg+Teubner, 2009.

[68] R. Haller. Fahrer-Assistenz versus Fahrer-Bevormundung: Wie erreicht man, dass der Fahrer Herr der Situation bleibt? In T. Jürgensohn and K.-P. Timpe, editors, *Kraftfahrzeugführung*, pages 31–38. Springer, Berlin, Heidelberg, 2001.

[69] P. A. Hancock, R. Parasuraman, and E. A. Byrne. Driver-Centered Issues in Advanced Automation for Motor Vehicles. In R. Parasuraman and M. Mouloua, editors, *Automation and Human Performance: Theory and Applications*, pages 337–364. Lawrence Erlbaum A, Mahwah, NJ, 1996.

[70] P. A. Hancock, L. Simmons, L. Hashemi, H. Howarth, and T. Ranney. The Effects of In-Vehicle Distraction on Driver Response During a Crucial Driving Maneuver. *Transportation Human Factors*, 4:295–309, 1999.

[71] P. A. Hancock and W. B. Verwey. Fatigue, workload and adaptive driver systems. *Accident Analysis and Prevention*, 29(4):495–506, 1997.

[72] J. L. Harbluk, P. C. Burns, M. Lochner, and P. L. Trbovich. Using the lane-change test (LCT) to assess distraction: Tests of visual-manual and speech-based operation of navigation system interfaces. In *Proceedings of the 4th International Driving Symposium on Human Factors in Driver Assessment, Training, and Vehicle Design*, Stevenson, Washington, USA, 2007.

[73] J. L. Harbluk, J. S. Mitroi, and P. C. Burns. Three Navigation Systems with Three Tasks: Using the Lane-Change Test (LCT) to Assess Distraction Demand. In *Proceedings of the Fifth International Driving Symposium on Human Factors in Driver Assessment, Training and Vehicle Design*, pages 24–30, Big Sky, MT, USA, June 2009.

[74] S. G. Hart and L. E. Staveland. Development of NASA-TLX (Task Load Index): Results of Empirical and Theoretical Research. In P. A. Hancock and N. Meshkati, editors, *Human Mental Workload*, pages 139–184. Elsevier Science Publishers, Amsterdam, 1988.

[75] Y. Hauß and K.-P. Timpe. Automatisierung und Unterstützung im Mensch-Maschine-System. In K.-P. Timpe, T. Jürgensohn, and H. Kolrep, editors, *Mensch-Maschine-Systemtechnik: Konzepte, Modellierung, Gestaltung, Evaluation*, pages 41–62. Symposion Publishing, Düsseldorf, 2nd edition, 2002.

[76] M. Häder and S. Häder. Die Delphi-Methode als Gegenstand methodischer Forschungen. In M. Häder and S. Häder, editors, *Die Delphi-Technik in den Sozialwissenschaften*. Westdeutscher Verlag, 2000.

[77] E. Hollnagel. Looking for errors of omission and commission or the hunting of the snark revisited. *Reliability Engineering and System Safety*, 68:135–145, 2000.

[78] W. J. Horrey and D. J. Simons. Examining cognitive interference and adaptive safety behaviours in tactical vehicle control. *Ergonomics*, 50(8):1340–1350, 2007.

[79] W. J. Horrey and C. D. Wickens. Driving and side task performance: The effects of display clutter, separation, and modality. *Human Factors*, 46:611–624, 2004.

[80] W. J. Horrey, C. D. Wickens, and K. P. Consalus. The Distracted Driver: Modeling the Impact of Information Bandwidth, In-Vehicle Task Priority, and Spatial-Separation on Driver Performance and Attention Allocation. Technical report, Aviation Human Factors Division, Institute of Aviation, University of Illinois, 2005.

[81] International Organization of Standardization. ISO26022:2010 Road vehicles – Ergonomic aspects of transport information and control systems – Simulated lane change test to assess in-vehicle secondary task demand, 2010.

[82] S. T. Iqbal, Y. Ju, and E. Horvitz. Cars, Calls, and Cognition: Investigating Driving and Divided Attention. In *CHI '10: Proceedings of the 28th international conference on Human factors in computing systems*, pages 1281–1290, 2010.

[83] B. Israel and H. Bubb. Augmented Reality im Fahrzeug – Möglichkeiten und Grenzen der Darstellung mit dem kontaktanalogen Head-up Display. In *Proceedings of USEWARE - Nutzergerechte Gestaltung technischer Systeme (USEWARE-2010)*, Baden-Baden, Germany, October 2010.

[84] G. Jahn, A. Oehme, J. F. Krems, and C. Gelau. Peripheral detection as a workload measure in driving: Effects of traffic complexity and route guidance system use in a driving study. *Transportation Research F 8*, pages 255–275, 2005.

[85] Japan Automobile Manufacturers Association. Guideline for in-vehicle display systems, 2004. ver. 3.0.

[86] H. R. Jex, J. D. McDonnell, and A. V. Phatak. A "Critical" Tracking Task for Manual Control Research. *IEEE Transactions on Human Factors in Electronics*, 7(4):138–145, 1966.

[87] E. Johansson, J. Engström, C. Cherri, E. Nodari, A. Toffetti, R. Schindhelm, and C. Gelau. AIDE Deliverable 2.2.1: Review of existing techniques and metrics for IVIS and ADAS assessment, 2004.

[88] P. Johnson-Laird. *Der Computer im Kopf*. dtv, 1996.

[89] D. Kahneman. *Attention and Effort*. Prentice Hall, Englewood Cliffs, NJ, 1973.

[90] R. Karsh and F. W. Breitenbach. Looking at the amorphous fixation measure. In R. Groner, C. Menz, D. F. Fisher, and R. A. Monty, editors, *Eye movements and psychological functions*. Lawrence Erlbaum, Hillsdale, NJ, 1983.

[91] M. Kienle, D. Damböck, J. Kelsch, F. Flemisch, and K. Bengler. Towards an H-Mode for highly automated vehicles: Driving with side sticks. In *Proceedings of the First International Conference on Automotive User Interfaces and Interactive Vehicular Applications (AutomotiveUI 2009)*, Essen, Germany, 2009.

[92] S. Kim and A. K. Dey. Simulated augmented reality windshield display as a cognitive mapping aid for elder driver navigation. In *CHI '09: Proceedings of the 27th international conference on Human factors in computing systems*, pages 133–142, New York, NY, USA, 2009. ACM.

[93] K. Kompaß. Fahrerassistenzsysteme der Zukunft – auf dem Weg zum autonomen Pkw? In V. Schindler and I. Sievers, editors, *Forschung für das Auto von Morgen: Aus Tradition entsteht Zukunft*, pages 261–285. Springer Verlag, 2007.

[94] C. Lank, M. Wille, and M. Haberstroh. KONVOI-Projekt: Einflüsse automatisierter Lkw auf Fahrer und Umgebungsverkehr. *Zeitschrift für Verkehrssicherheit*, 1:7–12, 2011.

[95] T. C. Lansdown, N. Brook-Carter, and T. Kersloot. Distraction from multiple in-vehicle secondary tasks: vehicle performance and mental workload implications. *Ergonomics*, 41(1):91–104, 2004.

[96] J. D. Lee. Can Technology Get Your Eyes Back on the Road? *Science*, 324:344–346, 2009.

[97] J. D. Lee and T. F. Sanquist. Maritime automation. In R. Parasuraman and M. Mouloua, editors, *Automation and Human Performance: Theory and Applications*, pages 365–384. Lawrence Erlbaum, Mahwah, NJ, 1996.

[98] J. D. Lee and K. A. See. Trust in automation: Designing for appropriate reliance. *Human Factors*, 46:50–80, 2004.

[99] L. Levitan and J. R. Bloomfield. Human Factors Design of Automated Highway Systems. In W. Barfield and T. A. Dingus, editors, *Humans Factors in Intelligent Transportation Systems*. Lawrence Erlbaum Associates, Mahwah, NJ, 1998.

[100] T. Lindberg, T. Schaller, and B. Gradenegger. Highly automated driving in Stop&Go situations or traffic jams. In *VDI-Berichte*, number 2015, pages 29–42. VDI Verlag, 2007.

[101] H. A. Linstone and M. Turoff. *The Delphi Method: Techniques and Applications*. 2002.

[102] T. Litman. Changing Travel Demand: Implications for Transport Planning. *ITE Journal*, 76(9):27–33, September 2006.

[103] M. Mangold. Bewertung des Einflusses von Nebentätigkeiten während einer autonomen Fahrsituation. Diploma thesis, Leuphana Universität Lüneburg, 2009.

[104] D. Manzey. Systemgestaltung und Automatisierung. In P. Badke-Schaub, G. Hofinger, and K. Lauche, editors, *Human Factors - Psychologie sicheren Handelns in Risikobranchen*. Springer, 2008.

[105] M. H. Martens and W. van Winsum. Measuring Distraction: The Peripheral Detection Task. Soesterberg, Netherlands, 2000. TNO Human Factors.

[106] S. Mattes. The Lane-Change-Task as a Tool for Driver Distraction Evaluation. In H. Strasser and Heiner Bubb, editors, *Quality of Work and Products in Enterprises of the Future*, pages 57–60. Ergonomia Verlag, 2003.

[107] S. Mattes and A. Hallén. Surrogate Distraction Measurement Techniques: The Lane Change Test. In *Driver Distraction: Theory, Effects and Mitigation*, pages 107–122. CRC Press, 2009.

[108] J. A. Michon. A critical view of driver behavior models: What do we know, what should we know? In L. Evans and R. C. Schwing, editors, *Human Behavior and traffic safety*, pages 485–521. Plenum Press, New York, 1985.

[109] P. Milgram and F. A. Kishino. A taxonomy of mixed reality visual displays. *IEICE Transactions on Information Systems*, E77-D(12):1321–1329, December 1994.

[110] N. Miličić and T. Lindberg. Menu interaction in Head-Up Displays. In *Human Factors and Ergonomic Society, Annual Meeting*, Soesterberg, The Netherlands, 2008.

[111] E. Mitsopoulos-Rubens, K. L. Young, and M. G. Lenné. Utility of lane-change test in exploring the effects on driving performances of engaging in additional in-vehicle tasks while driving. In *Proceedings of the European Conference on Human*

Centred Design for Intelligent Transport Systems, pages 401–412, Berlin, Germany, April 2010.

[112] N. Moray, T. Inagaki, and M. Itoh. Adaptive automation, trust, and self-confidence in fault management of time-critical tasks. *Journal of Experimental Psychology: Applied*, 6(1):44–58, 2000.

[113] K. L. Mosier and L. J. Skitka. Human decision makers and automated decision aids: Made for each other? In R. Parasuraman and M. Mouloua, editors, *Automation and Human Performance: Theory and Application*, pages 201–220. Lawrence Erlbaum Associates, Mahwah, NJ, 1996.

[114] M. Mouloua, R. Parasuraman, and R. Molloy. Monitoring automation failures: effects of single and multi-adaptive function allocation. In *Proceedings of the Human Factors and Ergonomics Society 37th Annual Meeting*, 1993.

[115] K. Naab. Automatisierung im Straßenverkehr. In *1. Nürnberger Symposium Fahrzeugtechnik*, 2000.

[116] W. Narzt, G. Pomberger, A. Ferscha, D. Kolb, R. Müller, J. Wieghardt, H. Hörtner, and C. Lindinger. Augmented reality navigation systems. *Universal Access in the Information Society*, 4(3):177–187, 2006.

[117] D. A. Norman. *The Design of Everyday Things*. Doubleday, New York, 1988.

[118] D. A. Norman. The 'problem' of automation: Inappropriate feedback and interaction, not 'over-automation'. *Philosophical Transactions of the Royal Society of London, B*, 327:585–593, 1990.

[119] D. A. Norman and D. Bobrow. On data-limited and resource-limited processing. *Journal of Cognitive Psychology*, 7:44–60, 1975.

[120] C. Nowakowski, D. Friedman, and P. Green. An Experimental Evaluation of Using Automotive HUDs to Reduce Driver Distraction While Answering Cell Phones. In *Proceedings of the Human Factors and Ergonomics Society 46th Annual Meeting*, pages 1819–1823, 2002.

[121] B. Oakley, M. Mouloua, and P. Hancock. Effects of automation reliability on human monitoring performance. In *Proceedings of the Human Factors and Ergonomics Society 47th Annual Meeting*, 2003.

[122] J. Oestlund, B. Peters, B. Thorslund, J. Engström, G. Markkula, A. Keinath, D. Horst, S. Juch, S. Mattes, and U. Foehl. Driving performance assessment methods and metrics, 2004. AIDE Deliverable 2.2.5.

[123] R. Parasuraman, M. Mouloua, and R. Molloy. Effects of Adaptive Task Allocation on Monitoring of Automated Systems. *Human Factors*, 38(4):665–679, 1996.

[124] R. Parasuraman, M. Mouloua, R. Molloy, and B. Hilburn. Monitoring of Automated Systems. In R. Parasuraman and M. Mouloua, editors, *Automation and Human Performance: Theory and Applications*, pages 337–364. Lawrence Erlbaum Associates, Mahwah, NJ, 1996.

[125] R. Parasuraman and V. Riley. Humans and automation: Use, misuse, disuse, abuse. *Human Factors*, 39(2):230–253, 1997.

[126] R. Parasuraman, T. B. Sheridan, and C. D. Wickens. A model for types and levels of human interaction with automation. *IEEE Transactions on Systems Man and Cybernetics – Part A: Systems and Humans*, 30:286–297, 2000.

[127] A. Pauzié. Evaluating Driver Mental Workload using the Driver Activity Load Index (DALI). In *Proceedings of the European Conference on Human Centred Design for Intelligent Transport Systems*, 2008.

[128] A. Pauzié and G. Pachiaudi. Subjective evaluation of the mental workload in the driving context. In *Laboratory Ergonomics Health Comfort, INRETS / LESCO, International Conference on Traffic and Transport Psychology*, 1996.

[129] I. Petermann and B. Schlag. Auswirkungen der Synthese von Assistenz und Automation auf das Fahrer-Fahrzeug System. In *11. Symposium AAET 2010 - Automatisierungs-, Assistenzsysteme und eingebettete Systeme für Transportmittel*, pages 383–403, 2010.

[130] T. Petzoldt, N. Bär, and J. F. Krems. Gender Effects on Lane Change Test (LCT) Performance. In *Proceedings of the Fifth International Driving Symposium on Human Factors in Driver Assessment, Training and Vehicle Design*, pages 90–96, Big Sky, Montana, USA, 2009.

[131] A. Popken, L. Nilsson, and J. F. Krems. Drivers' reliance on lane keeping assistance systems: Effects of different levels of assistance. In C. Brusque, editor, *Proceedings of the European Conference on Human Centred Design for Intelligent Transport Systems*, pages 301–310, Lyon, France, 2008.

[132] J. Rasmussen. Skills, rules, knowledge; signals, signs, and symbols, and other distinctions in human performance models. *IEEE Transactions on Systems, Man and Cybernetics*, 13:257–266, 1983.

[133] J. Rasmussen. *Information Processing and Human-Machine Interaction*. North-Holland, New York, 1986.

[134] K. Rayner. Eye movements in reading and information processing. *Psychological Bulletin*, 85(3):618–660, 1978.

[135] J. Reason. *Human Error*. Cambridge University Press, Cambridge UK, 1990.

[136] M. A. Regan, J. D. Lee, and K. L. Young. *Driver Distraction. Theory, Effects, and Mitigation*. CRC Press, Boca Raton, 2009.

[137] G. Reichart. *Menschliche Zuverlässigkeit beim Führen von Kraftfahrzeugen – Möglichkeiten der Analyse und Bewertung*. PhD thesis, Lehrstuhl für Ergonomie der TU München, 2000.

[138] T. H. Rockwell. Eye-movement analysis of visual information acquisition in driving: an overview. In *Proceedings of the 6th Conference of the Australian Road Research Board*, pages 316–331, 1972.

[139] D. D. Salvucci and K. L. Macuga. Predicting the effects of cellular-phone dialing on driving performance. *Cognitive Systems Research*, 3:95–102, 2002.

[140] N. D. Sarter and D. D. Woods. Pilot Interaction with Cockpit Automation: Operational Experiences with the Flight Management System. *The International Journal of Aviation Psychology*, 2(4):303–321, 1992.

[141] N. D. Sarter and D. D. Woods. Decomposing Automation: Autonomy, Authority, Observability and Perceived Animacy. In *First Automation Technology and Human Performance Conference*, April 1994.

[142] T. Schaller, J. Schiehlen, and B. Gradenegger. Stauassistenz – Unterstützung des Fahrers in der Quer- und Längsführung: Systementwicklung und Kundenakzeptanz. In *3. Tagung Aktive Sicherheit durch Fahrerassistenz*, April 2008. Garching.

[143] M. Schneid. *Entwicklung und Erprobung eines kontaktanalogen Head-up-Displays im Fahrzeug*. PhD thesis, Technische Universität München, 2009.

[144] T. B. Sheridan. *Telerobotics, automation, and human supervisory control*. MIT Press, 1992.

[145] T. B. Sheridan. Human Versus Automation in Responding to Failures: An Expected-Value Analysis. *Human Factors*, 42(3):403–407, Fall 2000.

[146] T. B. Sheridan. *Humans and Automation: System Design and Research Issues.* John Wiley & Sons, Hoboken, N.J., 2002.

[147] T. B. Sheridan. Next Generation Air Transportation Systems: Human-Automation Interaction and Organizational Risks. In E. Hollnagel and E. Rigaud, editors, *Proceedings of the second Resilience engineering symposium*, 2006.

[148] T. B. Sheridan and R. Parasuraman. Human-Automation Interaction. In R. Nickerson, editor, *Reviews of Human Factors and Ergonomics*. Human Factors and Ergonomics Society, Santa Monica, 2006.

[149] T. B. Sheridan and W. L. Verplank. Human and Computer Control of Undersea Teleoperators. Technical report, Massachusetts Institute of Technology, Man-Mchine Systems Lab, Cambridge, 1978.

[150] D. Shinar. Looks Are (Almost) Everything: Where Drivers Look to Get Information. *Human Factors*, 50(3):380–384, 2008. Golden Anniversary Special Issue.

[151] C. Spence and C. Ho. Crossmodal Information Processing in Driving. In C. Castro, editor, *Human Factors of Visual and Cognitive Performance in Driving*, pages 187–200. CRC Press, Boca Raton, 2009.

[152] W. Spießl and M. Farid. Vorausschauende Fahrzeugpfadanzeige, 2010. Application 102010028300.2 DE, patent pending.

[153] W. Spießl and H. Hußmann. Assessing error recognition in automated driving. *IET Intelligent Transport Systems*, 5(2):103–111, June 2011.

[154] W. Spießl and M. Mangold. ALCT - A Methodical Approach toward Evaluating the Influence of Secondary Tasks during Automated Driving. In *Proceedings of the Second European Conference on Human Centred Design for Intelligent Transport Systems*, pages 379–388, Berlin, Germany, April 2010.

[155] N. A. Stanton and M. Pinto. Behavioural compensation by drivers of a simulator when using a vision enhancement system. *Ergonomics*, 43:1359–1370, 2000.

[156] D. L. Strayer and F. A. Drews. Profiles in driver distraction: Effects of cell phone conversations on younger and older drivers. *Human Factors*, 46(4):640–649, Winter 2004.

[157] D. L. Strayer and W. A. Johnston. Driven to distraction: Dual-task studies of simulated driving and conversing on a cellular phone. *Psychological Science*, 12:462–466, 2001.

[158] M. Strobl. SPIDER: Das innovative Software-Framework der BMW Fahrsimulation. In *VDI-Berichte*, number 1745, pages 303–320. VDI-Verlag, 2003.

[159] J. Stutts, J. Feaganes, E. Rodgman, C. Hamlett, T. Meadows, D. Reinfurt, K. Gish, M. Mercadante, and L. Staplin. Distractions in everyday driving. Technical report, AAA Foundation for Traffic Safety, 2003.

[160] M. Tönnis, C. Lange, and G. Klinker. Visual Longitudinal and Lateral Driving Assistance in the Head-Up Display of Cars. In *Proceedings of the 2007 6th IEEE and ACM International Symposium on Mixed and Augmented Reality (ISMAR '07)*, pages 91–94, Nara, Japan, 2007.

[161] M. Tönnis, C. Lange, G. Klinker, and H. Bubb. Transfer von Flugschlauchanzeigen in das Head-Up Display von Kraftfahrzeugen. In *VDI Berichte Nr. 1960*. VDI-Verlag, 2006.

[162] W. Tomaske and T. Fortmüller. Der Einfluss von Wahrnehmungsschwellen auf die Auslegung von Bewegungssystemen in der Fahrsimulation. In K.-P. Gärtner and M. Grandt, editors, *Human Factors bei der Entwicklung von Fahrzeugen*. 2001.

[163] G. Traufetter. Captain Computer. *Der Spiegel*, 31:106–118, 2009.

[164] G. Traufetter. Geisterflug. *Der Spiegel*, 45:147, 2009.

[165] G. Traufetter. Allein über den Wolken. *Der Spiegel*, 36:138, 2010.

[166] A. Treisman. Selective attention in man. *British Medical Bulletin*, 20:12–16, 1964.

[167] T. Vöhringer-Kuhnt. Die Evaluation von Fahrerinformationssystemen mit dem 'Lane Change Test': Ergänzungen zum Normenentwurf ISO/DIS 26022. *i-com Zeitschrift für interaktive und kooperative Medien*, 2:25–29, 2009.

[168] M. Vollrath and F. Flemisch. Interaktionsgestaltung für hochautomatisierte Fahrzeuge. In *Informationssysteme für mobile Anwendungen*. 2006.

[169] P. Waldmann. *Entwicklung eines Fahrzeugführungssystems zum Erlernen der Ideallinie auf Rennstrecken*. PhD thesis, Technische Universität Cottbus, 2008.

[170] P. Waldmann, N. Kämpchen, M. Ardelt, and F. Homm. Der Nothalteassistent – abgesichertes Anhalten bei plötzlicher Fahrunfähigkeit des Fahrzeugführers. In *Proceedings of Ambient Assisted Living 2010*, Berlin, 2010. VDE Verlag.

[171] J. S. Warm, R. Parasuraman, and G. Matthews. Vigilance Requires Hard Mental Work and Is Stressful. *Human Factors*, 50(3):433–441, June 2008. Golden Anniversary Special Issue.

[172] C. D. Wickens. Attention, Time-Sharing, and Workload. In *Engineering Psychology and Human Performance*, pages 364–411. Harper-Collins Publishers Inc., New York, 2nd edition, 1992.

[173] C. D. Wickens. Automation in Air Traffic Control: The Human Performance Issues. In M. W. Scerbo and M. Mouloua, editors, *Automation Technology and Human Performance: Current Research and Trends*. Lawrence Erlbaum Associates, Mahwah, NJ, 1999.

[174] C. D. Wickens and J. G. Hollands. Signal Detection, Information Theory and Absolute Judgment. In C. D. Wickens and J. G. Hollands, editors, *Engineering Psychology and Human Performance*. Prentice Hall, London, 2000.

[175] C. D. Wickens and Y. Liu. Codes and modalities in multiple resources: a success and a qualification. *Human Factors*, 30(5):599–616, 1988.

[176] E. L. Wiener and R. E. Curry. Flight deck automation: promises and problems. *Ergonomics*, 23(10):995–1011, 1980.

[177] J. Wille, F. Saust, and M. Maurer. Stadtpilot: Driving Autonomously on Braunschweig's Inner Ring Road. In *IEEE International Conference on Intelligent Vehicles*, pages 506–511, 2010.

[178] H. Winner, S. Hakuli, R. Bruder, U. Konigorski, and B. Schiele. Conduct-by-Wire - ein neues Paradigma für die Weiterentwicklung der Fahrerassistenz. In C. Stiller and M. Maurer, editors, *4. Workshop Fahrerassistenzsysteme: FAS2006*, October 2006.

[179] D. D. Woods. Decomposing Automation: Apparent Simplicity, Real Complexity. In R. Parasuraman and M. Mouloua, editors, *Automation and Human Performance: Theory and Applications*, pages 3–18. Lawrence Erlbaum, Mahway, NJ, 1996.

[180] Y. Yamaguchi, T. Nakagawa, K. Akaho, M. Honda, H. Kato, and S. Nishida. AR-Navi: An In-Vehicle Navigation System Using Video-Based Augmented Reality Technology. In M. Smith and G. Salvendy, editors, *Human Interface and the Management of Information. Interacting in Information Environments*, volume 4558 of *Lecture Notes in Computer Science*, pages 1139–1147. Springer Berlin / Heidelberg, 2007.

BIBLIOGRAPHY 195

[181] R. M. Yerkes and J. D. Dodson. The relation of strength of stimulus to rapidity of habit-formation. *Journal of Comparative Neurology and Psychology*, 18:459–482, 1908.

[182] K. Young, M. Regan, and M. Hammer. Driver distraction: a review of the literature. Technical report, Monash University Accident Research Centre, 2003. Report No. 206.

[183] L. R. Young and D. Sheena. Survey of eye movement recording methods. *Behavior Research Methods, Instruments and Computers*, 7(5):397–429, 1975.

[184] M. S. Young and N. A. Stanton. Attention and automation: New perspectives on mental underload and performance. *Theoretical Issues in Ergonomics Science*, 3(2):178–194, 2002.

Scientific progress goes "Boink".

– **Bill Watterson** –

Die VDM Verlagsservicegesellschaft sucht für wissenschaftliche Verlage abgeschlossene und herausragende

Dissertationen, Habilitationen, Diplomarbeiten, Master Theses, Magisterarbeiten usw.

für die kostenlose Publikation als Fachbuch.

Sie verfügen über eine Arbeit, die hohen inhaltlichen und formalen Ansprüchen genügt, und haben Interesse an einer honorarvergüteten Publikation?

Dann senden Sie bitte erste Informationen über sich und Ihre Arbeit per Email an *info@vdm-vsg.de*.

Sie erhalten kurzfristig unser Feedback!

VDM Verlagsservicegesellschaft mbH
Dudweiler Landstr. 99   Telefon +49 681 3720 174
D - 66123 Saarbrücken   Fax   +49 681 3720 1749
www.vdm-vsg.de

Die VDM Verlagsservicegesellschaft mbH vertritt

Printed by Books on Demand GmbH, Norderstedt / Germany